ROBERT TAYLOR

ROBERT TAYLOR

JANE ELLEN WAYNE

St. Martin's Press
New York

Library of Congress Cataloging-in-Publication Data

Wayne, Jane Ellen.
     Robert Taylor : the man with the perfect face / Jane Ellen Wayne.
          p.   cm.
     ISBN 0-312-02972-1
     1. Taylor, Robert, 1911–1969.   2. Motion picture actors and
    actresses—United States—Biography.   I. Title.
    PN2287.T27W34   1989
    791.43′028′0924—dc19
    [B]   89-4069
                                                    CIP

First published in The United States by Warner Paperback.

First U.S. Edition

10 9 8 7 6 5 4 3 2 1

To my brother, Bob.

Acknowledgments

Ursula Thiess Taylor

Howard Strickling

Governor Ronald Reagan

George Murphy

Barbara and Art Reeves

Tom Purvis

Cal Clements

Irene Hervey

Dr. Ivy Mooring

Virginia Grey

Jim Merrick

Kay Mulvey

Katharine Hepburn

Robert Stack

Hall Bartlett

Henry Wills

Joe Santley

Bob Stapler

Helen Ferguson

"Nudie"

Ben Lane

George Nichols

The King Brothers

Deborah Kerr

Joan Crawford

Lloyd Nolan

Arvid W. Eyth

Sister Lucille Lang

The author wishes to express special thanks to the *New York Post* for the use of their files and to the *Beatrice Daily Sun* for their cooperation. Also to the Winchester-Western Company the author expresses her appreciation.

Introduction

I met Robert Taylor in 1962. He was doing a weekly television show "The Detectives" on NBC where I worked. By then Hollywood's golden years were memories on film and the legendary movie stars were forced to stoop from the great silver screen to the little boob tube. "I didn't own a TV set until recently," he told me. "I got it for my kids."

Throughout my life I had felt a mysterious affinity for this man. I never wrote him a fan letter or pasted his picture on my bedroom wall. Taylor was not a heartthrob to my bobby-soxer generation. At fifty-one he was old enough to be my father.

I'd been introduced to many celebrities, but I made a very special effort to meet the matinee idol who made love to Garbo in *Camille*, and defended Elizabeth Taylor's honor in *Ivanhoe*.

There he was, looking exactly as he did in his films.

"How many years ago?" he asked me with a chuckle.

"When you were MGM's knight in shining armor."

"That was almost yesterday, but thanks," he smiled.

We talked about his ranch, his horses and his fishing trips. Knowing he wasn't one for small talk, I asked him how he liked doing television. "There are fewer rehearsals and the pace is faster," he replied. "I prefer movies, but TV is the breeding ground for actors these days. I wish they could have the backing I did—a studio like MGM and a boss like L. B. Mayer. We were groomed by experts. One of a kind. No imitations. We were given roles according to our abilities. We did what we were told; it made us stars."

"But not all," I said as a subtle compliment.

"Oh, I had a couple things going for me," he said lighting a cigarette. "I was a good-looking kid with a good voice. But I couldn't act. Gable said we got the breaks because there was a shortage of leading men in the early thirties."

Members of the cast joined us for coffee. I remember thinking at the time that Taylor was one of the few Hollywood idols left. Bogart, Flynn, Gable, Power, and Cooper were gone. They were spared the transition from movies to television, and I wondered how many of those proud actors would have survived.

Taylor died in 1969. My proposed magazine article about him turned out to be a book because there was so much more to this man than even his close friends realized. Five years of research and interviews were devoted to this project. Bob's widow, Ursula Theiss Taylor, graciously welcomed me into their Mandeville Canyon home and she paved the way. To her I am most grateful.

The Egyptians had their temples and gods. Great Britain has its kings and queens. America's royalty reigned in Hollywood. They made us laugh during the Great Depression, and marched beside us during World War II. As we approach the twenty-first century, stars of the Golden Era will play a more significant role in American history and tradition.

Robert Taylor is a memorable chapter....

—JANE ELLEN WAYNE

ROBERT TAYLOR

Chapter I

"People seem to think I'm a millionaire, but I'm not. Every time a chance came along to really strike it rich outside the movie business, I was always a dollar short or a day late. It's the story of my life."

These were Robert Taylor's words after twenty-eight years as a motion picture star. He did not enjoy talking about himself but when he did he was known for his frankness. He never bragged about his accomplishments, and in fact rarely mentioned them. He had a habit of playing down his abilities or cutting a conversation off abruptly to talk about something else.

Few actors have equaled Robert Taylor's good looks, and certainly none his modesty. These two qualities do not make a star, but he represented more to audiences than the face they saw on the screen, he was a symbol of honor, strength, perfection, humility and sincerity.

Despite these old-fashioned virtues that no make-up, script or costume could conceal, moviegoers, fanatic for excitement, violence and sex, found him refreshing.

As a villain he was never truly despicable; in a bad movie he managed to keep the audience in their seats; as a lover he was innocent because of his integrity; in a Western he sat tall in the saddle and dismounted with natural ease; as the knight in shining armor he was the epitome of manhood.

As a human being he was a mystery.

Meeting this man for the first time was a startling experience, not so much because he was Robert Taylor but rather because of the realization that his face was flawless. His forehead, cheekbone structure, nose, chin and lips were perfectly proportioned. Then there was the always striking black hair and blue eyes.

Despite these facial attributes, his widow's peak was his most outstanding feature; it was a magnet.

His physique was lean but sturdy and he walked with graceful masculine determination.

However, there were those who were displeased with Robert Taylor's exceptional good looks, and the most vehement was Robert Taylor. As far as he was concerned, the mirror had never been invented. Any reference to his handsomeness embarrassed him, and he rarely accepted a compliment with a smile.

When he was introduced to John Derek, the actor, Taylor said, "I don't envy you, fella, not with those looks!"

People have always admired that which is real, and the actor who relates veracity is in tune with the public, as Taylor proved in *Magnificent Obsession, Johnny Eager, Waterloo Bridge* and *Quo Vadis.*

In the thirties he was MGM's biggest headache. Their other top stars were set in their molds: Gable was the tough romantic lead; Tracy and Garbo, the naturals; Jean Harlow, the braless sex queen; Joan Crawford was the broad with dignity; Loretta Young, the perennial soft-spoken lady; but Robert Taylor was a problem.

The studio had taken a shy kid and adopted him. They knew he would be the biggest name in pictures—if, that is, they didn't make a mistake.

If they continued to make him the powdered-down lover, it would ruin him. Make him a tough guy? Too soon. Give him a drama? No, there were too many other actors doing that. Put him in comedies, and the female public would be insulted.

Metro's strategy had been well-timed. America's Ambassador of Romance, commonly known as Pretty Boy, had just made his twentieth movie, *A Yank at Oxford.* He dispelled all the hot rumors that he was a sissy with his portrayal of a cocky athlete. His muscular, hairy chest was the talk of moviegoers everywhere. (Men who previously smirked at the mention of his name "ate their hats" and bought chest toupées, while the women begged for more romance in his next movie.)

MGM had spent four years building up Robert Taylor as the world's greatest lover, and he handled it too well.

13

But he was more than that to the public, and they could be swayed either way. He could have gone on being the kissing idol and nothing more, or his abilities as a personality could be directed elsewhere.

A Yank at Oxford was the appetizer audiences had been waiting for, but then they wanted more. When the film was released he was asked by an interviewer what his immediate plans were and he said, "None." Where would he go from there? "Search me." Did he have any special kind of role he would like to play? "No." What was all the talk about his changing from heavy lover to he-man in future pictures? "You know as much about it as I do. I don't pick my pictures. The studio does. They tell me what I'm going to play and I do what I can."

Wasn't he even consulted? "What for? I'm no producer. If they want me to be a Bull Montana, I've got to try. If they say be a swooning Romeo, I have to take it. I don't make any decisions because I wouldn't know how. But, if you ask me if we're getting anywhere with this interview, I'd say we're not."

Did it matter to him that they were getting nowhere? "Yes, it matters! It matters a lot to me. I don't like to sound like a lump. I ought to have a lot of quips to hand out so people would think I'm a great guy. But I'm just myself."

What did that mean? "I'm a guy who lives on an alfalfa ranch in San Fernando Valley thirty miles from here. This guy goes to work early in the morning and is in bed at nine at night. He doesn't say anything anybody would care about."

The reporters who had to write something about Taylor in their next edition often said, "I wonder what will happen to this kid who makes more money in one week than I do in a year?" But they were unanimous about one thing: he would be around for a long, long time.

The press would continue to make fun of his simplicity and obvious lack of self independence, but Taylor's realistic philosophy and integrity kept him a balanced, modest and unassuming man throughout his many years as a top Hollywood box-office favorite; he had "something" that can only be seen by the camera.

What irked the press was knowing Robert Taylor could

14

return to Nebraska any time, buy a farm with the money he was saving and have no regrets.

Hollywood to young Mr. Taylor meant getting up at 5:00 every morning ("I get up at dawn anyway!"), going to parties ("I hate them!"), hard work ("No problem. I can get plenty of that on a farm . . ."), and fame ("Nuts!").

What kept him going as a boy was his faith in L. B. Mayer and his contract with MGM. He liked money because it meant security for him and for his mother, because since his father's death he had taken complete responsibility for her.

Fortunately, they were able to live in separate houses, he in the country where he could keep his quarter horses, and she in town.

Taylor never got accustomed to the city, but his mother enjoyed it, especially Hollywood. She was easily able to forget Nebraska and had no intention of returning there except for an occasional visit to impress the folks back home.

As a child in Filley, Nebraska, Ruth Stanhope was never in good health and unable to enjoy normal physical activities. When she was sixteen, the doctors discovered her lack of strength was a result of a weak heart. They predicted Ruth would become an invalid within a few years and her life would be a short one. Her father was a grain merchant and could afford the best medical treatment in Nebraska, but even the specialists agreed that Ruth's condition was hopeless.

At eighteen she fell in love with Spangler Andrew Brugh and wanted to be his wife. Brugh was instantly attracted to the delicate girl who spoke quietly and walked slowly. He was as anxious as she to get married and though Ruth had not been told the entire truth about the seriousness of her heart ailment, Brugh knew.

Her father made it clear to Andrew that his daughter would be unable to function as a normal housewife and would undoubtedly have to spend most of her time in bed.

He also suggested that she remain in Filley with her family nearby and receive regular medical treatment which was expensive. If Andrew was willing to marry

15

Ruth under these difficult circumstances, he would accept him as his son-in-law.

Andrew was in his early twenties, spunky and ambitious. He was also a stubborn Pennsylvania Dutchman who was not easily discouraged. He made up his mind to marry Ruth despite the obstacles.

Stanhope gave him an equal partnership in his grain business and the young newlyweds settled down to a quiet life in Filley.

Being married and very much in love was excellent therapy for Ruth. She was full of laughter and enjoyed taking short walks with her husband in the evenings. After a year passed she stayed in bed more and more, unable to leave the house. She was breathless for no apparent reason. Andrew did the housework, shopping and cooking while Ruth tried to keep up with sewing and mending.

Her doctor recommended a warmer climate. He gave Ruth a few more years to live and stressed that the extremely cold winters in the Midwest were aggravating her health.

But despite these warnings she refused to leave Filley. She convinced Andrew that he was doing well as a grain merchant and she would feel safer being near her family and country doctor in whom she had great trust.

She was still not aware of the seriousness of her heart trouble and felt one day she would be strong enough to do light household chores.

As the months passed, Andrew found himself deeper and deeper in debt. The doctor bills were piling up. He told Stanhope that Ruth would lie almost lifeless in bed for days at a time and it seemed like every heartbeat shook her slim body. Then she would get up, sit in a chair, eat well, only to retire again for a week.

He consulted several specialists and they agreed that Ruth would continue this pattern until her death, which they predicted would come before her twenty-fifth birthday. They were doing their best with the medical knowledge available in 1909, but in circumstances like this they always advised a prayer or two.

Brugh did more than pray. He was fanatically devoted to Ruth and was convinced much more could be done

16

for her. At thirty years old, Brugh was well established in business, but the frustrations over the doctors' failures to help his wife became too much for him.

He decided to study medicine and find a cure for her. No one thought he would go through with his radical decision, but Stanhope was convinced it was worth a try and offered to back his son-in-law financially, which Andrew accepted as a loan.

He took Ruth with him to Kirksville, Missouri, where he enrolled for a regular four-year medical course. He specialized in heart diseases and was determined to learn what the other doctors did not know.

One thing he accepted—his wife was permanently ill, but trying to keep her alive and comfortable was better than sitting back and just waiting for her death.

To his surprise Ruth became interested in his new career. She wrote to her mother in Filley, "If anyone can save my life it will be Andrew and I feel better already."

One morning she had breakfast with her student husband and asked if she might attend classes with him.

"That's the damnedest thing I ever heard of, Ruth!"

"But look at it this way. If I do feel ill, just think of all the medical attention I'll get. When you look at it logically I am safer with you than I am at home."

She accompanied him several days a week and became so engrossed with the study of medicine she was seen taking notes in class. For the first time in their married life, Andrew found he could not control Ruth's limitations.

In his second year at school, Ruth became pregnant. It was a shock to both of them, and they had mixed emotions: after eight years of marriage, they silently accepted the fact that Ruth's health would be tested to the fullest.

They returned to Filley where Ruth was put to bed for seven months. Andrew took complete charge of her care. It took every ounce of courage and strength to pull her through this difficult period.

Brugh sat by her bedside trying to keep up his studies while Ruth read novels and spoke to him of how lucky they were.

At 7:00 A.M. on a hot August 5th, 1911, Spangler

17

Arlington Brugh was born and Ruth almost died. The baby was handed to a nurse immediately and all attention was given to the mother. The birth of her son made Ruth a complete invalid and Andrew doubted she would survive. For several weeks it was touch and go.

She remembered nothing about going into labor or hearing a baby cry. She had been in a deep sleep and very weak but when she was able to sit up the baby was brought to her; she said, "I'm so glad it's a boy because I didn't have a name picked out if it had been a girl."

Ruth in later years enjoyed telling about her long days and nights waiting for the birth and how she spent most of her time thinking of a name.

"I was very romantic and sensitive, a very impressionable girl. The hero's name in a novel I was reading was Arlington. He was dashing and inspiring, so much so that I decided if I had a son, Arlington would be his middle name."

Spangler was traditional in the Brugh family, handed down from generations of Pennsylvania Dutchmen. It was Robert Taylor's first name as well as his father's, though like Andrew he would be known to everyone by his middle name Arlington or "Arly."

From his mother he acquired the best in blood and tradition of Scotch and English ancestry, and she wanted her son to use her maiden name, Stanhope, on the stage. It almost happened.

Brugh continued his studies in Kirksville and from the day Arlington learned to walk he took the boy with him to classes. Ruth was hanging on but unable to care for him. He sat in the back of the classroom, listening and watching.

While other little boys were playing with colored blocks and wind-up trucks, young Brugh was given a small knife and whetstone. He sat in the corner of the laboratory sharpening his knife, expecting at any moment to be called upon to assist in the cutting up of a cadaver. Later he said, "I will never forget those dissection classes and the smell of dead bodies."

Being in medical school almost daily, wholly without association or companionship of other children, he attempted to learn Latin by himself. Unable to distinguish between English and self-taught garbled Latin, he became a stammerer. It reached a point where he could not communicate at all, making him withdraw into himself.

Ruth was improving physically but she became totally emotionally immersed in her affliction, using it finally as her identity before the world.

She rather enjoyed being pampered and took great satisfaction in pity. She "held court" at her home while her friends waited on her and praised her bravery during her pregnancy. Few women, they told her, would have sacrificed their lives for the sake of having a child.

She ruled everyone—her tactic being, "If you won't let me have my way, I'll get even for always—I'll die." And she used this threat with Andrew to excess. Her frailty was her greatest strength.

He, too, was undergoing an inner personality change. The study and practice of medicine as well as keeping his wife alive and cheerful, absorbed him completely. With the exception of dragging his son along with him every day, he had little interest in the boy.

Both mother and father decided that Arlington should be sent to the country. Neither parent was able to care for him properly and his speech handicap bothered and embarrassed them. With all of his medical knowledge, Andrew could not get through to his son. It angered him that Arlington could not talk except for a few words which he managed to stutter and stammer through. Ruth displayed him as one would a pedigree dog, and no one could deny his beauty, but when asked a simple question, he buried his head in his mother's lap.

He was sent to live with a Czechoslovakian couple, Ruth and Anton Tyser, who were friends of the Brughs. They welcomed Arlington with warmth and sincerity, accepting him as one of their own children.

He loved the country, learned to fish and hunt, and played with other children his own age. It was on their farm that he fell in love with horses and rode daily. This was also his first introduction to the comfort and easy atmosphere of normal family life.

Being with children his own age was difficult for a

time because he was unable to communicate even on their level. However, the patience that Anton had with the boy resulted in Arlington's chattering like the other youngsters—and he forgot his Latin.

When five-year-old Arlington returned home, his father had gone into private practice and the story of Mrs. Brugh's remarkable recovery swept throughout the small towns of southeastern Nebraska. Success came relatively quickly and easily for Dr. Brugh, for here was a grain merchant who had become a physician late in life and healed his own wife.

The family moved to the "big city" of Beatrice, Nebraska, when Arly was six. ("I really thought it was a metropolis," Taylor recalled, "all of 9,000 people!")

They rented the first floor of a little house on High Street. Their landlady, "Auntie Neuhauser," occupied the upstairs which consisted of a bedroom and kitchenette. There was one staircase and only one bathroom which served everyone. Mrs. Neuhauser was very exacting about cleanliness, which speaks well for the tidiness of the Brugh family.

Auntie's pancakes were a favorite of Arly's and he was often invited to have breakfast in the little kitchenette on the second floor.

Ruth did not believe in formal education for children at an early age and refused to send her son to school. Since the doctor was practicing day and night, she directed all her attention and love to her boy, who looked more like a little girl because of the way she combed his curly hair and fussed over his clothing. If he was permitted to go out and play with other children, he was told to keep his pretty white shirt free from dirt and grass stains. Mother and son spent their days reading together, having hot lunches and taking walks.

The doctor was very strict with Arly and if his son did not eat what was put before him he was sent to bed hungry. Because the doctor did not approve of the "temper tantrums" that Arly displayed occasionally, he did did not spare the rod! Ruth, of course, did not like this form of discipline, but would not defy her husband and said later it was just as well, she could have spoiled her son had it not been for the strong hand of his father.

20

Dr. Brugh, who called his son "Buddy," very often took the boy on house calls with him. The child witnessed everything from childbirth to death and he knew the smells of disease and saw the pains of amputation, but he adored his father and said he was going to be a surgeon, too. (As Robert Taylor he portrayed a doctor in five films and in 1935 his role in *Society Doctor* gave him the big push toward stardom.)

Ruth took "her baby" to school when he was seven years old and she cried all the way home. She felt she had lost him and wept, "I've lost my son!" clinging to him tighter than ever. She dressed him up in a little Lord Fauntleroy velvet outfit. Who suffered most that day is questionable.

Arly was chased home by his classmates because he looked so cute. The boys desperately wanted to see the velvet knickers covered with mud. This daily routine encouraged Mrs. Brugh's little boy to become the fastest runner in town! (His rosy cheeks didn't help the situation.) Being chased home from school became a game and the other boys discovered that Arly was having as much fun as they were.

As for girls, Taylor said he fell in love only once in his youth. She was the daughter of the physical director of the YMCA: "Guess she was pretty, but I don't remember. What intrigued me about her was that she could run faster than I could and we spent our entire 'brief courtship' trying to outrun each other. The day I finally caught up with her I lost interest."

A few friends called him "Doc" because he talked so much about becoming a doctor. If that didn't work out, he said he would be a cowboy "because I love to ride horses and to hunt," the latter being a characteristic he and his father did not have in common.

He was allowed to have a horse that he kept at the Tyser's farm a mile or so out of town. Riding "Gyp"— short for Gypsy—was one of his greatest pleasures.

Chapter II

At grammar school, the superintendent, who was also the leader of the school orchestra, persuaded Arly to take up the cello rather than the saxophone which he had been attempting. It was a relief to the Brughs when he took this advice because Ruth dreaded the noise of the saxophone and the "plunk of the banjo." Several students got together and formed a quartet. Arly took the cello seriously even though it was the object of some snickering.

In junior high school he became the first "elected" president of the student body, and in a letter written late in his life to a pal in Beatrice he said, "I shall never forget the fears that overcame me every time I had to preside over a meeting in that auditorium or introduce a guest speaker. Nothing else has ever frightened me so much."

He remained somewhat aloof—quiet, studious musical, handsome and quite a clothes horse. He was just *not* one of the crowd, possessing interests other than those of his classmates.

Arly was a member of the track team but said he was a faster runner when he wore knickers. On vacations he stocked wheat and mowed lawns.

When the doctor's financial condition improved—he was now an osteopath—the Brughs bought a brownish brick home at 901 North 6th Street. His neighbors described Arly as a fine-looking young man, always well-groomed and smiling. He especially enjoyed Mr. and Mrs. Clayton, the elderly retired farmers who lived next door, and considered them as close as his own grandparents who lived in Filley where he was born.

The Claytons were story-tellers, mainly relating tales of their early life in Nebraska, and Arly said he couldn't wait until he would be old like they were and have "lots of stories to tell."

Arly's closest friend was Gerhart Wiebe, a member of the string quartet and the son of a very respectable family of Menonites. The Wiebe family had always been well-to-do, but suffered a severe financial disaster. Arly stuck by his friend through this tragic time and in his quiet way let it be known that just because his buddy's family had lost their fortune, his esteem for Gerhart had not diminished. Arly and Gerhart shared the same interests: they belonged to the same high school organizations and both maintained high scholastic and moral standards. Gerhart Weibe went on to become a dean at the University of Boston.

Even as he grew up Ruth continued her strict dominance over her son, and because she was still a frail woman, he obeyed her without question. The doctor did not allow cross words to be uttered in her presence and insisted Arly help her as much as possible. In fact, he did more than his share of housework and cooking.

With this background he learned gentleness with women, treating each and every one as if she were his mother, weak, delicate and helpless; and later he was attracted to the motherly type of woman.

Except for his few close friends and neighbors, he was not sociable with the "party crowd," and rarely dated. Ruth would have objected anyway and he knew it.

Arly defied her for the first time when he appeared in the Dramatic Club Play, *Nothing But The Truth*, as the male lead, Mr. Ralston. He pacified his mother by continuing his cello lessons and joined the orchestra.

Always embarrassed about singing, he joined the Glee Club anyway, but his talent was most exceptional on the debating team. The Brughs' tongue-tied child had emerged into a brilliant speaker. He won the State Oratorical Championship for his speech, "The Peculiar Position Held by School Teachers in Public Society," and was awarded with a ten-day jaunt to Detroit.

He did not want to enter the contest because of the stiff competition. There were three ministers of the Gospel already enrolled and he told his parents, "I won't have a chance," but they encouraged him with the prom-

23

ise of a fur coat, the current rage. ("It was like raccoon but it wasn't real. It was one of the greatest things that ever happened to me. I'll never forget it!")

Ruth was prouder when Arly won a local musical contest playing "The Swan" on his cello. She told him she was sure he would be a famous performer one day. "Na! I'd rather take over Dad's practice right here in Nebraska!"

When he graduated from high school, underneath the 1929 Homesteader's Year Book picture of S. Arlington Brugh, it read—FEW THINGS ARE IMPOSSIBLE TO DILIGENCE AND PERSERVERENCE, and his credits listed were Dramatic Club, Glee Club, National Honor Society, Orchestra, Student Council, Homesteader Staff and Senior Social Chairman. As a member of the Senior High Operetta, *Captain Crossbones,* he is pictured in a sweater under his suit, while in the Dramatic Club Play photo he is the only one *without* a jacket: "The Dramatic Club Play, entitled *Nothing But The Truth,* was staged with great success. It was pronounced to be one of the finest productions ever rendered by a Beatrice High School organization. This was to be Taylor's first review.

In the Honor Society picture he is in the front row center, wearing his school sweater: "In election to this society, the faculty honors its members for the attainments already made and for the promise they contain of continued excellence in the ideals of the school—scholarship, leadership, character and service."

As a graduation present, Arly was given an old car. He had been hitching rides to Crete, Nebraska, every week to take his cello lessons from Professor E. Gray, an instructor at Doane University, forty miles from Beatrice.

Arly had great admiration for the professor ("He was my inspiration") and because of him he enrolled at Doane. He suddenly gave up the idea of following in his father's footsteps as a doctor and decided to dedicate himself to the cello and become a concert performer.

To help pay college expenses he played in a string quartet with his pal Gerhart Weibe, with Herbert Jackson, who went on to become a dentist in Beatrice, and Don Abbott, later to teach music at Loyola University

24

and dying a young man. The group performed over radio station KMNJ, earning forty to fifty dollars for each appearance. Arly continued to stock wheat during the harvest season, worked in a gas station part-time and painted cars for fun-money.

During Arly's sophomore year, Professor Gray announced that he was going to accept a better position at Pomona College in Claremont, California. This was a blow to young Brugh and at the age of twenty made the most important decision of his life—to follow the professor.

Ruth was opposed, but she wanted more than anything for her son to continue his ambition to be a cellist. It was she who convinced the doctor to let their son leave home.

On the long trip to California, he maintained a speed of thirty-five miles an hour—a promise he had made to his father when he got the car.

He had driven about one hundred miles when he stopped to telephone home. Ruth, who was still in tears after the front lawn farewell, put the doctor on. He listened for a moment then shouted, "All right, make it forty miles an hour!"

MGM, in its many biographical releases about Taylor, said he replied, "O.K., Pops, see you in the movies!" Actually, he never gave it a thought, except · for the weekly family outing on Saturday nights to see a picture show. And it is doubtful Arly would call Dr. Brugh "Pops."

At Pomona, the professor begrudged his protégé all outside activities save his academic work and the lessons on his cello. But Arly's public speaking became so polished he again was asked to join the Drama Club.

Not wanting to offend Gray, he declined, but despite the extensive music lessons, debating, tennis, orchestra and regular studies, he wanted to cram in still another activity and it narrowed down to the Glee Club or Drama.

Taylor said he cannot remember how he came to his decision, but the MGM Publicity Department insisted that it was an interesting story that put him on the stage.

According to them, he was taking a walk on the campus when he came across a cricket and a spider. A

25

silly notion struck him and he drew a line with the heel of his shoe.

If the spider crossed the line first, he would join the Glee Club, but if the cricket won, he would choose Dramatics.

The cricket won and Professor Gray was livid! "A concert performer is an artist. The public expects you to give total dedication to your art. A cellist is a musician, not an actor. The only thing Dramatics can possibly do is take time away from your practice, and your mind away from your total dedication. Dramatics! What a waste of time!"

Dr. Brugh received a letter from his son saying that he was confused: "At one time I wanted to study medicine, but I know how much you and Mother want me to master the cello. Yet I cannot deny my love for the excitement of debate and acting. What do you consider thè most important subject in the world?"

His father's reply came scribbled on a prescription slip: "Human Nature."

Arlington continued to play in the college orchestra but gave up his cello lessons.

His Phi Delta Theta fraternity brothers tried to fix him up with many girls but he seemed more interested in his school work than socializing. One of them said, "Every dame in town wanted to go out with Brugh but he turned them all down. He did show up at a few dances but always alone."

The college crowd at Pomona danced to jazz and be-bop music but Arly had mastered only the waltz and wasn't too impressed with the gyrating, wild steps of the jitterbug.

"What's the matter, Brugh? Why aren't you dancing?" a buddy inquired.

"Hell, this is all new to me. I'm still trying to figure out the fox trot."

"Tell you what you do. Find yourself a girl from Sacramento. They are *real* square up there. Bet she'll do a nice slow one with ya."

"But how do I know if a girl is from Sacramento?"

"Probably one of those wallflowers sitting over there . . ."

26

He approached one girl and she said she was from Los Angeles. Like a little boy he asked several until he found one from "up Sacramento way," and what started out to be a joke, turned out just right for Dr. Brugh's son. They danced every dance.

Someone said, "This is the first time I ever saw a couple doing a fox trot when the orchestra was playing boogie-woogie."

Taylor said in later years that he didn't "feel" popular in college because he wasn't "one of the gang" but thought his popularity—though not outstanding—was due to the fact that he went "smudging" with the other boys to earn extra money.

"The citrus growers burned smudge pots to keep the frost from nipping the fruit trees. It paid fifty cents an hour and the college allowed the growers to call out the guys during the night if necessary. If the cold was bone chilling and help was scarce, it might have even paid a dollar an hour.

"We'd shiver out of those warm blankets, put our oldest clothes on and ride up the baseline road into a special wind. It could freeze you down to the warmest part of your body and you'd shake for days afterwards thinking about it. The wind came off "Old Baldy," and when we got to the fields we felt lucky. We'd go around with a torch made out of a piece of burlap, dip it in oil and light up the pots.

"The smoke penetrated our eyes, lungs and every pore. Our nostrils and ears and lips and hair were filled with that sticky greasy soot and it was almost impossible to wash out.

"There would be times when all we got was an hour's sleep before making a seven-thirty class. I was the luckiest guy in the world—just to be working."

Dr. Brugh continued to pay the majority of Arly's college tuition, but he and Ruth were confused as to exactly what Arly would do when he had finished school. His letters were filled with details about his debating and how he was engrossed in psychology.

This seemed to be his favorite subject and he jokingly wrote that he wasn't very good in science so the world was spared a rotten doctor.

27

What he didn't mention to his parents was his growing interest in dramatics. A friend in Beatrice once described his acting. "In local plays and at college, others need not compete for any part in which Arly was interested. He always came through and stole the show. His appearance and spellbinding voice were always a part of *him*. He had it . . ."

He had appeared in *M'Lord the Duke, Camille* and *The Importance of Being Ernest,* yet he had no intention of making acting his career.

In his senior year he was picked to join Pomona's debating team in Oregon, but at the same time he was chosen for the lead in the senior play. He chose the play, and MGM's version of how Robert Taylor was discovered was a true one.

In 1932 there was a shortage of leading men in Hollywood. Clark Gable, Spencer Tracy, Robert Young and Fredric March were almost alone among the established male stars. Beautiful women were plentiful, but productions were actually being delayed because of the absence of talented, good-looking men.

Talent scouts were literally raiding the college campuses for photogenic male bodies who could be taught to act.

Ben Piazza, who discovered Harlow, Robert Mitchum and Rosalind Russell, was caustic, hard-bitten and hard to please, but still retained that willing suspension of disbelief that could look upon a starlet and see the glimmer of a star.

He could take one look at a girl, ask himself if he would enjoy going to bed with her, and if the answer was "yes," he approached her about a screen test. He was seldom wrong.

In December, 1932, he was in the audience at Pomona College to see *Journey's End,* and what happened that evening endowed a biographer with all the usual romanticizing: a legend and truth have become somewhat jumbled together.

Arlington played the part of the disillusioned Captain Stanhope in R. C. Sheriff's superb tragic World War I drama, *Journey's End,* but what was going on backstage

28

that night was rarely related properly as far as the future Glamour Boy was concerned.

" . . . everyone knew there was a talent scout in the audience . . ."

" . . . Arlington was alerted . . ."

" . . . Taylor put a movie contract in his pocket that very night . . ."

Actually the facts are simple. Piazza liked Taylor's performance, went backstage and asked him to come to his office the following day. Taylor said he didn't look very good the following day: there had been the usual after-the-theatre celebration and the excitement everyone felt about his being asked to make a screen test.

The receptionist at MGM's casting office expected him, but called him "Mr. Brugg."

"It's pronounced B-r-e-w."

Piazza questioned him about what his future plans were and Arly said he didn't know, but he would very much like to return to Nebraska after graduation. "California's OK, but I never did seem to fit in here. And the weather is awful—no change of seasons. I also can't get over not being able to ride a horse without going to a stable and renting one."

"Well, ah, what's your name again? Arlington?"

"Yes, sir."

"We thought you might like to take a screen test and if it turns out well, we'll give you free acting lessons. We have a fine school here on the lot, so . . ."

"Well, sir, I kinda want to finish college in June."

"Let's talk about that *after* we see what you look like on camera."

He photographed well, but when he read some lines from Noel Coward's *Private Lives*, Taylor said, "I was awful. I could see they were disappointed."

"Tell you what, kid, I think you're right. Better finish your education. Come back in June if you think you would like to try again."

("I guess that was the easiest way to break the bad news to me.")

The following June Pomona College conferred a degree of Bachelor of Liberal Arts upon Arlington Brugh.

29

His parents drove out to California for the graduation ceremony.

Ruth was the "Belle of the day," mingling with the other graduates and professors. One would never know she had been doomed to die over twenty years ago.

But the doctor looked pale and tired.

"What about the cello, son?"

"Wow, I haven't touched it in months, cramming for exams and all."

"Your mother's been talking to some of your classmates and they say you've been pretty good as an actor."

"Na. I thought I had a chance when some big shot talked to me about a screen test, but that never worked out."

"Not good enough, huh?"

"When someone says to come back and try again . . . shoot! That means forget it."

"I'd say it means to come back and try again."

The Brugh family talked it over later that day and Ruth was upset. She wanted Arly to come home to Nebraska for the summer and think things over. Then she took her son aside and whispered, "Your Dad isn't well. I think it would be best if you got a summer job in Beatrice. We'll work something out. It's a growing town, you know."

Arly was taken aback when he heard about his father's ill health, but Ruth and the doctor left for home without their son. Andrew felt the offer to try again at MGM was worth a try and gave Arly a check for $250. They agreed if he were rejected a second time, Arly would settle in Nebraska.

Although they were all surprised to see him back at Metro's casting office, they enrolled him in the acting school there. Oliver Hinsdell, the MGM dramatic coach, gave him private lessons on the side.

In October he was notified that his father had died of cancer. He went home for the funeral and was stunned to discover the doctor had little money left. His books showed that many patients owed him over $25,000.

The family managed to collect $1,000, which was enough for funeral expenses, and with a few dollars remaining, Arly returned to California, bringing Ruth with him.

The loss of his father broke Arly's heart. In Taylor's words, "I was twenty-two then and tried to be the head of a family. It's funny, always having everything you want, never thinking where it came from or wondering if you could have it. You sit down to dinner at night and there it is. It never occurs to you that the dinner and the bed won't be there.

"It's only when you are truly broke and don't know where your next meal is coming from or where you are going to lay the body down that night that you realize everyone doesn't have those things—that life isn't all beer and skittles."

When Dr. Brugh died, so did Arly's income. Aside from some property and a little insurance, that was it.

Arly rented a three-room apartment in Los Angeles for Ruth and himself, but he knew what little money they had would not last for very long.

When Arly told her that his acting coach, Oliver Hinsdell, was pleased with the results of his lessons and told him to try to stick it out a little while longer, Ruth encouraged him to continue his lessons at MGM.

The students in the studio school were rarely allowed to remain unless they showed promise. They teamed up and did scenes together. Front-office brass attended the skirmishes intermittently and if the glimmer of a star was discerned, a screen test was arranged.

Marcella Knapp, who worked in an executive office at the studio, caught Arly doing *When Ladies Meet*. She liked what she saw and arranged for him to be tested.

("When we went to the set to make it a few days later, in the middle of the scene, I looked at the camera and the lens was all cockeyed. It looked as though water were running over it, and I thought to myself, 'The camera is no good!' When they see this they'll throw me out of here for keeps.") It was bad. The actors kept going out of focus, but there was just enough decent footage to win Arly a contract.

Almost five years before he had earned $50 for playing with a quartet over KMNJ in Nebraska, and he could have gotten $85 a week as a concert cellist. But on

February 6, 1934, he signed a seven-year studio contract with MGM. L. B. Mayer offered him $35 a week—the lowest-paid actor or actress in the history of Hollywood.

When he received his first paycheck, he told Ruth he had only one debt he had to pay, and he was going to do it that very day.

He headed for a drugstore where he had been eating on a "pay-me-when-you-can" basis. Bill Schulhoff, the owner, congratulated Arly but didn't have the heart to take the entire check.

"Bill, I've kept track of every cent I owe you and it comes to exactly forty-one dollars and forty cents. I'll be back next week with the five-forty, OK?"

Robert Taylor never forgot Bill Schulhoff and showed up occasionally for years following to have lunch with him. "The food wasn't that good, but I got a kick out'a going up to the cashier and paying the check."

Arly's main concern at this time was his mother. He had never gotten over the fact that she had been gravely ill at one time and was still a weak woman with an unpredictable heart ailment. She was taking the present situation very well and did not complain, but Arly knew she was not accustomed to living the way they were.

"One night I realized I had to take stock of myself. What did the great stars on the lot have that I didn't have?

"Gable had sex appeal and looks. I thought about Nelson Eddy with that magnificent voice. And Spencer Tracy—the best actor in the business. By the time I got through analyzing myself, it seemed to me I had nothing and no prospect of getting anywhere.

"What I didn't realize was the things I envied were the result of years of hard work and experience that came with age. I made up my mind. I did not have any chance of becoming a success in movies. I had confidence in myself and knew I could find a job—something steady where I could compete with an equal."

"Clark Gable had told me that there were plenty of 'Gable' types selling shoes because they couldn't stand the constant rejection an actor faces. Part of being a star, he said, is having the guts to hang in there and refuse to take no for an answer."

32

The next morning Arlington asked to see the "Five-Star General of MGM" about breaking a contract.

L. B. Mayer was effusive, dramatic, calm, repressed and adaptable. He could rant, he could be patiently logical, he was harsh, merciless and often inept. As the head of the mightiest motion picture studio in the world, he dealt with the egos of the mighty, temperaments, feuds, box office balance sheets and the two Lord Gods who reigned in his Heaven—The Public and The Stockholders.

"I will go down on my knees to talent," he said, and he made no exception when it came to S. Arlington Brugh.

He sat down and talked to his lowest-paid employee . . .

Taylor would always remember that resignation session. "I asked Mayer to release me from the contract and I told him why. I'll never forget his kindness. He showed me how to budget so I could have money out of what I made. He advised me about clothes, how to cultivate patience . . . and that day he also gave me a new name.

"Actually, it was Ida Koverman, Mayer's secretary, who suggested the name 'Taylor.' I wanted 'Stanhope'— it was my mother's maiden name and I had been discovered portraying Captain Stanhope—but Mayer said 'Taylor' sounded more all-American.

"I couldn't argue with that, but when he insisted on 'Robert' I really felt like a nobody! Who the hell wants to have a common name like Robert Taylor when I had been Spangler Arlington Brugh for twenty-three years?

"I told Miss Koverman there were already too many Roberts on the lot, Robert Young and Robert Montgomery, but Mayer had already left his office.

"I honestly felt worse than I did the night before . . ."

He strolled down the hall to Kay Mulvey's office. Kay was a bright understanding girl who worked in the publicity department. She listened to Taylor and they talked it over. They came up with the name 'Ramsey.'

They were sure Mayer would go along. Taylor was going to demand they change his first name, but when he returned to Kay's office, he looked more Robert than Ramsey.

33

"Did he turn you down?"

"Hell," Taylor replied, "I waited for him in his outer office for two hours and didn't even get in to see him."

He might have tried again the next day and seen Mayer, who might have liked the sound of Ramsey Taylor. But he accepted the fruitless two-hour wait as a refusal and the subject was never brought up again.

When Taylor was an established star, he read in his hometown newspaper an article about the whys and wherefores of his taking the name of Robert Taylor.

He wrote to the editor:

Dear Earl:

You touched upon a subject which has always been kind of a "touchy" one in my career.

At the time when my name was changed I must confess that I wasn't in much of a position to argue with anyone. Jobs were scarce and I considered myself pretty lucky to be offered one even at the rather meager salary of $35 per week. I held out for the name of Stanhope as long as I could, but it was largely a matter of being out-voted. They had the job I needed . . . and they coulda called me Uncle Fud if they wanted and I'da accepted it! Nonetheless, I agree with you; Stanhope was a nice-sounding name and I wish I could have used it. At least I tried.

As Ever,
Bob

Robert Taylor, following his discussion with L. B. Mayer, found himself stuck with a contract he didn't want and now a name he didn't like, but the bit player stayed on. Seven days a week for six months he worked with dramatic coach Hinsdell learning "not to overact or mug."

For his first picture, Metro loaned him to 20th Century Fox for *Handy Andy* with Will Rogers. The choice was a good one. In any Will Rogers movie it would not have mattered too much if the supporting cast did not

34

show up, but Taylor did. He portrayed the swain of one of Will's daughters, played by Mary Carlisle.

For his second picture he was loaned out, again— this time to Universal for *There's Always Tomorrow* in which Binnie Barnes made her American debut.

In the same year, 1934, Metro finally used him in *Wicked Woman,* starring Jean Parker. It was in this movie that the director *and* his own studio termed him as awkward, stiff and clumsy . . .

He was so ungainly in *Wicked Woman* that Metro decided to use him as a "test horse," an actor who does a day's work playing opposite potential female stars in their screen tests. Sometimes he was on camera, but more often he was a sound-effect man. When Tamara Geva was tested he was the background noise.

In 1935 MGM produced a series of featurettes called *Crime Does Not Pay.* These films were training ground for unknown actors and Taylor "starred" in the first of them, *Buried Loot,* as a bank clerk who embezzles $200,000.

The role called for him to have a scar across his face, and despite this ugly deformity, several letters were received by MGM asking about "the handsome newcomer," and they decided to give him one more chance.

He was sent to San Antonio to play a flying cadet in *West Point of the Air.* The picture had a noteworthy cast—Wallace Beery, Robert Young, Maureen O'Sullivan and Rosalind Russell.

Taylor had one speaking line and his name appeared last on the long list of credits. However, he received a telegram to return to Hollywood immediately. He finished his one-line part in *West Point of the Air* and rushed back to California.

Lucien Hubbard, an astute producer, had seen *Buried Loot* and wanted "the young man with the scar on his face" for the part of *Society Doctor.* Taylor's co-stars were Chester Morris, Virginia Bruce and Billie Burke.

The director, George Seitz, was able to bring something out in Taylor and it was in this picture that he relaxed for the first time.

Chester Morris worked with ease and some of it rubbed off on Taylor.

He attended a sneak preview of the movie and when the lights went up, Mayer obviously was pleased. He said he would go down on his knees to talent, and he walked up the aisle smiling at Robert Taylor.

Clark Gable was seated a few rows in front of Bob, and he turned around with a wink of approval.

The reviews said Robert Taylor, with his strikingly beautiful face, was headed for eventual stardom, and a few more letters trickled in.

In *Times Square Lady* he again worked with Virginia Bruce, and Jean Parker joined him in *Murder in the Fleet,* in which he impressed the ladies wearing a Navy lieutenant's uniform.

Though Taylor's social life was uneventful, he and Virginia Bruce dated quietly. Some said their secret meetings were Bob's idea; some said MGM did not approve. Yet others thought it was because Miss Bruce had been going through divorce proceedings; to make matters worse, she had received kidnap threats regarding her daughter and she preferred to stay as close to the child as possible.

Regardless of why they kept their relationship from the public, except for studio publicity purposes when they had to attend benefits, premières and the like, Virginia Bruce and Robert Taylor *were* involved. She was his first romantic interest.

Though she was the same age as Taylor, Miss Bruce had been an actress for some time and made her screen debut in 1929. She had been married, was a mother and now divorced. Her maturity was far greater than that of Taylor, and the sophistication that only Hollywood can produce was well handled and maintained by the lady.

Insiders said simply it was a "fling" and nothing more.

For the first and last time in his career, Taylor sang in a musical, *Broadway Melody of 1936.* He serenaded "I've Got a Feelin' You're Foolin' " to June Knight, and he danced with Eleanor Powell. Even though he was uncomfortable, the critics said he gave an easy, natural and creditable performance.

Universal Studios agreed and asked if they might borrow him to play opposite Irene Dunne in *Magnificent Obsession*.

Miss Dunne recalls, "I remember sitting with John Stahl, who was to be our director, looking at some film of Robert Taylor. Neither of us knew much about him. I did know John, however, and he was the kind of director, who if he were in heaven, would tell God where to sit, and then complain about the lighting.

"But I like to remember that I told John I thought Taylor would be entirely right for the part of Robert Merrick."

In the movie based on Lloyd C. Douglas' novel, Taylor portrayed a playboy who gradually awakens, through a great love, to a new meaning and purpose in life. He becomes engrossed in the fine ideals and unusual teachings of a famous physician, after the latter is drowned, at the very moment that Merrick himself, having tumbled off the deck of his yacht in a state of drunkenness, was being saved by the only available pulmotor. In time he develops his own latent powers and carries on the profession and the humanitarian message of the great doctor.

It was his performance in *Magnificent Obsession* that lifted Robert Taylor to certain and instant stardom. Almost twenty years later, the same role made Rock Hudson famous in the 1954 remake of this film.

Not only was this movie the professional beginning for Taylor, it was also the beginning of his being called "cute," "pretty," the "It Boy" and "The Darling of the Girls" by the press, which was a burden he would carry for a long time.

Nevertheless, the moviegoers had a different impression of their new "object of adoration and attention" because they had been starving and crying for an idol since Valentino left them without an imaginary lover.

Women admitted they were too busy looking at him to appreciate what role he was playing. The men tried to figure out if he had an imperfection, like a wart on the tip of his nose that the make-up men were cleverly concealing.

Taylor himself was trying to be only one thing—a good actor. He really could not understand what all the fuss was about and would be the first one to admit that he was still a kid who admired Gable's good looks and Tracy's acting.

But on the screen Robert Taylor was different.

Valentino's appeal was to the lower side of woman's nature—slick and dangerous. They had wanted him to kidnap them, beat them and then make violent love to them. Gable's rough and rugged approach was also attractive to the girls. Both Valentino and Gable were considered members of the "new undiscovered sex" that was now a matter of public interest.

Taylor, however, was all-American, innocent and gentle. Women wanted to mother "Pretty Boy." Their dreams of him were clean: their search for male kindness, loyalty, softness and perfection ended in Taylor's image.

He was Norman Rockwell, *Reader's Digest*, a church picnic, white slacks and blazer; while women wanted him, they knew he was above sex but they liked him that way!

He weighed 170 pounds, was twenty-four years old stood almost six feet tall. He had a tiny scar over his left eye and he also had a widow's peak, which was the object of debate:

One reporter wrote, "Robert Taylor had such a squared-off forehead that MGM told him they would have to attempt to shave his hair. He objected but was taken to the barber and they almost had to tie him in the chair. Delicately his hair was plucked out one by one to create a widow's peak."

Critics and reviewers unanimously harked back to *his face*—his talent was beauty and that beauty was his talent.

Taylor told a friend, "This may sound conceited of me to confide, but I'm almost ashamed to tell you about a party I went to recently.

"When I arrived the room seemed to be filled with women and they stared at me as if I were somebody aside from the norm. They made remarks about my looks, but my inferiority complex was sticking out like a severe case of the mumps. I guess by trying to hide this complex, I give the wrong impression—that I'm a snob or I like myself too much.

38

"I never know whether people are trying to encourage me or whether they are laughing at me. Should I behave like a gentleman or be aggressive. I don't know. . . .

"Success is frightening when it happens as fast as it did to me. You say to yourself one day you'll mix with the right people, the big shots, but then you find out they are only interested in you for business reasons.

"They give you advice—how to invest your money, what kind of movies to make, how to dress for a preview, how to zip up your fly—everything but, 'Are you happy?' You see, they think they know the answer because anyone who is rich has to be happy."

Taylor's salary, needless to say, had jumped considerably from $35. He was now earning $750 a week.

Ruth figured it would be a good time to visit old friends in Beatrice and MGM agreed. Although there was a good deal of publicity connected with his returning home a success, Taylor was sincere. In his humble, almost naïve way, he thought things back home would be the same.

Instead, as could be expected, the people in Beatrice put on a big welcome home celebration in his honor, that included a parade, a reception and a banquet.

The Ritz Theatre's marquee read *Magnificent Obsession* starring SPANGLER ARLINGTON BRUGH and Irene Dunne. The manager had bowed to the demands of the township that their most famous citizen be billed properly. No one could get used to "Arly" being called Robert Taylor.

Taylor made a brief speech: "I know this thing might be just a flash in the pan. Don't know, but for some reason my looks caught on, but that can't carry you far. I don't know much about acting—I realize that better than anyone—but I'm going to work hard at it, and before the bloom wears off, maybe I can learn something and make a career out of it.

"If I don't, so what? I'll go back to school and get my medical degree, just like I had planned to do in the first place."

Ruth told her friends in Beatrice she was very proud of her son but she would always think of him as Arlington and was disappointed that she would not see his real name in lights instead of that dreadfully common Robert.

Still a frail woman weighing only 100 pounds, Ruth was changed by Hollywood in several ways. For one, she dyed her hair, saying, "Arly likes it this way."

Mrs. Anderson, Ruth's close friend, said, "Mrs. Brugh was always a delicate, somewhat shrill, unusually pretty woman. Arly had her eyes and mouth exactly. We had not seen her since the doctor died and I hardly knew her. I asked her if Arly had fallen in love with a beautiful movie actress yet and she stared at me for a moment and said that he came straight home from the studio every night and never went out with girls."

The day they left Beatrice, Bob thanked everyone for remembering to use his real name on the theater marquee. Ruth interrupted and said she had made up her mind to live in Nebraska several months every year to be near her "dear, dear friends," but that she would maintain residence in Hollywood: "The climate is so delightful there, you know."

Taylor took an old pal aside and said, "Hey, will you send me the *Beatrice Sun*. I really miss it. It would be great to subscribe to it. Don't forget, OK?" And for the rest of his life he received his hometown newspaper every day—by regular mail.

Chapter III

Reporters were waiting for him when he arrived back in Hollywood. One asked Taylor what he thought was the driving force behind his performance in *Magnificent Obsession*.

His reply was rather like that of a college sophomore: "A screen metamorphosis is more psychology than histrionics. The thing is to analyze the character you are playing and then the various stages of self-development become a logical outgrowth of that individual finding himself."

The reporter looked at Taylor: "Would you mind repeating that?"

"Yea, sure. You see, a screen . . ."

"Never mind, Bob. I was never good at spelling!"

L. B. Mayer called Taylor to his office after the interview hit the press. "Did you actually say that, son?"

"Yes, sir, I did. Anything wrong?"

"Yes, you sounded like your jockstrap was on too tight! For the time being, keep your mouth shut."

Louella Parsons said she thought Taylor was the most promising actor of the day and the progress he had made in one year was unusual.

Magnificent Obsession was thrilling thousands of women in 1936. Even the blind wrote letters to him. "I go to the movies, mostly musicals, of course, but I can appreciate Robert Taylor even though I cannot see him. His voice is musical and deep. He has a symphonic voice."

Bob showed the letter to Ruth, who sighed, "I know. You have assimilated the vibrations of the cello."

Taylor was beginning to find his mother a little depressing. He missed the privacy that he had enjoyed when he was in college and in Hollywood before his father's death. He found his days at the studio tiring enough. Then the reporters were always waiting for him as he left at night. To come home to Ruth, who treated him like a little boy who had just won a beauty contest, was too much. She kept an unusually close eye on him, still calling him Arly or Buddy.

Another change that Ruth underwent since coming to Hollywood was that she was becoming a religious fanatic, a strict Methodist who hated Catholics, Germans and Democrats. Her philosophy was that sex was evil and girls were little devils in disguise. Every time she thought Arly was straying, she used her old tricks and pretended to need him: "I don't feel well. I'm weak. Take me to bed."

There were many times when she even made him sleep with her and keep his hand over her left breast to make sure her heart was still beating.

It was difficult for Bob the day he came home to tell Ruth he was moving into his own house on the outskirts of town. "It's only a short drive from here, Mother, and you know how much I love the country. I can even keep some horses there."

Ruth froze for a moment, then walked very slowly over to the couch and Bob sat down beside her. He'd get her a companion or a nurse, and during the week he'd spend a night or two with her.

"But can't you borrow a horse from the studio on your lunch hour? Besides, animals have an awful odor even if they are kept away from the house!"

Bob stood up, trying to avoid her demanding eyes and said firmly that he had already signed the lease and that was that.

"You can't afford two houses, Arly. We'll end up in the poorhouse!"

As he was leaving he said he would check with a reliable agency about getting someone to stay with her, adding, "And don't worry, Mother, I'll make sure she isn't anyone but a white Protestant."

He moved into a moderate-sized white New England house overlooking the San Fernando Valley, and bought a cocker spaniel that he called Rumba, a tiger cat, several kittens and two riding horses, Garbo and Speed.

There was a garage, barn and corral. A barbeque pit in the backyard was one of the first things he made sure was ready before he moved in.

Though Taylor was always a do-it-yourself person, he hired a man to take care of the place when he wasn't there. Harold had little to do since Taylor took personal care of his horses, loved to do the gardening and was meticulous about his clothes.

The house itself was informal. The large living room overhung the valley; the dining room was done in deep blue and white; the kitchen was a bright yellow; in the back was the sunroom and hidden bar. His bedroom was actually a suite, complete with a large dressing room and bath all done in brown and cream.

The guest room was used by Ruth, for her quilting frame which was too big for her tiny place.

She told him she hoped he would not "get too wild" now that he had his own dwellings: "Keep yourself clean, son."

And that's exactly what Taylor did. After his affair with Virginia Bruce, he did not date. He did, however, frequent the "cat houses" near the MGM lot, as did many of the other male stars.

He joked about these visits during his later life. He intimated that L. B. Mayer had arranged for these women to be available for his famous employees saying, "L. B. probably hand-picked each one and made sure they were clean. I wouldn't doubt if they were studio rejects but I do know one thing—they made more money than I did!"

Though Taylor was still boyish and shy, he was known for being a cocksman. He wasn't known as the great lover in his personal life as yet, but that would come later.

Throughout his life, he was extremely discreet when it came to women. There was no doubt that he "got around," but with whom and when, no one ever knew. He could have had any of the cute little starlets tripping around the lot, but it is doubtful he did his playing that close to home.

His personality was still "prairie style." He lacked sophistication, but was well-liked and though hardly a good actor, he was admired for his punctuality and for always knowing his lines.

Easily influenced, he was impressed with Janet Gaynor, his new co-star in *Small Town Girl*. She always made it a practice of falling in love with her leading men, claiming she gave a better performance that way.

While they were filming she tried to change Taylor's way of dressing, urging him to wear conservative suits. She told him, "Your looks make it unnecessary for you to dress conspicuously."

One day he showed up on the set wearing a banker's gray, double-breasted hard-worsted suit with faint chalk stripes, dark colored tie, cordovan wing-tipped shoes and a gray snap-brim hat. The other members of the cast were a bit more than surprised because they were used to seeing him in odd-colored slacks and sweaters. Rumors about Taylor and Gaynor swept the gossip columns and movie magazines and the MGM publicity department built up a romance between the two.

When the picture was completed, Miss Gaynor followed her usual pattern and immediately fell out of love with her leading man. Taylor went back to sports clothes.

Quite unnoticed on the set of *Small Town Girl* was an attractive young girl who was an extra in the film—Pat Ryan—today known as Mrs. Richard Nixon. She said, "I had an awful crush on Bob Taylor. You might say I had my eye on him. We had quite a laugh when I told him about it thirty years later." [1]

On Taylor's first trip to New York he felt the personal sting of the press. They seemed to have a private war going with him, calling him their "popular headache" at the office as well as at home.

The day after he arrived the New York newspapers waved this bulletin: TAYLOR SAYS HE'S RED-BLOODED.

In case you care, Robert Taylor of the movies has hair on his chest, regards himself as a red-blooded man and

1. Winzola McLendon, "The Nixons Nobody Knows," *McCalls,* May, 1971, p. 116.

resents people calling him beautiful! As he came into Grand Central Station yesterday where hundreds of screaming women were waiting, the curly-haired screen star was asked point blank, "Do you think you are beautiful?"

He smiled and said he thinks people are belittling him when they refer to him as beautiful. Pressed for an answer he said, "Well, I am a red-blooded man and I resent people calling me pretty—and for your information, I'VE GOT HAIR ON MY CHEST!!!!!"

It was a youthful outburst, but the expression "hair on my chest" caught on and was included in every article about Taylor from then on for a long time. The press was dissatisfied with Taylor's answers about his beauty and manliness of his chest.

The whole situation was degrading to him and led to untruths. Men were growling that their women were idolizing a homosexual. They labeled him once and for all "Pretty Boy." They asked their wives, girl friends, sisters, daughters, mistresses and grandmothers what they saw in this male American beauty.

Their replies were, "Just because he's so good-looking." "He would treat me like a princess." "That widow's peak gets me." "He's all American, if you ask me!" "His voice makes my ears tingle."

Taylor, always the gentleman, tried hard to contain his anger. He told of having a persistent dream: "I'm trying to fight somebody and I can't get my arms up. They never hurt me and I never hurt them, so I can't call it a nightmare . . ."

As much as he tried to respect the press, later he was finding it more and more difficult to say anything sensible. He remarked about this period, "I think my innocence was showing."

MGM did much of his talking for him, but there were few places he could hide.

He was driving down Sunset Boulevard one day and stopped for a red light. Someone ran over to his car and said, "Hey, Bob, what is your definition of love?"

"What? Oh, love. Guess admiration and respect."

45

"No sex?"

"The light's changing . . ."

"What about the physical side of love?"

"Oh, that's different!" Taylor stepped on the gas and found himself having been interviewed in the morning paper.

By 1936, Taylor was receiving 3,000 fan letters a week. It had only been two years before that Mayer raised his salary from $35 a week to $50 because Taylor needed a secretary to handle his mail. The years proved that he would have little trouble increasing his wages. As his popularity grew so did his income.

Getting a new contract, which meant more money, was almost unheard of in those days. The only star whose rise was as sensational as Taylor's was Shirley Temple.

The usual procedure was rather simple but discouraging. An unknown actor would usually be put under a seven-year contract with a beginning salary of $50 to $75 a week, with gradual increases to the seventh year when his salary would be $1,500 more or less.

The studio retained the right to drop the player at the termination of certain intervals. The actor, however, had no such privileges. He *had* to stay with a studio until the end of the seven years.

Most of the players did not become a success, but those who did found themselves making thousands for their studio and just a few dollars for themselves.

There were many *stories* about Robert Taylor and Louis B. Mayer and the best was concerning money. It was the one and only time Taylor asked for a raise and his agent said, "See him yourself, Bob. He likes you, but he would surely battle with me."

Mayer listened to Taylor and said, "Sit down, Bob, let me talk to you. You know, God gave me two lovely daughters and they are a great joy to me. But for reasons, in His infinite wisdom, He never saw fit to give me a son.

"But if I had a son, Bob—if He had blessed me with such a wonderful gift—I can't think of anything I would have wanted than that son to be exactly like you.

"And if that son came to me and said, 'Dad, I

am working for a wonderful company, Metro-Goldwyn-Mayer, and for a good man, the head of the company, who has my best interests at heart. But he is not paying me much money, Dad. Do you think I should ask him for a raise?'

"Do you know what I would have said to my son, Bob? I'd say, 'Son, it is a very good company and it will do great things for you. It will make you a star and give you an exceptional career. Why, you'll be famous. Now, that's much more important than a few extra dollars.' Don't ask him for a raise right now, son."

Taylor's agent was waiting for him outside: "Did you get a raise?"

Taylor replied, "No, but I got a father!"

The studio also made another decision for him—far more dramatic than the one about money. . . .

Irene Hervey was a contract player at MGM when she met Robert Taylor. It was love at first sight, but their romance was doomed from the beginning. Although they became engaged to be married, the persisting rumors that Taylor was still involved with Janet Gaynor embarrassed them. MGM continued to print items linking the two stars for months after *Small Town Girl* was released.

One evening Irene and Bob were dining out. Several reporters approached their table and asked Taylor about Miss Gaynor. They ignored Irene completely. Bob laughed it off saying he admired Janet, etc., but that he and Irene were officially engaged. Yet the following day there was no word in the papers of his answer—rather an item about Gaynor and Taylor.

Irene and Bob ignored it, planning marriage, until MGM intervened. It was made clear to Taylor that single and available, he was a good investment; married and possessed, he would not be swooned over by women.

Taylor was crushed. Ruth, of course, was delighted. Irene was depressed. When he accepted the studio's decision, she became more and more critical of Bob. Why didn't he stand up to MGM? Why was he always talking about Nebraska and how—if it hadn't been for Mayer—he would be a soda jerk back in Beatrice? Why didn't he grow up?

After almost two years of waiting for marriage, Irene, too, gave in to the studio's demands. She broke her engagement to Taylor and began seeing the young tenor Allan Jones.

After that, Taylor dated Ginger Rogers, though not seriously, because she and Jimmy Stewart were involved.

Today Irene Hervey recalls: "Bob was a very sensitive young man. I do believe that during the years we shared our beginnings in the motion picture business, his career moved so fast he needed—as everyone does—a good shoulder to cry on, God knows, but whatever, I believe I was that shoulder.

"By the time the studio came through with permission for us to marry, I had about become convinced that he should not marry at that time of his career.

"I had met Allan Jones and I really wanted to be married. So did he."

It took Robert Taylor quite some time to get over Irene. She was his first serious love and it hurt him to see her with Jones even after their marriage. But being a gentleman, he made a point of going out of his way in a night club to go over to their table and say "Hello."

Rather than retaliate and nurse his wounds by dating other women, he stayed by himself or went to parties alone. He had no desire to be involved for a long time . . . until, that is, he met "The Queen."

It was at the old Trocadero in Hollywood late in 1936 when Marion and Zeppo Marx invited Barbara Stanwyck and Robert Taylor to dinner. He arrived right on time and when she came in they sat down. Every time the door opened, she would look around. She seemed to be preoccupied and did little talking.

"Would you like to dance?" he asked.

"No, Zeppo wants me to meet someone—a Mr. Artique."

"Never heard of him. What's his first name?"

"I don't know. The Marxes want me to meet a Mr. Artique."

"Artique . . . Artique . . . that's a peculiar name."

Suddenly it hit Taylor and he yelped like a puppy! "Artique is R.T.—R.T.—don't ya see? That's me!"

Though Barbara was downhearted over her impending

48

divorce from Frank Fay, and Taylor was still carrying a torch for Irene Hervey, one would never have known watching them on the dance floor that night . . .

Private Number opened at Grauman's Chinese Theatre on Hollywood Boulevard. Across the street a couple stood looking up at the marquee.

It was the first time he had received top billing and the first time he had seen his name in lights: ROBERT TAYLOR—LORETTA YOUNG. ("I was terribly impressed!")

Barbara remarked quietly but firmly, "Don't let it go to your head, buster. Loretta has been working for years to get her name up there. You've only been at it a short time. The trick is to keep it up there!"

Taylor said that was the best advice he ever had.

This time MGM reversed its outlook and decided to exploit Taylor's close relationship with a woman. They invited Barbara to co-star with Bob in *His Brother's Wife*. It was obvious to everyone on the set that their love scenes were sincere. Every day they lunched together in her dressing room and he never let her start the day without a basket of flowers.

The critics were favorable. *His Brother's Wife* was good and the romantic lines spoken well, but Taylor was not accepted in his role: "We are either bold enough or cowardly enough to admit that words are of no weight against the enormous popularity of Mr. Taylor. However we have reservations about the star's personification of a lab scientist. He is just not the type to be exposed to heat, fever-bearing ticks and Metro's special effects!"

Mayer said, "Seems to me, Bob, you are just too pretty to be a doctor, too handsome to be a brain surgeon and too delicate to trudge through the jungle and certainly too sweet to be bitten by bugs.

"Keep up the good work!"

Next he assigned "his son" to do *The Gorgeous Hussy* with Joan Crawford, Barbara's closest friend. (The press asked whether the title role was played by Crawford or Taylor.)

Taylor said, "Miss Crawford has driving ambitions unlike any actress I have ever known."

49

Of him she remarked, "Robert Taylor will always remain one of the beautiful people in my life."

They were all close socially also. Miss Crawford was married to Franchot Tone at the time and Saturday nights were devoted to cozy gatherings of the happy foursome.

Bob and Barbara were accepted everywhere as a very close couple, belonging exclusively to each other, but at that time they never discussed marriage or even becoming engaged, for that matter.

Love was excluded from any interviews, Barbara protecting Bob for the sake of MGM and he respecting her position with Frank Fay whom she had yet to divorce. They were seen together often; then suddenly he would appear at a party without her and she somewhere else without him. Sometimes they dated others and the press admitted they were confused.

But the Queen and her Prince remained silent.

Ed Sullivan gave it a go: "You're from Nebraska, Bob?"

"Yes, and someday when I get my hands on enough money I want to go back to the farm."

"And take Barbara with you?"

"We're not planning marriage, Ed. That's all I can tell you. Just between you and me, she's the grandest person I've ever met. She has helped me an awful lot, believe you me. I've always liked the girls, but I wish some of them wouldn't make saps of themselves—or of me!"

"Getting back to Barbara . . . do you think she'd like Nebraska?"

"Don't know, Ed. Why don't you ask her?"

Taylor never did take Barbara Stanwyck to Nebraska. Whether she would have wanted to is unknown, but from all indications, he was not about to at this time.

He had enough instinct even then to know she would not have fitted in. She had always been a city girl and was bored with country living. Small-town folks had little in common with her and vice versa.

She could have easily insulted someone without realizing it. Her outlook was straightforward, and she let it be known. Barbara's vocabulary would also be a problem in

50

the Midwest. Her adjectives were explosive and few could be found in the dictionary.

Although she was careful with Ruth, the two women clashed from the beginning. Both were domineering and possessive, and Bob was in the middle. They told him what to do and how to do it, but in different ways.

If Ruth liked blue sweaters on Bob, Barbara didn't . . . so he tried to avoid blue. Ruth liked her son to use her handmade quilts on his bed; Barbara thought blankets were more masculine. So he used both.

Ruth took advantage of her position as Robert Taylor's mother and gave out interviews at will. She was quoted as saying her son had no intention of getting married until he was well over thirty years old. Further, she made it clear that though her son was not living with her, she was quite content in her little house at 1063 Selby Street; Arly called her every day and often spent the night with her.

Despite the influence that Ruth and Barbara had on Taylor, L. B. Mayer was still the ultimate boss of his career. He had promised "his son" great things and now he was preparing to keep his pledge.

He called Bob into his office and said, "How's your wardrobe, son?"

"Well, I have a couple suits."

Mayer sent him to the best tailor in Hollywood and had him back in his office to inspect them. "Maybe you can't act very well, Bob, but at least you can dress decently."

Taylor also got his first dinner jacket, white tie and tails and even a top hat. The first time he wore the formal clothes was to an Academy Award dinner. He wasn't invited but slipped in when the guards weren't looking.

He said, "I just stood there and watched the stars come in and as I watched, my mouth hung open further and further until you could have stuffed an Oscar in it!"

Actually, Mayer had more in mind than making Taylor *look* like a star. He was casting for one of his greatest films—a classic in the film industry—*Camille*. Greta Garbo had accepted the lead, playing the Lady of the Camillias, but the part of her lover, Armand, had not been filled. They were looking for an actor who was young, innocent and immensely attractive. There were numerous conferences in Mayer's office to discuss *Camille* and who would support Garbo as Armand.

Irving Thalberg suggested Taylor, but the others were opposed. They felt he was too inexperienced to match the quality of Garbo. Thalberg disagreed and pointed out that he was not looking for a superb actor for the romantic role of Armand but rather an established star who was extremely handsome and "peppy"—which Taylor was—and who could portray great love for Garbo, which Taylor could. Thalberg got his choice and Mayer had kept his promise.

Taylor was scared to death!

The Lady of the Camillias was the vehicle that would allow him to reign even stronger on the MGM throne, temporarily take Gable's crown away and conquer not only the heart of a nation, but the world as well.

The year was still 1936 when George Cukor, who was to direct *Camille,* introduced Greta Gusafsson from Sweden to Spangler Arlington Brugh from Nebraska, U.S.A.

"How do you do?" she said without raising her eyes.

Not another word was said and after a painful moment of silence, Bob, slightly embarrassed, walked away in a sweat. He had been prepared for the Garbo treatment, but when he got it, he was hurt.

"She never spoke another word to me after our introduction, except on camera. I gave up trying to guess what was wrong when one day suddenly she started talking to me; then slowly, as Marguerite (Camille) warmed up to Armand in the script, Garbo's attitude toward me off the set changed completely.

"By the time Marguerite fell in love with Armand, Garbo was as friendly and delightful as anyone could possibly be.

"I realized that out of the range of the camera Garbo lived her part just as intently as she did when she was 'on.'

"During the last part of the picture we used to talk for hours, sometimes on the set, sometimes in her dressing room. Between takes once she looked down and saw a small ant hill near her chair. For the next half hour the two of us discussed ant hills in particular and ant life in general."

Garbo never allowed anyone other than the crew on the set when she was filming. Her reason—"It destroys the illusion."

She could spot an outsider even if he were disguised as one of the extras or crew. She would stop a scene and point to the intruder: "Out!" It was an uncanny sense she had.

She didn't believe in giving her autograph. When she became ill during the filming of *Camille*, several people in the cast sent flowers. Her reply cards simply said. "Thanks." No signature.

Taylor said the other members of the MGM *"Stable"* —Crawford, Harlow, Gable, Garland, Shearer, the Barrymores, Rooney—were all pals. No jealousy existed between the male stars and none between the female notables.

Only Garbo was aloof. She would arrive alone in her chauffeured Packard, do her work on the set, then leave alone in her chauffeured Packard.

Everyone was impressed.

Even though, as Taylor said, she warmed up to him during the filming of *Camille,* he was extremely on edge. During rehearsals he paced the floor. He had been told to show up regardless if he was on camera that day or not.

On one of these days he sat watching Garbo and became so tense over a scene he was going to do with her the following day, he wandered off the set onto another soundstage.

He spotted Gladys George, who was doing *Marie Antoinette,* and she noticed his nervousness. "Relax, Bob. C'mon, let's have some fun. Why don't you sneak on our set as an extra?"

He put on a costume and white wig and mingled in with the others ready for the scene to be shot.

The director, Woody Van Dyke, spent almost an hour setting things up, telling everyone where to stand, etc. Finally he shouted, "All extras remain in place. As for you Taylor, get off this set!"

53

Taylor, stunned and blushing, was amazed that he had been discovered among 200 extras.

"Jerk," said Van Dyke, "gentlemen of Marie Antoinette's court did not wear black and white buckskin sports shoes with crepe rubber soles. Wear shoes of the period next time you want to play, little boy!"

Taylor left the studio and stopped off to see Ruth. He told her he was tired of *everything*. MGM should have known better than to have put him in the same movie with Garbo.

"During the first love scene we slipped off the divan and fell on the floor. Can you imagine? She was laughing and I was stumbling all over myself trying to help her up."

The next day he faced the camera again and this time Garbo's dress caught on fire. Smoke emerged everywhere.

Taylor pushed her away, got a bucket of water and poured it on the actress.

There was silence.

Knowing Garbo's temperament, the stage crew waited for lightning to strike. Instead she calmly asked if they could conclude shooting for the day since it would take hours to re-do her hair and prepare another dress.

Taylor said he didn't know what to do when he saw her on fire and followed his first instinct. He was doing a bad job with his role and everyone felt sorry for him.

Barbara tried to calm him down. She said it took guts to play Armand under any circumstances.

He complained that he wasn't allowed in the sun because Garbo wore little make-up and he had to be very pale. He loved the sun and was always in it, playing tennis, falling asleep or swimming, but during *Camille* he had to give up any exposure to the elements.

For the first and last time in his career, his nose, which was slightly pointed to the left, was cosmetically straightened with putty. He hated it, saying he felt like Pinnochio. "The one thing I dislike most about this business is having to take 'womanish care' of myself!"

The re-takes of *Camille* went on and on . . . Garbo continued doing the unexpected. She startled Bob when on one occasion she was supposed to kiss him once, but instead kissed him all over his face. She was the aggressor in her love scenes—reaching first, but *never touching* —just pretending she might.

In a later scene, while Taylor was kissing her, she giggled. Cukor told her politely that she was supposed to show anger, not mirth.

She laughed. "I try to get angry, but he does not give me a chance."

Taylor never knew if she was laughing at him or just diverted for the moment . . .

But the worst was when he almost dropped Garbo during the final death scene. ("I don't know why I was so frightened of her because her acting was as natural as her breathing. She thought with her eyes—they expressed exactly what was needed. I considered working with her my greatest acting lesson, but I confess it didn't teach me anything because what she had was inborn—not method.")

When the picture was finished, they never spoke to each other again!

Alexander Dumas, author of *Camille*, based his novel on the life of Albhonsine du Phesis, a girl with a dresdin china figure and long enameled eyes like a Japanese woman. He created the impression also that she wore scentless camillias because she could not endure the odor of flowers. He wrote the book to pay his debts and called it a "potboiler." Yet it set the pace for his career and had an extraordinary influence on modern literature.

Garbo was nominated for an Oscar, but did not win.

Robert Taylor was re-elected the King of Romance, love-making and Hollywood.

Men were more positive than ever that he was Pretty Boy and women were more positive than ever that he was the man of their dreams.

But one of the best-kept secrets during the filming of *Camille* was Robert Taylor's date with Miss Garbo. It was not for publicity and Bob did not mention it until many years later—which was typical of him. He frustrated his friends by confiding something, yet never giving details and often not finishing what he had started out to tell.

One evening when her name was brought up he casually said to a close buddy, "Yeah, I will always remember the one and only date I had with Greta Garbo. When I arrived at her house there she sat, all dressed up, in the middle of the floor, her long full skirt surrounding her as if she were posing for a picture. When I walked in she made no attempt to get up and though she was aware I was there because her eyes acknowledged my presence, she remained in that position until she had finished meditating."

But you could get nothing more out of Taylor about that evening. Twenty years later he saw her in the MGM commisary and when someone asked why he didn't go over and say "Hello," he replied, "I respect her privacy and would never approach her. Besides, she probably wouldn't remember me anyway . . ."

The reviews of *Camille* were superb. Frank Nugent of *The New York Times* wrote: ". . . Camille is Garbo's best performance. Robert Taylor is surprisingly good as Armand, a bit on the juvenile side at times, perhaps, but certainly not guilty of the traditional sin of the many Armands of the past—callowness."

Other critics acclaimed the movie also—"You could hear a few tear drops in the Capitol Theatre during the exquisite pathetic scene when Camille dies in the arms of her lover. Robert Taylor plays Armand with considerable reserve and modestly steps away from the center of the stage, allowing Miss Garbo to bask in the full glory of the limelight."

Taylor was said to have been wholesome in his role; his final visit to the dying Marguerite (Camille) was hailed with balcony cheers precisely like those that greet the arrival of the United States Cavalry to the settlers besieged by the Indians, except they were uttered by ecstatic females instead of small boys. This, it was said, was a spontaneous tribute to Taylor.

One newsman said he didn't know why so many people spoke ill of the handsome Robert Taylor: "He seemed all right to me."

Their kissing was highly praised: one reporter called it "pretty hot stuff," and there were times the audience thought the screen lovers were going to bite each other.

A famous hairdresser in New York obtained a photo of Garbo's hair-do in *Camille* and had an artist do a

56

sketch of her three feet high showing off the *Camille* coiffeur. To make it look even more authentic, the head of Robert Taylor wearing his costume was placed below the sketch of Garbo. The hairdresser anticipated a rush of Garbo fans. He was sure to do big business with the ladies who were so greatly influenced by Garbo in her performance. They came to his salon, all right, but not because of Garbo's fuzzy, long rope-like curls, but because of Taylor's sleek pompadour.

Taylor hated it all, but MGM would make millions!

Chapter IV

"The Queen," Barbara Stanwyck, was born Ruby Stevens on July 16, 1907, in Brooklyn, New York. Her mother was killed while getting off a streetcar when Ruby was four years old. Her father, a bricklayer, had been working on the Panama Canal for many years, and when she was ten years old she was told he had died at sea returning home.

Exactly when she became an orphan she never knew.

Her older sister, Mildred, became head of the family, but Ruby was sent to live with neighbors, the Cohens, during the remaining years of grammar school.

She remembers they were so full of love that it overcame the stigma of being called an orphan by the other children.

She worked at several odd jobs to bring in a little money, but when the hurdy gurdy man came around to the Brooklyn tenements, she would run with the other children to dance. At sixteen she enrolled in night school to learn stenography and later worked as an operator for the New York Telephone Company in downtown New York.

For a brief spell she worked with Condé Nast Patterns and at Remick Music Company, where she practiced her clerical skills.

Ruby entered show business as a chorus girl in a revue on the Strand Roof in New York. She moved into a cold-water flat with two other girls, all making a pact to "stick together."

Billy LaHiff, who owned The Tavern, a popular restaurant with the theatrical crowd, was unusually generous: he fed young girls who were out of work and unable to pay for their meals. Ruby stopped in one night to take advantage of Billy's hospitality. When she finished her dinner, Billy took her over to Willard Mack's table and introduced her to him.

At the time Mack, playwright and star, who was casting for *The Noose*, a broadway show, offered her a part in it. She said she would accept on one condition—that he hire her two roommates also. He agreed.

They opened in Pittsburgh and the play was a "turkey!" Mack decided to revise the script and do some readjusting in the cast. He gave Ruby a "juicy" part in the third act—that of a girl pleading for her brother's life—but he said, "Ruby Stevens is no name for an actress!"

He glanced over to the wall and noted an old English theatre program listing Jane Stanwyck in *Barbara Frietchi*. Almost immediately he said, "You will now be known as Barbara Stanwyck."

Mack took her to the producer's office to sign a contract. The producer, however, was not keen on an unknown taking on such an important part, although he said later that it was her "tough poignancy" that overwhelmed him.

As she was about to sign the contract, she got as far as "Bar," looked up at Mack and said, "How do you spell Barbara?"

Throughout her lifetime she would use two capital B's in her first name—BarBara.

On opening night in New York she invited her family to attend. Her sister, Mildred, looked at the theatre program and didn't see the name Ruby Stevens listed. She stayed, thinking Ruby had a very small part, probably just a walk-on, but before the last act the Stevens family left. They missed her short but very effective performance at the end of the play.

Ruby had neglected to tell them about her new name.

The Noose was a success and remained in New York. During this time, Barbara was introduced to Frank Fay, one of the most famous personalities in show business. Not only was she excited about meeting Fay, but she was attracted to him as well. After a brief courtship, twenty-one-year-old Barbara Stanwyck married Frank Fay in St. Louis in August, 1928.

It was in the smash hit play *Burlesque* that she became an established stage actress.

Willard Mack had coached her while she studied, practiced and worked. Along with Fay's help and encouragement, she became a polished performer.

Fay, who billed himself "Broadway's Favorite Son," took his wife to Hollywood where he had several offers to do films. Barbara took a screen test at Warner Brothers without result, but Fay spoke to Harry Cohn at Columbia, offering to pay her salary and expenses, if they would give her a break. She spent hours at the zoo watching the panthers so that she could learn to walk like them.

She appeared in *Mexicali Rose,* a low-budget film, but Fay again helped her get another role in Frank Capra's *Ladies of Leisure* for Columbia, which convinced the studio to put her under contract.

One critic said, "Her accent is unattractive and her acting stilted," but in *Ten Cents a Dance,* released in 1931, the critics were unanimous. They agreed her talent was worthy and she sued Columbia for more money. The matter was settled when the studio allowed Warner Brothers, who wanted her, to share her contract.

With Adolphe Menjou in *Forbidden* she was acclaimed as "great," and this movie put her over the top, professionally and financially.

Frank Fay, however, was on the decline. He drank heavily and gave up his brief career in the movies. He decided to produce a musical revue, *Tattle Tales,* and Barbara declined to appear in several scheduled pictures to be part of her husband's new stage show. They went on the road heading eastward, but when the play opened at the Broadhurst in New York, it was a flop.

One review said: "It was hardly worthwhile. The show was sluggish, which suggested that very likely Mr. Fay's and Miss Stanwyck's collective effort was that way a little, too."

After the play closed, they returned to Hollywood and adopted a son, Dion. Barbara was very much in demand then and she picked up where she had left off. The Fays moved into a lavish Brentwood Heights estate in Los Angeles, but neither the child nor the luxurious way of life that Barbara was now able to afford, could make up for Fay's behavior.

He had made his wife a star but in the process destroyed himself.

Their neighbors remember that at least once a week the police were called to the Fay home. Their violent quarrels sounded as if there were more than two people involved, but the smashing of dishes, breaking windows, screaming, doors slamming and cars screeching off into the night were the results of bitter arguments between Barbara and Frank alone.

There were many separations and it was Barbara who usually begged her husband to return. She wrote letters to him: "No need to tell you that I felt blue when you left. I can't stand your being unhappy in any way at all. Whatever you want to do I am with you 100 per cent only I do not want you to sacrifice yourself in any way. I can live any place or go anywhere with you.

"I love you just as much as it is possible for a woman to love a man. If I was born with anything fine in me, and I choose to think I was, from what I know of my mother and father, you have brought that fineness to the surface.

"I cannot imagine life without you and I am not being melodramatic.

"I probably do not give you that impression at any time—that of not being able to imagine life without you, I mean. However that is due to my lack of education and not being able to express myself clearly in speech.

"I can write it, however. You are always right about everything so you must be right about what you want to do. Only, please, Frank, love me—whatever you do. And wherever you go, take me. For there I shall be content."

In another letter dated November 17, 1934, she wrote to him on his birthday: "Dear Kid: I haven't any grand present to give you this year, no diamonds, no watch, no nothing!

"I feel rather funny not sending you anything, but it just has to be.

"And so, Frank, all I have to give you today is my prayers that all will go well with you. And whatever you do shall be right, and that God will keep your path well-lighted so that you will never hurt yourself. God bless you and spare you. Barbara.[2]

In August, 1935, she left Frank, but this time it was the end of their marriage. She gave him possession of their house and did not take with her the choice antique pieces and the silver she had been collecting.

She and Dion moved into a ranch in the valley outside of Los Angeles. They had 140 acres to themselves and stables nearby where she bred racehorses in partnership with Zeppo Marx. The grounds were called Mar-Wyck (Marx and Stanwyck).

Early in 1936 she filed for divorce and was awarded custody of Dion. One of her complaints 'was that there were "too many women who were attracted to Fay and he enjoyed it too much."

When she left the courtroom she told reporters, "I hated to have to do this, but it seems the only salvation for both of us. Frank is better off alone and so am I. I want our divorce to be free of bitterness."

Unfortunately, there were many battles to follow . . .

The five-foot-five-inch, auburn-haired Barbara Stanwyck had blue eyes and weighed 115 pounds. She was four years older than Robert Taylor, and they had little in common.

When they met, he was still a kid, while Barbara had never really been a child. He was a top box-office attraction, but lacked the well-developed genuine talent she had. Taylor was well-educated, Barbara was not. He was soft, she was hard. He was and always would be a country boy—she could only breathe in the city. He liked the femininity of frilly blouses, soft colors and flouncy skirts. She liked tailored clothes—suits, sports outfits and slacks made out of men's materials. He liked to treat a woman like a lady. She lit her own cigarettes and fixed her own chair. He was discreet, she was brutally frank, and made remarks about herself before anyone else could get around to it.

He loved to hunt. She thought it was cruel. He loved guns. She was terrified of them. He loved dogs, but she was allergic to them. She allowed her son to have one,

2. *New York Herald Tribune*, January 12, 1938.

but when the dog was in the house, she sat on a step-ladder.

He was the master in bed, but inexperienced and an unsophisticated lover. She had been around.

Though Taylor could hold his liquor, he didn't care for it. Barbara was a good drinker and liked to put her feet up on the table, chatting in her characteristic New York accent.

Then what, if anything, did either see in each other? Barbara Stanwyck was the motherly type despite her masculine traits, and Taylor needed to be mothered, to be told what to do and how to do it. Everyone who knew them both at that time agreed.

And there were similarities. They drank gallons of coffee, both were chain smokers, *and* both were on the rebound.

They disliked night clubs and parties in general, though they were obliged to put up with them because of publicity. Taylor once said, "When I walk into a crowded room, sometimes I say 'Hell,' turn around and find someplace quiet where I can drink lots of coffee." Then, of course, he was very shy and did not like small talk.

Barbara had never forgotten that early in her career she had been rudely snubbed at several Hollywood parties and now that she was a star, could afford to snub them back.

Taylor had always remained himself, never really changing despite his fame and money.

Barbara was once asked what "going Hollywood" meant and she said, "It should mean working your head off, but in the popular sense it means going to the right places with the right people."

Neither did.

"I envy Barbara more than any other person in the world!" Taylor once remarked. "I wish I were one-tenth the person she is. She rarely shows her emotions. She has been through so much, and she is so grateful for everything life has given her.

"She considers it a weakness to give way to every mood.

"If going through things gives one Barbara's tolerance and appreciation, I wish it could have happened to me.

"I am very awed at what has happened to her. She practically brought herself up.

"Why, one night we took a drive to the beach and just sat there in silence. Barbara was crying and I had never seen her show any emotion before."

Barbara always gave Bob the spotlight. Ironically it was a privilege to be seen with Barbara Stanwyck, but she purposely remained in the background. When they were mobbed by fans, she stepped back, letting him sign autographs and say a few words in the microphone. One time she stepped too far back, became one of the crowd and was almost trampled to death. Taylor looked over his shoulder and yelled for one of the policemen to help her. They had been assigned, however, to guard Taylor, and when he saw her being pushed to the pavement, he grabbed an officer and screamed, "You get her out of there or I'll kill you!"

She came out of it bruised and frightened. For a few minutes she sat on the curb trying to pull herself together.

No one recognized her.

Barbara was undoubtedly the stronger one, yet like a parent, she gave into Bob's whims.

Afraid of height and excessive speed, she allowed herself to be talked into a roller coaster one night. "He always had to be someplace in the sky. The highest he could get then was on a roller coaster. I hated it! I hated it! My stomach is still up there. I never told him that because I was in love with him—so I went along."

Taylor, in later life, said, "There were two traits I admired in Barbara and Garbo. Barbara turned off anyone who crossed her just once. Garbo demanded her privacy and got it. I was too young to understand how they 'stuck to their guns' and never relented."

These two characteristics, however, were to be the keystone of his character when he matured . . .

In 1936, before the release of *Camille*, Taylor wanted to get away from Hollywood for awhile and was given a few weeks off. He took a boat to Hawaii alone. When he arrived the pier was filled with tourists and he panicked. Having no protection, he had to fare for himself, and tried to disappear in the crowd, leaving the boat.

He found himself in the middle of herds of people. They pulled his hair, grabbed for souvenirs (buttons, handkerchiefs and the like) and no one came to his aid. The few policemen who tried to help were unable to get through the mob.

Taylor tried to pacify the crowd by promising to sign autographs and pose for pictures, and asked them to give him some breathing room. There was so much noise and confusion, his voice could not be heard. Women fainted and pushed each other into the street.

An attractive woman—very determined—elbowed her way into the mess and yelled loud enough for Taylor to hear, "I'm a reporter. Can I help?"

This was probably the only time Taylor was glad to see a member of the press. She tugged at his sleeve. "Do you want me to get you out of this?"

"Please, for God's sake, yes!"

"My paper wants a story and I'm going to get it."

"Just get me out of here."

"Will you give me that story?"

"Yes . . ."

"When?"

"Just get me out of here!"

"I want that story now—not tomorrow."

"Lady, do something. Damn, I'll give you the best story you've ever written!"

"Is that a promise?"

"Do you want an obituary? Lady, this is the worst mess I've been in. Yes, I promise, but hurry."

The determined small girl reporter grabbed his arm and literally yanked him through the crushing stampede to her car and shoved him in.

Within seconds she was on her way with Robert Taylor beside her.

They drove to a remote beach and she said, "Stay right here!"

He sat for fifteen minutes looking out at the ocean wishing he were homeward bound.

When she returned she had a basketful of food and a bathing suit for him. They went swimming, had lunch and talked.

Taylor said he didn't have the feeling he was talking

to a reporter. "After spending time with her she was a woman—simple as that—and I enjoyed her company.

"I guess she got her story, don't know. We stayed on the beach long after dark and later she drove me to a small hotel.

"I really think she forgot I was Robert Taylor. Because of her I would have stayed in Honolulu as planned. She could have 'made' my vacation, but after that scene at the pier, I knew it would be impossible."

The next day he took the same boat home to California.

The public had awaited with great anticipation the release of *Camille* mainly because of Garbo. But Robert Taylor was voted the number-one popular male star in 1936 . . . and was also considered the "prettiest" face on the screen.

A woman reporter asked him for an interview, saying she was going to call her article "Has Robert Taylor Changed?"

"She had written a story about me over a year ago and she wanted to compare notes—yesterday and today. When she realized I hadn't changed, I guess she was disturbed that she didn't have a story after all.

"She had made up her mind that I *was* different and I had made up my mind to prove to her that I wasn't.

"Then she got on the subject of Garbo. What did I think of her and all that hogwash. I said I didn't want to talk about Garbo. No one talks about Garbo.

"The woman accused me of hating Garbo. When I told her I had no reason to hate her, she accused me of being in love with her! The interview ended with this dame telling me whom I liked and whom I disliked; how I had changed from an easy-going guy to a 'tough' interview-type.

"Well, at least it was nice to know what and who I am . . ."

Whatever was written about him did not alter what his fans thought. Letters were pouring in at 30,000 a month and he was drawing a salary of $2,500 a week.

Gordon Kahn, Hollywood staff reporter for the New York *Daily Mirror,* met with Taylor for lunch. Kahn did not know what to expect as he waited for him to arrive

66

at the restaurant. He glanced at the menu thinking, "Wonder what Pretty Boy will order? Breast of guinea-chicken Virginie, *sous cloche?* or perhaps an *omelette au confiture* with a pint of Chateau Yquem?

"Hell, no. He sat down and said he wanted a steak as thick as the Bronx telephone book and a tall glass of ice water. On the side he had a huge order of potatoes and the biggest batch of succotash I've ever seen!

"I offered him some hors d'oeuvres—caviar—and he said he never liked the stuff. Then he asked, 'What the heck is that thing?' I said it was the heart of artichoke. He prodded it with a fork and said—'I don't think I'm going to like that either.' He ate a piece—nope! He didn't like it!

"He told me he had tasted his first glass of champagne a few weeks ago and innocently commented that 'it wasn't too bad.'

"He ate every bit of the meal and then he admitted he was a bit nervous when he first saw me waiting for him, but after his second harvest helping of succotash, he felt at ease.

"In between gulps he said he was going to get away for a few days to go fishing with Spencer Tracy . . . but this time he would tell the studio brass where he was going."

"When I was doing *Camille* I 'ducked out' of Hollywood and Mayer really bawled me out," Taylor admitted.

"Where did you go?" quizzed Kahn, who was watching Bob attack more succotash.

"I called the airport and asked them if there were any planes going anywhere that day. They wanted to know where I wanted to go and I told them I'd go anywhere the plane went.

"They reeled off a list of places and the sound of Salt Lake City hit me just right. I took my stand-in along. Anyway, we rented an old Ford—terrible piece of junk, with every useless thing hanging on it. That's why we liked it.

"We drove until we came to a ranch and we stopped, made friends with the farmer and his wife. When they finally recognized me, instead of hysteria, we all sat

67

back on the front porch and talked about anything but Hollywood—politics, gangsters, so forth. After a few hours we flew back to Hollywood. Nice place, Salt Lake . . ."

"What happened when you got home?"

"Yipes! Barbara was frantic. She had been driving all over town looking for me. Mayer thought I had been kidnapped or something! The make-up men were terrified I had been exposed to the sun and all in all, it was a mess. Whatever pleasure I got that day in the country was ruined." [3]

Kahn said he thought, after talking to Taylor, that the kid would be happier on a farm in Nebraska.

Talking to the current Heart Throb of the Nation was like talking to your next door neighbor. He was so simple, yet so puzzling.

Barbara felt sorry for Bob, and though she never guided him with his career, she was in there pitching for him. He had complete and utter faith in her.

She had been chosen for the lead in *Stella Dallas* through the efforts of Joel McCrea, a friend of Taylor's.

McCrea, also a graduate of Pomona, had met Taylor in the men's room at the Coconut Grove. Bob came up to him with a letter of introduction and said, "This is a terrible place to do it, but I'm scared of all those big stars you're sitting with."

McCrea was dining with Marion Davies, Norma Shearer and Mary Pickford that night. He said, "Not long after that meeting, Bob was a bigger star than me." (Forty years later when McCrea came out of retirement, he said he particularly remembered Robert Taylor above all of his contemporaries.)

But in 1936 he was working at Paramount with Barbara and he told her that Goldwyn was going to do *Stella Dallas*. When she heard about it, Barbara said she would give anything to get the part.

He went to Goldwyn, but though she was given a screen test, she had three strikes against her: Goldwyn didn't think she could handle the part because she was too young and inexperienced with children.

3. Gordon Kahn, *New York Daily Mirror*, 1936.

However, when he saw the results of the birthday scene in *Stella Dallas* that Anne Shirley did with Barbara —taking all day to do it rather than the usual few hours—he gave her the part.

With this role, she got her first Oscar nomination and when she lost to Luise Rainer (*The Good Earth*), she said it was the only time such a failure hurt: "I really poured my blood into it."

Barbara let few things get her down, which was another attraction she had for Taylor. Though always doing something to rid herself of her nervous energy, she appeared relaxed and composed on the surface.

She could balance Bob's personality, laughing at his disappointments, urging him on, yet putting him in his place when he displayed any sign of being impressed by his increasing rise to stardom.

She had never worn jewelry, except for a fourteen-carat diamond that Fay had given her during their marriage. Bob did not like anything ostentatious but he loved to give her simple expensive pins and rings, so that for the first time in her life, she wore jewelry and loved it.

Barbara also began wearing clothes that were more feminine and became quite a collector of frilly negligées which Bob loved. She let her hair grow and wore high heels rather than the drab walking shoes she liked previously.

Taylor was impressed with Barbara's determination and will-power. He compared her to Ruth, who had built her life on weakness, dependence and bigotry.

Barbara was now Bob's confidante, and his relationship with her was upsetting Ruth, but she knew she had one very important person on her side—L. B. Mayer. MGM would not allow Bob to marry, but she did not realize that Barbara's influence over her son had become a substitute for her own sheltering and dominance.

"The Queen" was guiding Taylor in the ways of love, humor, sex and human nature. Taylor's classic understatement to the press was that "Miss Stanwyck is not the sort of woman I would have met in Nebraska."

As usual, the reporters had a circus with another Taylor quote, and to this one they added, "That's for sure!" Barbara Stanwyck taught Robert Taylor everything she knew . . .

Though actresses both here and abroad were asking to be cast opposite the "It Boy," MGM was in a quandary as to what to do with him next. They worried about the type of publicity he was getting. His being called "beautiful," "dainty," "cute," and a "sissy" could only lead to one conclusion—he was not a man. The press had convinced the male public that Taylor was "queer," and his heavily powdered complexion on the screen only confirmed their beliefs.

Mayer did not know how long the moviegoers would accept this "virgin idol" nonsense, though its effect was making his studio millions of dollars. He had a plan, but not now. *Camille* was a victory and would tranquilize his fans for the time being.

MGM's greatest worry of the day was Jean Harlow. Mayer knew she was seriously ill and he feared it might show up on the screen. When he signed her for *Personal Property,* a giddy comedy, he also assigned Taylor as her leading man—for box-office insurance.

When the movie was released the studio sent Jean and Bob to Washington to attend President Roosevelt's Birthday Ball for the March of Dimes.

Though they both had a touch of the flu, they managed twenty-two appearances in one day. They had lunch at the White House with Mrs. Roosevelt, who said the President didn't mind taking second billing to Taylor during the star's visit to Washington.

"In fact," she said, "he admitted romantic appeal is more persuasive than statesmanship. He likes the movies and is a big fan. He told me they do the world just as much good as any politician in the long run."

On the night of the President's Ball, Jean and Bob were told they had to attend still another function in Baltimore. J. Edgar Hoover accompanied them in a bullet-proof limousine escorted by roaring motorcycles proudly handled by state troopers.

On one personal appearance, Taylor was making his way to the stage when a woman ripped his tie off, tearing it into bits, distributing it to her friends.

It was an exhausting whirlwind trip.

70

When they returned to Hollywood, Jean Harlow made what was to be her last movie, *Saratoga Trunk,* with Clark Gable. She died just before the picture was completed.

Bob said Jean looked like the shadow of death in Washington, but he had no idea the end would come so soon. "I don't know why everyone made such a monster of Jean Harlow. She was a kind and amusing child."

Personal Property was not a good movie, but the Harlow-Taylor billing made it a hit. Mayer's fear about Taylor's image was beginning to grow. Several fan letters were brought to his attention and he knew he would have to execute his plan very soon:

To whom it may concern at MGM:
Why not give the Bob Taylor fans a break? Now, for instance, in that scene in *Personal Property,* where the thrilling heart throb of millions of American Women sat serenely in the bath tub! Just think of how much nicer it would have been if Bob could have been taking a shower with that handsome head thrust out of the top of the curtains and his shapely (I hope) legs peeking at us from underneath?
I held my breath hoping he would show his legs at sometime or other, but he did not. I would like to know just why we are deprived of seeing those two very important features. Maybe it is for the best, though, as they might not be so perfect as he, and I will never admire a man with bowed legs.
I lost interest in Warren Williams after seeing him running around in a pair of shorts and maybe it would be that way with Bob! I will continue to see all the Taylor pictures hoping some day to see him in trunks!

Another letter came from a gentleman who said he was one of the "sufferers from Taylor-itis":

Dear Robert Taylor:
Who controls your publicity? Why so much emphasis on

romance? Every picture we see of you shows Barbara Stanwyck. The rest show you in the company of prominent people—Hollywood and otherwise. We know they are trying to build you up into the great "luvver," but it is tiresome to see nothing but Bob and Barbara hitting the high-spots. Why don't they get married?

In other words, we are getting tired of this Bob and girl hooey. Loosen up! Let a few pictures at least show Robert Taylor as he is, not Taylor, the ladies' man. Prove to us you are a real guy and that there is something in your life besides dames. We know there is, so why not let us know about it?

Mayer told his staff to keep Taylor's fan mail from him for the time being. "He wants two things—a solid manly role and to marry Stanwyck, but he can't have either right now. Arrange a meeting with Twentieth Century immediately!"

He arranged for Taylor to co-star with Barbara Stanwyck in *This Is My Affair,* a sensational title considering the circumstances. The public was anxious to see the two unmarried lovers having "an affair" on the screen, but they were disappointed. It was far from a romantic movie, rather the story about a government undercover agent (Taylor) who tries to crush a wave of bank robberies in the Middle West during Theodore Roosevelt's Presidency.

One critic wrote, "It is impossible to disguise Mr. Taylor, even though he assumes a hero's stature and has a 'reservation' in Arlington Cemetery. Mr. Taylor is still Mr. Taylor.

"He did, however, make love to Miss Stanwyck persuasively."

Like mosquitoes on a hot summer night, the buggy reporters bit into their "Crown Prince of Charm" constantly:

"Mr. Taylor, do *you* think you are beautiful?"

"Really," he said, gritting his teeth, "do you expect a man to answer a question like that?"

"What would you prefer to be then, 'Mr. Taylor?"

"Just Robert Taylor, a guy with a job in the movies!"

72

"Mr. Taylor, what about . . ."

"Ask me anything except about Miss Stanwyck and about the hair on my chest!"

"C'mon, Bob, are you beautiful?"

"Can't you understand I object to people making remarks like that? It's sarcastic. If you said I was a lousy actor, I'd feel better."

"Mr. Taylor, why is it you never take a vacation?"

"Hell, why should I? I like my work."

Ruth read the interview and told her son it was no sin to be beautiful so why not admit to it? But he calmly explained to her that those reporters were trying to pick a fight, to get him mad enough to say things he'd be sorry for. "Besides, a man is considered handsome, not beautiful. . . ."

Ruth mentioned Valentino and how he had *used* his good looks. Everyone adored him because he acted as if he were proud of his face.

"I'm no Valentino!" But she disagreed saying that he, Robert Taylor, was better looking and it was about time he began to realize it. Then she asked him why he didn't hold a press conference about the Barbara Stanwyck nonsense.

"I'm not allowed to hold press conferences, Mother."

"Then ask that nice Mr. Mayer to meet with the reporters *with* you and let *him* do all the talking. He'll tell them once and for all you are not going to marry *anyone* right now."

"That nice Mr. Mayer would give me a good swift kick in the ass if I asked him to do such a thing . . ."

Ruth scolded him about using vulgar language in a God-fearing house, and asked what had happened to his excellent vocabulary. "Hind-end would have been more appropriate!"

Taylor did go to Mayer, however. It would be impossible for him to take much more abuse from the press. Would MGM *please* try to eliminate any publicity that made him a laughingstock?

"We'll do our best, Bob. Now you know damn well I wouldn't do anything to hurt you. Why, I've spent thousands of dollars to make you a star. I won't let you down now. Be patient."

"Yes, sir . . . I'll try. . . ."
"I think you'll do better than that, am I right?"
"Yes, sir!"
     Headlines—Oklahoma City, August, 1937

BOB TAYLOR'S KISS NO THRILL TO HER
Robert Taylor sleeps with his mouth open and snores!
Ruth Robinson, a reporter on orders from her city editor, kissed the actor on a flight to Kansas City—"This
hurts me worse than it does you," she told Taylor. He
yelped, dodged and tried to escape when Miss Robinson
leaped into his lap.
She also kissed him as he slept. That, however, was before his mouth dropped open and began to snore! [4]

Taylor flipped! His rage turned into depression. He was
disappointed in Mayer. Miss Robinson was only *one* reporter and from Oklahoma City, no less. Yet her story
appeared in every major newspaper in the country.
"Things are getting a little tough when a guy can't fall
asleep on an airplane without being attacked!"
Mayer laughed and explained that his publicity department could not control the press entirely. He reminded
Bob that with or without MGM, he was still a popular
Hollywood star, and if his publicity crew did not release
another word about him, he would still be written up
almost everyday in some newspaper.
Taylor always described Mayer as fatherly, kind, protective and above all, understanding. "Some said he was
cruel. Don't know, but he surely knew how to handle me,
and most important he knew my abilities better than I
did and assigned me to the level of my talent."
He put Taylor in *Broadway Melody* of 1938 (released
in 1937) with Eleanor Powell, Buddy Ebsen, Judy Garland and George Murphy, and immediately followed up
with *Lest We Forget,* a Will Rogers Memorial.
Then Mayer kept his promise. His timing was just in
time.

4. Ruth Robinson, *Oklahoma City News,* August 19, 1937.

MGM announced that Robert Taylor was through with tender roles and he was going to prove himself without "any dames around."

They scheduled him for *A Yank at Oxford,* to be filmed in England.

Chapter V

Taylor's second trip to New York on his way to Europe was a mass of confusion. Multitudes of women, camped out with food, blankets and small valises, greeted him at Grand Central Station. As they waited for his arrival on the curbs surrounding the terminal, their vigil was known as The Robert Taylor Picnic.

As he tried to make his way to his hotel from the station, women and children leaped on his car. One young boy got his foot caught between the spare tire and the bumper. Taylor looked around and saw the boy being dragged down the street, begging for help.

Taylor stopped the car and with the aid of the driver, they got the boy free. He wasn't injured and after Taylor looked him over, he yelled, "You damn kids! And I thought those girls were nuts. I don't know whether to worry about idiots like you getting hurt or worry about myself getting killed!

"It's not worth it, fella—not just to see me . . ."

It took him over an hour to get through the lobby of his hotel and up to his suite. He had lost his tie, as usual, but this time he had no buttons on his suit, was minus his pockets and one sleeve was hanging by a thread.

A young energetic Chinese girl climbed thirty-eight flights of stairs to his room, but when she was spotted the police grabbed her by the arm to escort her out of the hotel. Taylor intervened and invited her into his room for tea.

Taylor's being in New York caused many disturbances and he was lucky to go to the bathroom without someone peeking. In fact his fans actually did wait in the men's room if he was anywhere nearby and before he was able to relieve himself police had to search the washrooms.

76

Wherever he went the taxi or limousine had to drive up on the sidewalk and park as close to the entrance as possible. One time 1,000 fans were waiting for him at Loew's State Theatre Building, and though he had only two feet to walk to the door, he was hoisted in the air until the police rescued him. When he left he was told the crowd had doubled and he would have to leave via the fire escape. Some fans had taken off his shoes. "And if you think it's easy going down a fire escape without any shoes on, you're nuts!"

In the same building where he was doing a series of radio shows he was trapped on the seventeenth floor because of the crowds of people in the street. He took one look out of the window and said, "God damn, what I need is a parachute!" Instead it was decided that he walk down the seventeen floors and escape through the service entrance.

He started down the steps but found them lined with women and was obliged to sign autographs as he made his way down the seventeen flights of stairs. ("It was then I was convinced I wasn't safe anywhere—20,000 feet in the air on a plane or seventeen flights above the street. . . .")

Girls sat outside his hotel with sandwiches and knitting needles, but the worst event of the few days he had in New York was when he was leaving his hotel. From nowhere a mob of women appeared and came at him like a bunch of cannibals!

He was helpless. They tore off his clothes and he ran back into the elevator with his shorts, undershirt and socks. How they managed to get his shoes was always a mystery to him.

The day he sailed for England he found two young girls under the bed in his stateroom. Twelve women fainted and the departure of the *Berengaria* was delayed for over an hour.

"PUBLIC HEART THROB SAILS TODAY"
"DOZEN GIRLS COLLAPSE AS TAYLOR SAILS"
"TWO BRONX GIRLS

One weary Hollywood correspondent was glad to see Taylor out of the country. "Now I can take a vacation," he said. "I'm going to paste a large picture of Robert Taylor on the side of my car, drive out into the country and when someone says, 'Who's he?', that's where I'm stopping."

The news of Taylor's arrival preceded him when an English newspaper had a girl telephone Taylor from their office "ship-to-shore."

Sitting by her side was a prominent Harley Street physician who took her temperature, pulse rate and blood count and found them all normal. But immediately after her conversation with Bob, the doctor discovered that all three had risen! A complete chart of the girl's reaction was published in the paper.

Though the majority of people who mobbed Taylor consisted of fans who truly wanted to get a glimpse of him, MGM could certainly take the blame or credit for the "excess."

They had built up Robert Taylor as the greatest romantic hero of the thirties and his popularity as "Pretty Boy" had gotten out of hand. They had a top star who had practically been turned into a freak!

However, now they were attempting to accomplish a difficult transformation. They were out to prove that Robert Taylor *was* a man, and *A Yank at Oxford* was their method of succeeding.

He had been heckled and insulted, adored and praised, but MGM was getting the public steamed up for a bigger and more startling campaign. The enormous budget they were allotted to spend on Taylor's trip to England was well worth it—they were paid back a thousand times over.

They preceded him on his trip to England and it didn't take too much advance publicity to create another stampede there.

When the *Berengaria* docked in Southampton, 3,000 people were on hand to greet the ship. By the time Taylor was to disembark, the Bobbies estimated 5,000 had gathered to welcome him and he had to be smuggled out in a "goods lift." He settled down in the Claridge Hotel.

A crowd gathered outside and they caught a glimpse of him standing on his balcony. Casually he flicked a cigarette butt to the ground below and the mad scramble for it injured several people.

Taylor wasn't in Hollywood, but the cigarette butt incident made a jolly bit of news in London's morning press releases.

Even the Queen said it was a trifle quiet around Buckingham Palace. Taylor's "Queen" was in California, and one of the first things he did was call her. He said he thought the English people were wonderful, even the reporters, and he "prayed to MGM and God"—in that order—that they would remain that way.

From London he asked Barbara to marry him regardless of the consequences, but she prudently said they should wait. She agreed that six months was a long time to be apart, but she suggested he concentrate on doing the one film that would relieve him once and for all of the abuse he was suffering.

A Yank at Oxford was not only an experiment with Robert Taylor's new image, but also the first American movie to be filmed in Metro's new studio in Denham, England. Motion picture executives from all Hollywood studios followed with interest the new developments, for this would be the beginning of American actors and actresses going abroad to face the camera.

Bob moved to the little village of High Wycombe. He loved the fog and rain, hoping to see snow before he completed the picture.

He became so accustomed to tea at four that it was he who was the first to clamor for his hot brew. It amazed everyone on the set since he was noted for his extreme fondness for coffee.

He loved England and England loved Robert Taylor, and for many years after, he was remembered there. They respected him for coming in the first place, for no other American movie star had crossed the Atlantic to do a movie in their country.

Lionel Barrymore and Vivien Leigh supported Taylor. During the filming of *A Yank at Oxford,* he said, "I've always been a nice guy in pictures and I'm glad to be a louse at last!" As Lee Sheridan, a young, conceited, cocky, loud-mouthed American lad, completely oblivious to Oxford tradition, he proved himself as an athlete.

To prepare himself for the rigors of the cold weather and the outdoor racing scenes, Taylor started each day with a cold bath filled with ice. The river work, in fact, turned out to be an endurance contest between him and the hired professional crew to see who could stick it out the longest.

As Lee Sheridan he surprised his fellow students by excelling at track and rowing in the bump races, but as Robert Taylor he shocked every male from Texas to Tibet—for he had fine legs, solid arms and *hair on his chest!*

Paris was one of the first to announce the "hairy news." They published a picture of Taylor in athletic trunks and shirt. Underneath his photo, dated August 28, 1937, they printed, *"Mon Dieu Quel Homme!"* "My God, what a man!"

The American Press announced ROBERT TAYLOR BARES CHEST TO PROVE HE-NESS!

A man's chest became the topic of the day everywhere!

Hollywood was especially concerned and the news of other actors and their chests spread about town.

Errol Flynn, Tyrone Power, Charles Boyer, Andy Devine and even Buck Jones had little to offer in the way of hair on their chests. However, Gary Cooper, Joel McCrea, David Niven, Randolph Scott, Fred MacMurray, Clark Gable, Dick Powell and Edward G. Robinson were ready to match hairy chests any day.

Cary Grant needed a magnifying glass, and Douglas Fairbanks actually had to shave his chest for a movie.

Doctors wrote in medical journals (picked up by movie magazines and other periodicals) that the amount of hair on a man's chest had nothing to do with masculinity. Lou Gehrig, Iron Man of Baseball, did not have one hair to show, yet Roland Young had enough on his chest to share with a dozen men.

A "chest toupée" show opened in Hollywood to take care of those men who were afraid Robert Taylor's exposure would embarrass them, especially since men's bathing suits were passé and trunks were the style!

The colossal amount of publicity affected Taylor very little. He was relieved that the advance notices about *A Yank at Oxford* proved that he was as rugged as the next man. Most of all, he wanted Barbara to join him in England.

They called each other almost every day, and he never failed to ask her to take the next ship leaving for Europe. But when she met with the press in New York on her return from Canada, she said, "No, I am not going to England to see Bob. He told me yesterday that the weather was not good and the filming was being delayed because of rain and he might not be home for Christmas.

"We have no plans for marriage and I have no intention of visiting Bob in Europe. Can you imagine what would happen if I went? It's bad enough here alone with you reporters. We wouldn't have a moment's peace!"

She went on to say if it continued to rain in England—and it really rains in England!—their six-month separation might be extended: "Our transatlantic telephone conversations will have to do for now. Guess you think it's silly talking about the weather, but at the moment our seeing each other depends on it . . ."

During the time production of *A Yank at Oxford* was halted due to weather, Taylor spoke to Barbara again about getting married. In fact, he begged her.

She confessed she was lonely, too, but her obligations to her son and to her career came first. Bob hung up "in a huff" several times.

In motherly fashion, she confided to a friend that Bob was still growing up and perhaps shouldn't be tied down. She said she wanted Bob to experience fame and fortune. "Then he will have a better sense of values and will be capable of judging what is best for him."

It is doubtful that MGM would have allowed Taylor to go through with the marriage at this time anyway, and though Barbara's remarks about Bob's being too inexperienced with life made sense, she was wise enough to know that Mayer would change Bob's mind.

81

She was more career-minded than Taylor and knew what marriage would do to his image. Like Irene Hervey she realized the importance of Bob's remaining single, but unlike Irene Hervey, Barbara was willing to wait. She simply had to make Bob think it was she who was not ready and take the blame instead of MGM or his popularity standing.

Taylor, bored with the delays because of bad weather, asked MGM for a private plane—with no advance publicity—to take him to Amsterdam for a few days.

The plane circled the field several times and finally landed. By the time he caught sight of the gate, he saw hundreds of women waiting for him.

They broke through the police cordon and tied up traffic for hours.

"I couldn't figure out how they knew I was coming. This same thing happened time and again—everywhere I flew somewhere in Europe. Sightseeing was impossible and once I told the pilot to turn around and go back to London.

"I spoke to the publicity men and they said they had not wired ahead or given out any releases about my traveling.

"They were right. But I was flaunting my own arrival.

"I discovered that on the belly of the plane was a huge picture of the MGM lion and my name in bold letters. The pilot confessed he had been told to fly over each city two or three times before attempting a landing.

"By the time I reached the ground the whole city was at the airport! I never did get to see Europe!"

On December 14, 1937, Taylor returned to New York on the *Queen Mary*. The ship pulled into New York harbor early in the morning. A few fans were there, but the press outnumbered them.

He granted a brief interview in his stateroom before leaving the ship, looking relaxed in a dressing robe and smiling throughout the conference.

"Did the great crowds in England bother you, Mr. Taylor?"

"There weren't any great crowds. Just little ones."

"One of our wire services said 5,000 people came to see you off."

82

"Just saw a few."

"How did the reporters treat you, Bob?"

"Polite! They didn't grab you on 'the street or interrupt you while you were eating dinner. *And* they weren't allowed on the set."

"Well . . . you're back in the United States now, Mr. Taylor."

"Yeah, and don't think I don't remember reading your releases about my trip to England and how I was 'through' in the movies. You boys buried me! Maybe I was dying a slow death, but you coulda given me one last chance."

"You mean *A Yank at Oxford?*"

"Hopefully, yes."

"What do you think is more important, Bob—brains or beauty?"

"Why don't you boys answer that one yourself! Thanks for coming out so early . . ."

As the reporters left Taylor's room they saw Lionel Barrymore, who had also made the crossing on the *Queen Mary.* They asked him about his drinking and what his opinion of Robert Taylor was. "I haven't had a drink in a long time. And it's not Bob's fault he's so damn handsome. Good day, gentlemen!"

The reporters who were allowed on board ship were a chosen few. They had been carefully selected by the MGM publicity staff on hand to escort Taylor back to Los Angeles. While they waited to get some pictures of Taylor disembarking, one of them commented, "I think Bob is still a little bewildered by what has happened to him and inclined to be a bit sheepish over his designation as the male American Beauty."

Newsmen were unusually conscious of Robert Taylor at this particular time to see whether his new image on the screen had any effect on him personally. They knew he wanted to be himself with them, but were also aware of the fact that he was probably still naïve enough to believe that what the press said or thought about him could affect his popularity and career. One reporter wrote that "Taylor didn't know what to do with his hands. Gable was the same way except he had a good reason. They were unattractive and he knew it, but Taylor didn't know whether to stand at attention, keep his hands in his pockets, which he had been told NOT to do, wave them in the air when he was trying to make a point during an interview, or use them for a better purpose—to shove newsmen aside."

And on this cloudy morning in December, the press waited to see if Pretty Boy had matured. The MGM publicity men waited also and wondered if their fair-haired boy would be able to handle himself on this most important day, without their intervening. One of them suggested they get Taylor off the ship quickly—no interviews—but it was decided to let him handle the press himself. "Just keep your eyes and ears alert when those other meatheads get ahold of him . . . God!"

Taylor came down the gangplank in a hurry, but was laughing at something Barrymore was saying. The two said good-bye and Barrymore was helped into a waiting car and drove off.

Bob saw his friends from the studio and briskly walked in their direction when a dozen or more members of the Fourth Estate crowded around him, cameras in action.

"Hey, Bob, do you *still* think you are beautiful?"

"I resent that question." Taylor still smiling.

"Who was the hairdresser who created your widow's peak?"

"It runs in the family!"

"How does it feel to be more beautiful than Garbo?"

"For God's sake, that's ridiculous and I've said it a hundred times, how can you compare me to Garbo or any other woman, for that matter? If we *have* to continue this, let's get off the subject of my face *and my chest!*—and I know God damn well you'll get around to that! Why the hell don't you ask me how the voyage home was—or about *Yank at Oxford?*" Taylor was *not* smiling now.

"OK, Bob, when do you plan to get married?"

"I don't know . . . GooooooooD DAMN! Someone's trying to take off my shoe!"

"It wasn't your shoe we wanted, Bob—just a picture of the hair on your legs!"

"That's enough, *damn it to hell*—I have a train to catch!"

Though Taylor did not swear in public often, his favorite expression was God damn—he used it all the time.

On the train ride back to Hollywood, however, he said to a friend in the MGM publicity department that for six months he had been calm and relaxed in England, even with the reporters there. Then in less than ten minutes back on U.S. soil, he had lost whatever tranquility he thought would remain with him when he returned home. He said in England "everyone does whatever they want to do but they don't go around talking about it," which was the way he wanted to live.

"I shave twice a day because I *have* to. I don't wear my mother's dresses when she's not at home. I ride a horse better than Gary Cooper, and shoot straighter than Randolph Scott.

"I like to get laid and can screw better than Errol Flynn!"

Then he thought for a minute: "Trouble is I can't act as good as Spencer Tracy or drink as much as Bogart. . . ."

The publicity man looked at Taylor seriously: "First of all, Bob, I don't think anyone will argue with you about your skills with guns, horses and even women, but you yourself said what you did in bed was no one's business . . . Flynn is just the kind of guy who likes to flaunt it. You don't care for booze, so forget Bogart. As for Tracy, he just happens to have been born an actor—simple as that. You weren't—simple as that. But you *were* born with an unusually handsome face and a helluva good voice, and I think the public recognizes more than that in you . . . they sense realism and truth, and something that is fine, touchable and believable. These qualities may not make you number one, but they will always keep you in demand . . . so, stop downgrading yourself!"

On the day when Taylor left New York, one newspaper came out in defense of him with an article written by a woman reporter

THE PRESS AND MR. TAYLOR

Our sympathies go out to Mr. Robert Taylor, the young personable motion-picture actor, for being forced again to submit to the severe questionings, not to say heckling, on whether he regards himself as beautiful. Some months ago when he arrived here from Hollywood on his way to England to make a picture, he was asked questions several times by our enterprising journalists. Today upon his return from England he was forced to undergo a similar ordeal. One of the reporters, seeking to explain this phenomenon, said that apparently men did not like Mr. Taylor and ascribed this unfortunate state of affairs to the fact that Mr. Taylor is so good looking.

This is so much bosh! New York has some of the handsomest journalists to be found anywhere in the world and there is no reason why they should be jealous of Mr. Taylor's looks. Perhaps the reason is to be found in the shifting of news values in this country.

It used to be big news when Stanley found Livingstone, when a crown Prince was born, or when a great economic or political upheaval shook the world. Apparently we are now past all that.

Today's news is whether Mr. Taylor thinks he is beautiful and just how he feels, if at all, about Barbara Stanwyck!

When Taylor arrived in Hollywood Mayer told him he had seen the rushes on *A Yank at Oxford* and remarked, "Now you are a man, Bob." He said he would publicize the movie to the hilt and from then on not to worry about concentrating on being the lover anymore.

"Nothing happens overnight, son, but you'll see a change—not only in your fans, but in yourself."

Taylor was satisfied with the results of *A Yank at Oxford* and knew Mayer would keep his promise.

What he wanted now more than anything was to see Barbara, who was waiting for him at her ranch.

Again he asked her to marry him and again she said they had to wait. But she agreed to a secret engagement. He gave her a good luck charm engraved: "Luck to you from Lucky Me."

Barbara told him that while he was away Frank Fay had obtained a court order to compel her to let him see their son, Dion, and that Taylor was mentioned as a consort. "It's going to be messy," she confided. "But I'll fight him all the way."

86

The court battle went on for weeks. On December 29, 1937, Barbara went on the stand to deny Fay's allegations that she would not allow him to see their adopted five-year-old son, Dion, for sixteen months so that the child "would become accustomed only to Robert Taylor."

She said Fay was not in his right mind—that he had once struck her when she went to a burlesque show and also he had felled her with a "wallop to the jaw." On another occasion while on a drunken spree, he threw the boy into their swimming pool.

Fay's attorney, Philip Stein, asked her, "Isn't the reason you are barring Mr. Fay from visiting the child because you want the boy to become accustomed to someone else—say Robert Taylor, for instance?"

Stiffening in the witness chair, Miss Stanwyck answered, "No."

"Wasn't it a fact that you were having Mr. Taylor to your house frequently so that the child would forget Fay?"

"Mr. Taylor was at the house frequently, but it was not so the boy would forget Fay."

"Did not Mr. Taylor give the boy gifts on numerous occasions?"

"Yes."

Stein asked her about a check for $50 that had apparently been made out to the child and signed by Taylor. The judge, however, made him withdraw the question.

There was no objection. Stein said he was trying to show that a deliberate attempt was being made to alienate this boy's affections from his foster father.

The judge sustained the objection and said, "I don't care how many times Mr. Taylor came to her house. This is her personal life and has nothing to do with this proceeding!"

On January 10, 1938, Barbara went back on the stand and said she demanded a psychiatric examination for Frank Fay. She portrayed him as a man who mingled prayers wtih profanity. She submitted ten affidavits in her attempt to show Fay to be of "unsound mind."

She told of his peculiar habits. "When he passed a

87

church, Frank would remove his hands from the wheel and pray, endangering the lives of others."

He cried "Amen," "Lord Help us" and "Have mercy on us" while he was reading the newspapers.

He got into fist fights with the late Ted Healy, but had to stop to look for his false teeth when Healy knocked them out!

Once at the Trocadero, Miss Stanwyck said, Fay accused her of drinking too much champagne and knocked her down. "I'd only had one glass of champagne," she told the judge.

"He is an unfit guardian for the child. He drinks too much. Why, he even fell into Dion's crib once and fell asleep, keeping the boy awake with his snoring. As far as I'm concerned he loves his new store teeth more than his son."

She was asked whether it was true that she owned fifty race horses and Barbara gave an affirmative answer.

"Is it true that you spent most of Christmas Day at the races instead of at home with your child?" was the next question.

Barbara lowered her head and nodded.

Two days later came the headlines—TAYLOR CITED: FIGHT IS LOST BY STANWYCK. "Robert Taylor's name was dragged into the Frank Fay-Barbara Stanwyck custody fight today when attorneys for Fay attempted to cast the Number One Heart Throb of the Screen in the role of a villain in the Santa Claus suit."

The judge ruled in favor of Fay who would be allowed to visit his son twice a week and on alternating Saturdays, provided he was completely sober and always in the company of the child's nurse, Nellie Banner, who would report his conduct to Miss Stanwyck.

Barbara commented as she was leaving court that her ex-husband was an all-the-time-drunk and told her lawyers to appeal.

To add to her problems, she was suspended by her studio for refusing to take a part assigned to her in a forthcoming picture.

Before Taylor had left for England he bought property next to Barbara's in Northridge located in the far corner of the San Fernando Valley fifteen miles from the MGM studios. He built a house and stables within walking distance of the Mar-Wyck ranch. Movie magazines printed stories about Bob's running over to Barbara's for a swim in her pool, or Barbara hopping over to Bob's to borrow something and usually ending their articles with "Why don't they just live together?"

Bob raised quarter horses because they felt solid under the saddle while Barbara continued to breed thoroughbreds. They were seen riding together at all hours, though she was not known for her ability on horseback.

While he was in England, Barbara completed the decoration and furnishing of Bob's place and when he returned to California it was finished. They spent most of their evenings on one another's ranch . . . putting them in the same category as Clark Gable and Carole Lombard, Paulette Goddard and Charlie Chaplin, as well as other un-married couples who lived next door to each other, shared each other's family, food and lawn mowers.

Taylor's three years before the camera and especially his experience with the press sent him deeper into a quest for privacy. Now his "acquaintance" with Barbara made him withdraw even more. MGM no longer felt he needed to be seen so much in public and slowly they allowed him to live his own life. Their strategy to make S. Arlington Brugh into the famous one and only Robert Taylor was one of the most expensive and biggest publicity campaigns known to Hollywood.

The audiences who viewed *A Yank at Oxford* admitted they had been wrong, though many said it was not his screen characterization as the spunky Lee Sheridan that proved his virility—rather his remarkable restraint in the face of biting and unjustified criticism and his all-around ability to take punishment from the crowd without wavering or turning a hair that proved conclusively that everybody was wrong.

But WAS it so wrong to bring happiness to old maids and plain ugly ducklings who get their romance by way of the silver screen with its Clark Gables and Robert Taylors?

Women upheld the fact that seeing a handsome man on the screen satisfies that secret desire of theirs to be loved by someone the whole world admires—not just an ordinary sort of man who takes a shine to them. Any pug can pick a fight and become involved in a brawl, but not every man can be the personification of woman's dreams.

When Taylor went to New York to promote *A Yank at Oxford,* there was little confusion. He slipped in quietly and remained in seclusion—except for one night when he attended a Broadway show.

He managed to get to his seat without being seen but just before the lights went down, a teenager spotted him and within ten minutes—while the play was beginning—there could be heard a constant buzzing in the audience. People were pointing, standing up on their seats and girls were screaming from the balcony.

This continued throughout the first act. During intermission he sat with the program in front of his face. People filed by him like a funeral procession.

Apparently the whole thing annoyed him so much, he opened the theatre program, leaned back in his seat, put the pages over his face, hat on top and fell asleep!

He missed the second act.

Who woke him up, no one knows. The theatre emptied out ever so slowly, girls trying to get a peek but afraid to move the theatre program or his hat.

A mob waited for him to leave, but apparently he slipped out—and not by the stage door.

Several teenagers spent the night outside thinking he would sleep undisturbed until breakfast-time.

After doing several radio programs, he returned to Hollywood to do *Three Comrades* with Robert Young, Franchot Tone and Margaret Sullivan—the story of three young veterans in post-war Germany.

Miss Sullivan did not show up for work for six days claiming she never started a picture until it rained, because of an old superstition.

The script was changed at the last minute to make the locale of *Three Comrades* undefined, but unfortunately Franchot Tone had already had his hair cropped German-style. Young and Taylor escaped the clippers.

The film was acclaimed "splendid." "Robert Taylor,"

critics said, "had never been happier in a role for which he was obviously not suited."

Taylor disliked *Three Comrades:* "I'd like to forget it!" He never explained why, but one thing is sure: He was a staunch patriot and though the theme of the movie did not specify that the three comrades were Germans, anyone who saw the picture assumed they were and Hitler was not exactly Taylor's idea of what democracy stood for.

He was scheduled at once for *The Crowd Roars,* to play the ethical boxer, Killer McCoy. The public was still getting used to Taylor's rowing and running at Oxford, then his seriousness and forcefulness in *Three Comrades,* but now they were going to see him as a tough boxer who used rough language and rarely combed his hair.

He was put into the hands of the studio's physical director to obtain the "solid effect" and had a gym set up in his house.

Actually Taylor had been working out for years. When he started his career in movies, he was thinner, but MGM went out to prove that their wonder boy had developed remarkably:

1935		1938
5'11"	Height	5'11½"
37"	Chest	43"
29½"	Waist	30"
37½"	Hips	37"
20"	Thighs	23"
13½"	Calf	15"
12"	Biceps	14¾"
10¾"	Forearm	12"
6½"	Wrists	7"
14"	Neck	16"

"That's a hell of a thing to read over your morning coffee," Taylor told Mayer.

"Better your measurements than mine!" came the reply.

The Crowd Roars was acclaimed as one of the greatest prize fight pictures made to date. "Mr. Taylor plays the pug seriously and with a good deal more command than he has mustered in the past." "As a human hero, he takes his place with Gable among the screen greats. Everything MGM had hoped to accomplish with Taylor has been more than achieved in this story and from now on there will be no stopping him with male as well as female audiences."

Shortly after the film was released he had lunch with Max Baer.

"You oughta see Bob punch an air-bag," Baer said. "He's better at it than most professionals. Why, if he didn't have so much going in the movies—I mean so much interest there—he'd make a darn good fighter."

Baer was eating a dainty chicken salad and ruggedly attired in a white silk shirt, open at the neck, with a vivid bandana knotted around his big neck.

Taylor, in contrast, wore a brown tweed suit and brown tie. He was tearing into six slices of bacon with eggs.

While being interviewed the two said they had been friends for three years and often sparred together. Baer held up his two broken thumbs for a laugh. Taylor had only one, but not as twisted as Baer's—"Broke it during rehearsal . . ."

As they were leaving the restaurant, Taylor was asked about *The Crowd Roars:*

"Bob, was that *your* hair on your chest?"

"It was my own."

"Did you wear a wig?"

"The hair on my head was mine, too . . ."

"How come it was so long?"

"It grows just like yours does . . ."

"What about your chest . . . was . . .?"

"Yeah, that was mine, too . . . Goooood damn!"

Ruth didn't like her son mussed up and walked out of the theatre when she went to see the movie. She thought it was disgusting and told him so. "You could have gotten hurt, son."

Bob quietly explained to her how movies were made and that most of the punches were faked. She wanted to

92

know why a stand-in wasn't used, just in case, and he said there was no need for one and preferred doing all his stunts himself, but assured her the studio would not let him take any chances. "Anyhow, Mother, people better get used to the idea that I am not going to trip daintily into a room, kiss a lady's fingertips, hand her a rose and speak softly into her ear."

Ruth was stunned. How could the public appreciate his "lovely profile" that was so very perfect, especially when he was doing a love scene, if he bounced around in a boxing ring? Furthermore, if she did not *have* to go to a prayer meeting that night, she would call Mr. Mayer and rush to the studio for a long talk with him. Did he know what his studio was doing to her son? And if so, why?

Bob was silent for a moment. He knew Ruth was genuinely concerned and didn't know quite how to go about putting her mind at ease.

His next movie was *Stand Up and Fight*. The title alone made her gasp. "O, dear God, dear God . . ."

Taylor put his hands gently on her shoulders—"Please don't worry about the name of the movie—it sounds awful, that's all. It has nothing to do with boxing. I'm gonna play the part of a guy who just wants to build a railroad. Mr. Mayer picked me, Mother, and he knows exactly what he's doing. Anyway, so far he's kept us out of the poorhouse . . ." And he laughed.

So did Ruth.

Wallace Beery teamed up with Taylor in *Stand Up and Fight* and it was Taylor who was seen with blood streaming down his classic face.

The picture was good, but the best thing that came out of it was a lasting friendship between Taylor and Wallace Beery.

Ruth was right about the type of pictures her son was making. He was getting acclaim because the public enjoyed seeing him roughed up rather than appreciating his acting ability.

Yet, throughout his long career with MGM he never turned down a role offered to him. He took what they gave him without protest.

Barbara, on the other hand, was an independent,

93

rarely under exclusive contract to any studio. She picked her pictures carefully and though not temperamental, she did her fighting beforehand. If the script could not be changed to her liking, she refused to do the movie.

At this time, friends wondered why she did not influence Bob in his career. They felt she could have talked him into or out of anything.

She claimed she was too busy with her own professional problems to worry about his. If he wished to be MGM's property, she had no right stepping in. But she had no intention of being owned by any studio, and she had the spunk to handle it. Bob did not.

Chapter VI

In February, 1939, during the production of *Lucky Night,* with Myrna Loy, Barbara and Bob announced their formal engagement. Louella Parsons predicted it two months earlier when Bob gave his "secret fiancée" a diamond and ruby bracelet for Christmas. He also included a St. Christopher medal (The Saint of Travel) engraved "God Protect Her Because I Love Her."

They put both ranches up for sale, but otherwise did not discuss marriage.

Clark Gable told Bob, "Baby, betcha Carole [Lombard] and I beatcha to the preacher!"

Taylor took the bet but even *he* did not know when MGM would give him permission. He had been seeing Barbara for three years and there was no doubt in his mind that he truly loved her, but unlike his frantic begging in 1937, he wasn't terribly anxious to go through with it now.

He felt very much alone on his trip to England and he knew that *A Yank at Oxford* was his last chance: his career was gliding nicely at last and he wasn't afraid any more.

But Barbara had done many favors for him and through her he had learned something about sophistication and what life was all about. He would be the first one to admit he had a long way to go, but she definitely had helped put him on the right path.

In fact, she had done more for him than his own mother ever could. When he *really* needed Ruth she was too engrossed in the spotlight and excitement of being Robert Taylor's mother to speak to him logically.

MGM was using reverse psychology. Taylor had been seen with the same woman for a long time and though never spelled out, it was taken for granted he and Barbara were "living together"—an unaccepted and naughty arrangement in 1939.

The cameras were rolling on Robert Taylor and Hedy Lamarr in *Lady of the Tropics* when Mayer stopped production for twenty-four hours.

MGM had made arrangements for a wedding and on May 13th, Barbara and Bob eloped.

They drove to San Diego to the home of Mr. and Mrs. Thomas Whelan. Joining them were Mr. and Mrs. Zeppo Marx; Ida Koverman, L. B. Mayer's secretary; Buck Mack, Barbara's godfather; and Dale Frantz, a friend.

The wedding party had a buffet supper and after midnight, to avoid being married on the unlucky thirteenth day, the ceremony began in a room filled with roses.

Barbara was dressed in a new blue silk dress and borrowed hat from her hairdresser, Holly Barnes, whom Barbara had stood up for the day before. Buck Mack gave the bride away.

She was very calm and spoke distinctly.

Taylor, in a brown business suit, was visibly shaken and he mumbled.

Judge Phil Smith was so nervous he cleared his throat several times and by the end of the ceremony he could hardly talk.

The bride's wedding ring was a slender gold band circled with rubies which matched the bracelet Bob had given her for Christmas.

At 2:00 P.M. that day the Taylors met the press at a reception at the Victor Hugo Café in Beverly Hills. Joel McCrea was the first to telephone congratulations and William Holden sent a telegram—GOSH, WHAT A BLOW! and signed it "Golden Boy."

The Taylors said they had taken out their marriage license three days earlier under their real names, Ruby Stevens, age thirty-one, and Spangler Arlington Brugh, age twenty-seven. They admitted that at the time they did not know exactly when or where the marriage would take place.

Taylor confessed years later that when MGM eventually gave in to his getting married, they masterminded the whole affair and he wasn't sure what was happening. "I wasn't even sure I was in love . . . The only thing I

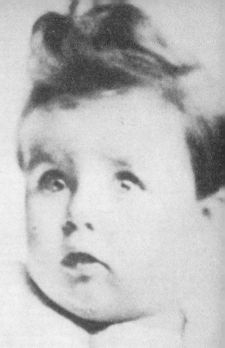

Ruth, Arlington and Andrew — the Brugh family.
The large picture was taken in 1914

Spangler Arlington Brugh. Pomona
College graduation yearbook, 1933

The young hopeful

A scene from Taylor's first movie, *Handy Andy*, with Mary Carlisle, 1934

Irene Hervey and Taylor dining out in 1935 during their engagement

MGM

Society Doctor (1935), with Chester Morris and Virginia Bruce, made Taylor a star

The perfect Taylor profile — and that of Irene Dunne, in *Magnificent Obsession*
UNIVERSAL PICTURES

was allowed to say about the whole thing was 'I do.' "

The *Daily News* wrote, "The Number One Heart Throb of the movies eloped with Barbara Stanwyck leaving the set of *Lady of the Tropics* and the beautiful Hedy Lamarr. There, there, girls, bear up and try not to take it too hard. You know it was ordained by fate."

The unwritten consensus of the press and the feelings of those who were close to the newlyweds were that it was Barbara Stanwyck who married Robert Taylor— not the other way around.

Their wedding took place less than a month after Clark Gable and Carole Lombard cracked the ice for the little group of Hollywood stars whose long and close relationships recently caused a fan magazine to describe them as "unmarried husbands and wives."

After the press reception, Barbara returned to her ranch, and Bob went to see Ruth, who was hysterical, sobbing quietly but constantly. She had called the doctor, who said if she continued to refuse food he might have to put her in the hospital. He gave her a sedative, but when Bob walked in the door she covered her face with her hands and wept.

They talked—finally—but the word "wedding" was not mentioned: rather, they referred to it as "it."

Bob knew he would find Ruth depressed and ill. He assured her nothing would change and tried to joke about it. "Gosh, Mother, you know when I'm working sometimes I get so tired I don't feel like driving all the way out to the ranch. I'll stay here often!"

They had coffee, but Ruth complained that she truly felt sick and very weak. She'd get some rest but, "Will you check my heartbeat every so often during the night . . . just to make sure?"

The following morning he was back on the set with Hedy Lamarr, going through another wedding in *Lady of the Tropics,* and Barbara returned to the filming of *Golden Boy* with William Holden.

With both ranches still up for sale, the Taylors settled down at his place temporarily with Dion Fay who adored his stepfather and referred to him always as "Gentleman Bob."

Lady of the Tropics was Hedy Lamarr's great accomplishment. Critics said, "She is more beautiful than Robert Taylor—if you can believe that!"

Remember?, a light comedy with Greer Garson, followed, and Taylor labored at it. With this film came a decided change in him—restlessness, quiet displeasure, lonely valiantness, gallant hopefulness.

The film was *so* bad that the Hollywood press said, "It may have been the very desolation of *Remember?* when it was released that began appealing to our sense of fair play. We have it if you dig down deep enough!

"Whatever it was, we know you could feel Hollywood's mood toward Robert Taylor changing from that day on. What lies in the future for him, none of us can prophesy, but it does seem that he has taken too much punishment."

Mayer agreed with the press. He told Bob, "You're in a slump, boy, but it happens to every top star. Spencer Tracy couldn't get a job when we put him under contract. Some said he was finished and not a God damn soul thought he was any good. Twentieth Century Fox fired him because he refused to do a film, and I didn't want him because he had been arrested for drunkenness and resisting arrest in Arizona.

"Hell, nobody wanted Spence. He was a trouble-maker like Berry, but Thalberg thought he knew what to do with him. I sure didn't!

"So, there's your great idol, son. If it can happen to Spence, it can happen to you. Have I ever failed you?"

"Nope!"

After a brief honeymoon with Barbara at the Bucks County, Pennsylvania, home of playwright Moss Hart, Taylor made his next movie, *Flight Command,* with Walter Pidgeon and Ruth Hussey. He took the part of a cocky Navy Ensign and became so involved with his role as a flier, that in 1940 he decided to take flying lessons.

Barbara was terrified of airplanes, but Taylor spent every minute of his spare time in the air with instructor Max Constant. This new hobby was the beginning of many disagreements between Bob and Barbara. She felt he was already spending too much time fishing with Spencer Tracy or at the Hunt Club with Clark Gable.

She was afraid of guns and was upset every time Bob handled one. Now it was airplanes: "He's not happy on the ground anymore." But no matter how much he pleaded with her to fly with him, she cringed at the very thought.

When they moved into a house at 400 St. Cloud Street in Bel Air, an exclusive area in Los Angeles, Bob felt very much "fenced in." He had not sold his ranch in the valley and kept his horses there, but it wasn't the same. He enjoyed riding at will in the country.

The Taylors' home was rented to them furnished by Coleen Morris' mother, and though this was a temporary arrangement, it did not please Bob. He preferred having his own belongings, furniture, gun rack and kitchen designed to his liking.

Barbara was delighted to be back in town. Her career was flourishing and she was among Hollywood's top ten money-makers in the 40's. Such movies as *The Lady Eve, Meet John Doe* and *Ball of Fire* were all Oscar material and she was nominated again for the latter, in which she played a flashy night club singer. However, she lost again, to Joan Fontaine in *Suspicion.*

Taylor's career was sporadic, and at long last he spoke out about what was happening to him. "I've kept my mouth shut because there was nothing I could do. I hoped that *A Yank at Oxford* would solve my problems and that the tempest would blow over, but when I returned from England, the reporters were there poking their camera at every part of my body.

"My impulse was to poke someone in the nose.

"I think I would have pulled out of *that* all right if my pictures hadn't started going to pot. I did what the studio wanted, but I can only blame myself for *Lucky Night.* I picked that one myself and it was a flop!

"Several times I snuck out to the studio and got them to run off *Magnificent Obsession* for me. I sat watching the picture that I had made in 1936 trying to figure out what I had then that I'd lost.

"What baffled me was that it had been an instinctive piece of acting when I didn't know any better. I'd sit there in the darkness, getting myself all pepped up and then the picture would end and—boom!—down I'd go again!"

He emphasized that Barbara had been loyal to him in so many different ways during this period. She knew Hollywood. He did not. There was no explaining why, she said, one gives a polished performance in one picture and yet with a good script is rotten in the next. Bob's problem was that his career was never on an even keel— rather very good or very bad. Actors, if they are lucky, go along doing "well" and the critics say "good performance" about anything they do, but Taylor was just not destined to follow this pattern.

Bob concluded his statement: "After Barbara and I were married and settled down on the ranch, I'd go walking around the place—God damn happy to be so lucky to just be living there—stop by a flower patch and do a little gardening or exercise the horses. Then I'd be back at the studio—mentally, that is, and I'd go crazy trying to figure out my future . . . if any . . ."

Taylor's form of courage was "survival"—at least that is what *he* called it and Barbara agreed. He was taking a beating, but he had survived the initial attack in the Pretty Boy Era, the continued newspaper bombardments that went on for years, and then radio commentators' poisonous bits. But now he would somehow have to survive the lemons that bore his name on marquees, all coming without any time for one decent breath of fresh air.

When Barbara managed a few days off, she liked to curl up with a good book or script. Bob felt obligated to stay home with her, staring at his fishing equipment and guns.

"He made me so nervous," she said. "If he couldn't use his rifles, he was cleaning them. I thought I'd go crazy watching him aiming those things at every dish in my china cabinet so I 'shooed him out of town to Wyoming to try them out. It was self-protection!"

Yet it was she who added a pair of superb hunting rifles to his collection.

When Taylor wasn't up in an airplane or courting the forests and streams, he was at the typewriter jotting notes to himself—or he was in the kitchen. It was his favorite room in the house. He always knew what was going on "in there" and loved to cook. He made the meals for himself and Barbara when the cook was off and bought every cookbook, foreign and domestic, that he came across. He could not resist kitchen gadgets. If it had been invented, he had it!

Barbara was good at opening cans.

Some of Bob's friends suggested that he and Barbara do a movie together. When they were single, *His Brother's Wife* and *This Is My Affair* were both very good and the audiences and critics agreed they liked them together on the screen. But Bob said he didn't think the public would pay to see a married couple make love to each other in a picture. "Barbara's a wonderful actress though, and she coaches me for all my pictures. You know something? She's the only actress I ever heard of who learns all of the script before they start shooting. She just learns it like a play so on the set if they want to add or change a line, she is able to tell them whether it will fit in with the rest of the story."

Taylor admitted he always had an inward fear of not knowing his lines, but rarely did he forget one word of dialogue. He gave Barbara credit for that, even though at everything he did, he was a perfectionist.

"When I was just about convinced I had been forgotten, MGM handed me the script of *Waterloo Bridge*," Taylor said. "It was an actor's dream and the role fitted me better than a pair of custom-made shoes!"

The movie was a cinematization of Robert E. Sherwood's play, the bitter-sweet story of a British soldier who falls in love with a ballerina. He is reported killed in action, and his sweetheart, who has lost her job and is desperate for money in war-torn London, turns to prostitution.

When her lover returns, she feels unfit for his love and rather than reveal her past to him, she throws herself in front of a truck on Waterloo Bridge, where they had met for the first time.

Today the film stands out as one of the greats. It was this movie that made "Auld Lang Syne" a love song, and no two people looked better on a dance floor than Vivien

Leigh in a white flowing chiffon gown, and Robert Taylor in his British dress uniform.

Perhaps it was the opening scene: Taylor standing in a heavy London fog on the bridge looking down over the Thames, reflecting his dead love—his hair sprinkled with gray—that told the audiences this was the Taylor they had been waiting for—the Taylor he was—Taylor, the actor, the man, the professional.

Since it was the custom of all English officers during the First World War to wear a mustache, he was required to wear one—the mustache he was to shave off and grow again with monotonous regularity through the years. It did, however, give him distinction and maturity and transformed a juvenile pretty face to one of character.

Waterloo Bridge was the second movie Taylor had made with Vivien Leigh. He always mentioned her as one of the most talented and most beautiful women in motion pictures. "How well I remember," he said, "one day between scenes in *A Yank at Oxford* her asking me, in a most interesting manner, what an American Southern accent sounded like.

"When I saw her a few years later giving that magnificent performance in *Gone With the Wind,* I couldn't help wondering if, even then, she wasn't rehearsing for the Oscar she so validly won."

With the release of *Waterloo Bridge* Taylor's popularity was restored. He was back on top, but this time as an established motion picture performer. The reviews were excellent.

More important, his appeal was no longer limited. He still maintained his popularity with the younger crowd, but their parents also flocked to see him, including the fathers! *Waterloo Bridge* would always be his favorite movie and was the beginning of a series of successes for the nearly forgotten Robert Taylor.

Mervyn LeRoy, who directed *Waterloo Bridge,* was assigned to *Escape,* in which Taylor co-starred with Norma Shearer. It was released only a few months after the première of *Waterloo Bridge* and proved to be a good follow-up.

In 1941, *Billy the Kid* was reborn on celluloid. It was Taylor's first of many Westerns and his first color film.

The only problem he faced was making his blue eyes steely enough in the technicolor close-ups.

Taylor loved playing Billy and said he was damn careful to see to it that everything was as perfect as possible. "Billy gets killed in the end and when we reached the final death scene I wanted the audience to realize and to feel just how tough Billy was. I wanted the camera to pick up the look of hatred and contempt in his cold piercing eyes.

"I wasn't satisfied. My blue eyes were a handicap, but I wouldn't give in.

"I went to a doctor and got some drops that made my pupils contract, and when the camera rolled and the lights were trained on me, the camera-man saw my pupils contracting into tiny, needle-steel points. Perfect! Only trouble was I couldn't see a thing! The lights had made me temporarily blind and we were unable to finish the picture until the next day. I played it straight—blue eyes and all —and died on schedule.

"I'll tell ya—if I could have lived in another century, I'da chosen somewhere in the West. I'd be a cowboy, and maybe that's why I liked Billy. I'd probably have been shot to Kingdom Come if I'd lived then, so it may be just as well I was born in the twentieth century."

He handled his guns and horses as well as Billy, despite the fact he had to learn a fast-draw with his left hand.

Many said Taylor should not have played Billy the Kid, mainly because—although his playing the outlaw was extremely well done—he was just too likable! The public couldn't hate him. At the end of the movie when he allows himself to be killed in a duel with his friend the sheriff, portrayed by Brian Donlevy, drawing with his right hand deliberately, the audience was actually disappointed when the despicable renegade was rightfully shot to death.

Warner's had made Errol Flynn America's Robin Hood, Twentieth Century's hero was Tyrone Power as Jesse James, and MGM put Robert Taylor in movie history books as Billy, and with the one exception where a critic wrote that Taylor looked like a little boy with a new cowboy suit, the reviews were excellent.

103

Barbara had given him the horse he rode in the movie and from then on he would try to use his own guns, saddle and horse in each and every Western he filmed.

In *When Ladies Meet* he was reunited with Joan Crawford and Greer Garson. Though comedy was not Taylor's forte, he came across well as the conceited, frisky and lovable playboy. It was not a difficult movie to make and there was more laughing on the set during rehearsals than in the script.

Within two years Taylor had made four top-rated movies, and Mayer did not cease being generous with both money and good roles for "his son."

During 1940 and 1941, both Barbara and Bob were busy, she in Hollywood, and he on location somewhere else. Because they were separated most of the time, divorce rumors started. Bob was in Palm Springs when the news hit the papers and Barbara met with the press in Hollywood saying, "Bob is tired. He has made several pictures in a row with no time off in between—and he's resting now.

"He wanted to take some extensive flying lessons and took his instructor to the Odlum Ranch in Palm Springs. We are by no means separated but there are people, I suppose, who are jealous and would like to see me take a fall. Since my career has been successful lately, they attacked my marriage."

When asked if she were going to have a baby, Barbara looked the press straight in the face and said she would shout it to the world if it were possible.

"Bob and I are building a house in Beverly Hills," she said, changing the subject. "Does that sound as if we were getting a divorce? The new house will be small and cozy with a living-room, a small den, a dining room and kitchen downstairs; upstairs, four bedrooms—one for Bob and me, one for Dion, one for Buck Mack (Barbara's godfather) and a servant's room."

Bob sent a letter to Jim Reid of *Motion Picture* magazine. It was dated March 14, 1941:

Dear Jim:
Thank you for the opportunity of replying to the rumor

104

which seems to have been circulating around recently. Unfortunately it is an opportunity which is too seldom granted people in this business.

Barbara and I were married two years ago for reasons which are common, I believe, to any two people who decide to take that step, namely love, mutual interests and a pretty good understanding of each other. So far as we are concerned these elements still exist.

The rumor, though unfortunate, did not come as a surprise to either Barbara or myself. Actually we have been expecting it. It seems most inevitable that when picture people have been married over a year, rumors of this sort arise. Why, I do not know but the fact still remains . . .

May I assure you and hope that you will assure your readers, in turn, that all such rumors are entirely unfounded and untrue.

Thanks again for Barbara and myself. . . .

Sincerely,
Bob [5]

Though the public was satisfied with the Taylors' statement, their close friends saw a strained marriage.

Barbara continued her maternalistic instincts, calling Bob "Junior," and he still referred to her as "The Queen." One acquaintance said, "Maybe they forgot each other's real names, they're apart so often."

Actually the reverse was true. These separations held the Taylor marriage together as long as it did. If they had been forced to live under the same roof seven days a week, neither could have tolerated the other for very long.

When Barbara spent time at home she studied her scripts and read a great deal; Bob was not a reader and longed to be on a horse or in a plane.

Ernest Hemingway used to kid Taylor about having never read one of his novels and Bob, having no defense, said, "Everyone is always telling me to buy this and that book—usually a best seller—and with all good intentions I make a special effort to go into a book store, but whether I end up with what I went in for or not, I always—and I

5. *Motion Picture Magazine,* April 1941.

105

mean always—walk out with a cookbook—can't resist them!"

He loved to whip up a new barbeque sauce or meatloaf—anything but sit still. He was very restless and because of this was bored easily.

Taylor did not like to answer the telephone for fear he would get involved in a conversation or have to give an answer to a party invitation.

If he were sitting by the phone and Barbara was in another part of the house, he would yell for her to pick it up. His excuse was that she was a better liar than he was.

"Bob could not just say something like, 'We're busy that night,' because if he attempted a lie, he'd stammer and stutter. The only time he will use the telephone is when he is 15,000 feet in the air in a plane—then he calls everyone just to say 'hello.'

"But if a buddy calls him about going hunting, he'll talk on and on, making plans in detail."

Taylor's quirks regarding the telephone used to puzzle everyone. He always identified himself, "Hi, this is Bob," even to his closest friends, including his mother. Whether he just didn't trust Bell's invention or was modest enough to think no one would recognize the voice that was unique and unmistakably his is debatable. (Though many actors are impersonated—Bogart, Cagney, Cooper and Gable—it is almost impossible to do Tracy and Taylor.)

Western Union was a good customer of his. "Bob, we were supposed to go to dinner tonight with so and so."

"I'll send a telegram!"

"Why don't we just call and tell them we can't make it?"

"Nah! They'll try to convince us we should come. I'll just wire we won't be there!"

Barbara complained that she was a "telephone wife" because Bob was usually away someplace. Under those circumstances he was one to call regularly—just as long as he was far enough away.

Since Barbara was not a traveler, the majority of her movies were made in Hollywood, and if she had to get anywhere it was usually by train. On the very few trips she and Bob made together, he would fly and she would find other means of transportation to meet him at their destination.

She liked to be close to her work and liked the conveniences of city living. She never took vacations and concentrated all her efforts on her career. Bob talked often about getting another ranch, but they remained in town.

During these first few years of their marriage, he did not see much of Beatrice, Nebraska, and did not take Barbara home to meet his old friends. Ruth divided her time between California and Nebraska. She no longer dyed her hair, saying "Arly likes it natural." But no matter where Bob was, he kept in touch with her every day.

There was no warm affection between Barbara and Ruth.

Barbara never forgot that Mrs. Brugh was not in favor of the marriage, and Ruth still considered her daughter-in-law a threat to her influence over Bob. There was little suffering, however, since the three were rarely, if ever, together.

In 1941 Lana Turner entered Robert Taylor's life. She was his co-star in *Johnny Eager,* the story of a gangster who destroys himself when he falls in love with the girl he framed.

Taylor was physically attracted to Miss Turner instantly. She was only twenty-one years old, held the title of "Sweater Girl," and was suing Artie Shaw for divorce after less than a year of marriage.

She was not terribly career-minded and preferred men and jewelry over anything else.

Taylor remarked that Miss Turner was perfectly proportioned and not as "busty" as her pin-up pictures. "Her face was delicate and beautiful. I have never seen lips like hers, and though I was never known to run after blondes, Lana was the exception. I couldn't take my eyes off her and there were times during the filming of *Johnny Eager* that I thought I would explode!

"Her voice was that of a breathless little girl. I don't think she knew how to talk without being sexy. When she said a simple thing like 'Good morning,' I melted. She was the type of woman a guy would risk five years in jail for rape."

107

Acting daily with Miss Turner fascinated Taylor. He took it as long as he could and when he discovered she was making no effort to ignore his attentions, and in fact, was physically drawn to him, he knew he had to be with her alone.

"She became an obsession. I HAD to have her . . . if only for one night. . . ."

Van Heflin in *Johnny Eager* won an Oscar as supporting actor for his portrayal of the drunken Jeff Hartnett.

Taylor was awarded with excellent reviews, though critics were not about to write anything about him without bringing up his past. "It is hard to figure out why MGM wanted to flash another facet of its already faceted Mr. Taylor.

"Let it be said right away that it is Mr. Taylor's best 'facet' to date! Such fatal beauty as his is much better taken with mussed up hair and a convincing snarl.

"In fact, Mr. Taylor, though the admiration comes grudgingly, you're okay!"

In Norma Shearer's last movie, *Her Cardboard Lover,* she shared top billing with Taylor. The script was weak (a fable about a lady who employs an ardent gentleman to pose as her personable male secretary in order to pique the bounder she loves.)

Her Cardboard Lover was bad. Taylor could afford one failure, but it was a bitter disappointment especially since it was Miss Shearer's farewell to movie-making.

With World War II in full bloom, battle films were popular. Taylor was scheduled for *Battleground,* but didn't look the part of the tough war correspondent. The make-up and costume department tried everything, but nothing worked. John Hodiak replaced him. However, he and Charles Laughton appeared in *Stand By for Action,* a worthwhile picture, but unfortunately it was compared to its English counterpart, Noel Coward's *In Which We Serve.* Critics said, "It would be better to laugh this picture off, but too many folks will take it seriously."

In 1943 a cast of male stars gathered on the set of *Bataan:* Lloyd Nolan as a wise-guy corporal, Robert Walker (his movie début) as the scared kid from someplace in the Midwest, George Murphy as the even-tempered Air Force lieutenant, Thomas Mitchell as the old Army man, Desi Arnaz with his unusual interpretation of the English language, and Robert Taylor as the hard-bitten sergeant who buries his buddies and digs his own grave at the end.

George Murphy said, "It was a good thing we were supposed to be a motley crew because that is exactly what we were.

"I'll never forget the scenery. The movie was filmed entirely in the Hollywood studio and somehow, some frogs decided to make the *Bataan* set their home.

"We arrived one morning and they were everywhere. We had to stop production so the studio could be fumigated."

The end of the movie was a vivid one. Taylor, the last alive—no place to go, no place to hide, no sleep, waiting to be killed by the hundreds of Japanese who were quietly watching him from not too far away—prepares his own resting hole, where he knew his body would fall.

From out of the mist came one, then ten, then hundreds of the enemy.

"C'mon suckers . . . Ha! Ha! Come and get it! What's the matter with ya? Whatya waitin' for? Ha! Didn't think we were here, did ya? You dirty rotten rats . . . We're here. We'll always be here. C'mon suckers . . ."

His machine gun aimed at the camera, Taylor goes mad and the shooting fades into the camera-haze until the last bullet is fired.

Bataan was unusual—a movie that did not "prettify" the facts of war and was true and ugly in every detail.

Taylor's performance was generally regarded as magnificent, and it was said that his excellent acting "will remain in our memory for a long time without a doubt."

But as usual, not letting him forget, one critic commented, "His role as the Sergeant is by far the most intriguing without a trace of the softness his roles once allowed him.

"Handsome Bob looks with disdain from the beginning to the end."

Lloyd Nolan, who appeared with Taylor in several movies, including *Bataan,* said he thought Bob was a very sensitive man, but that life could have awarded him more than he received.

"I think Bob Taylor had to fight two things—his great beauty as a man (which he couldn't help!) and his lack of confidence in his talent as an actor.

"I don't think he realized that handsomeness is a great segment of the acting art. Valentino to this day commands the attention of both men and women, and he had a minimum of talent.

"Bob knew he was regarded as one of the top box-office names—that his salary was one of the tops, and he wanted to deliver the best."

Lloyd Nolan summed up his friend very well when he said, *Taylor did not realize that handsomeness was a segment of the acting art*. Instead he regarded it as a detriment and spent too much time playing it down rather than concentrating on his talent. He went too far to cover up his face with beards, blood, dirt, hats or helmets.

There is no doubt that Taylor would have accomplished more in his career if he had allowed himself to use his good looks to their greatest advantage. Though he was able to adapt himself to any role, it was just impossible for moviegoers to dislike him. He could scowl, murder, demoralize, brutalize, irritate and curse, and yet he came across as a nice guy. If he hit a woman, that was all right. She deserved it! If he killed a man, that was all right, too. His victim deserved it!

In Ruth's pitiful and prejudiced way, she was right. Her son was meant to be the playboy, the lover, the distinguished and gentle lover of a younger woman.

When Taylor said he was trying to figure out why he had been so outstanding in *Magnificent Obsession* when he didn't know any better, he never did come to the right conclusion. He was *meant* to be Robert Merrick, the carefree doctor who fell in love with a blind woman. He was supposed to be handsome, rich and spoiled—the traits were written all over his face.

But instead he chose his own destiny. Never let it be said that MGM held him back, for Mayer would gladly have given him back the title of America's Ambassador of Romance, even though Taylor's movies always made

110

money for the studio. It was Bob who wouldn't allow himself to be greater than he was unless he did it *his* way—by not exploiting his widow's peak and blue eyes.

Except for a guest appearance in *The Youngest Profession,* Taylor's last film before enlisting in the Navy was the controversial *Song of Russia.*

He did not want to do this movie for political reasons, saying it was pro-Soviet, and if there ever was anyone who was pro-American, patriotic and hated Communists, it was Robert Taylor!

He had many meetings with Mayer, explaining he did not find it in his heart to do the picture.

"But it's just a boy-girl story set to Tchaikovsky's music, Bob."

"As far as I can see, it's 'Commie' from beginning to end!"

Mayer sent for an aid to the late President Roosevelt who was the head of the Office of War Information's film division to talk with Taylor. He said the United States Government was interested in having the movie made and wanted other producers to film similar themes in order to influence the American people in favor of Russia.

Taylor replied that he had been waiting for his orders to report for Navy duty and was more interested in getting in uniform than "trying to promote some 'pink' propaganda shit for loyal Americans to watch."

Mayer tried to remain calm: "Son, it's just a lovely story about an American symphony orchestra conductor who tours Russia and falls in love with a Russian girl . . ."

"L. B., why can't you get someone else? Why me?"

"The role was made for you," Mayer argued.

"It stinks and you know it. I'd feel more at ease playing Jack the Ripper or bleaching my hair and standing by as Shirley Temple's double. And you know what else? I think you're trying to delay my going into the service!"

"There will be a delay—if you do the movie!"

"No, I do not want any part of it and that's it!"

The head of OWI, however, managed to convince Taylor that if it was important for the U.S. Government to step in, he should reconsider.

Reluctantly Taylor gave in, and Mayer won as usual.

Taylor was supported by Susan Peters and John Hodiak in *Song of Russia*.

He was upset for the many reasons stated in Mayer's office, but he also felt left behind since Clark Gable, Jimmy Stewart and Tyrone Power were already in various branches of the service and he was stuck in Hollywood.

Chapter VII

In February, 1943, when *Song of Russia* was released, Taylor was sworn into the United States Navy under the name of Spangler Arlington Brugh, even though he and Barbara legally adopted their stage names a few days before.

He applied for active duty but was turned down because he was thirty-one years old and too old for combat. Instead he was assigned to the Navy's Aviation Volunteer Transport Division as a Lieutenant (jg), the customary rank given to men over thirty who have a civilian pilot's license. Taylor had 110 flying hours to his credit.

"The day I was ordered to report for duty I walked into a barber shop and ordered a butch-cut and came out with about a half-inch of bristle all over my head. I left my own car in the garage and drove down to the Navy base in a beaten-up old station wagon.

"I figured I had two strikes against me before I came to bat. I was an actor and an officer.

"The CO had been tipped off I was coming and I'm proud to say that when I reported under the name, Lieutenant S. A. Brugh, the CO was the only one who recognized me."

Taylor took his basic training at the Naval Air Station in Dallas, Texas, then was transferred to the Naval Instructors' school in New Orleans as a student.

He feared he might not make the grade and refused comment or publicity until the tests were taken and he knew he had passed. When he graduated, *again* he asked for active duty and was told *again* his age made it impossible.

The Navy sent him to Livermore, California, to make seventeen training films for the Naval Air Cadets. During these few months he felt, because of his theatrical background, he was being used. He loved to fly, but he was grounded and in front of a camera.

When the films were completed, he tried for the third time to get permission to get into action, even if it meant transporting men or freight overseas, but was turned down. The Navy reminded him *again* that his age was the biggest drawback, but also they felt he was too valuable as an instructor.

He settled down in New Orleans and made several films to be used in the instructors' training program. He hadn't been flying for almost a year.

When this assignment was finished, he was told he would begin his regular duties as flying instructor and was asked to prepare to take cadets up in a plane the following day.

Taylor went directly to the Chief of Flight: "Do you think it is wise for me to go up there when I haven't been flying for so many months? To tell the truth, I'm not too confident at this time. I request a refresher course, sir."

"No problem, Lieutenant. I'll get one of the boys to go up with you for a few days!"

Taylor looked a little embarrassed and said, "If you don't mind, I don't want to go up with one of those twenty-one-year-old kids and have them run all over the base telling everyone I can't do a slow roll or inverted spin properly."

The Chief of Flight said he would assign an older instructor to Taylor. "There's a guy named Purvis. He's about your age and he'll keep his mouth shut about your being a little rusty. Think you'll like the guy!"

Tom Purvis became Taylor's co-pilot and this was the beginning of a lasting friendship between the two men.

"Taylor was nervous the first time we went up together," Purvis said. "He was concerned that I was thinking to myself, 'These handsome Hollywood stars don't take anything seriously except their box-office ratings,' and he was very quiet.

"We got up to five thousand feet in an open plane and I said, 'Get ready for a right slow roll.' It was perfect, but when we came out of it Taylor looked like he was going to throw up. I asked him what was wrong."

" 'Hell, I just lost my cigarette lighter. It's down there in the Mississippi River!' "

Taylor had forgotten to button his shin pocket of his summer khaki coverall. He told Purvis the lighter had been a gift from Barbara—a solid gold Zippo bearing a raised gold replica of his Naval Station Emblem and the date (1943).

"Barbara will flip her lid! What do I tell her? A three-hundred-dollar lighter is at the bottom of the Mississippi River?"

"Yeh," Tom said, "tell her just that. If you ask me, it's almost funny!"

"You don't know Barbara!" was Taylor's reply.

However, when she came to see him on her one and only visit while he was in the Navy, she gave him another. Taylor arranged a party for her at the Roosevelt Hotel in New Orleans.

She had been nominated for another Oscar for her performance in *Double Indemnity* with Fred MacMurray, but lost to Ingrid Bergman (in *Gaslight*) and she said, "I'm beginning to feel like one of Crosby's also-ran horses."

While Bob was drawing his lieutenant's pay and loving it, Barbara was the highest salaried woman in the movies—$323,333 in 1943—out-earning the other cinema queens—Bette Davis, Greer Garson and Betty Grable.

There was no publicity about her visit to Taylor. He wouldn't allow it. He was all Navy now and cared little about what was happening in Hollywood. On one of his furloughs to California he agreed to pose with Barbara in their home. He looked very young with his butch cut and Barbara very mature and sophisticated in her dressing gown and upswept hair. The pictures released were "very-much-posed" with Bob in uniform trying to look interested in the domestic scene.

He said he felt more comfortable in New Orleans and that somehow he resented any publicity when he was in Navy dress.

Mayer called him and said, "You'd better keep yourself in the public's eye, Bob. There's a whole new crop of young guys taking over here and the kids are crazy about them. And before you say anything about not returning to the movies, let me tell you something . . . You'll be back!"

"Not until the war is over, L.B."

"Sometimes I think you'll never grow up. What I can't figure out about you is that you never let fame go to your head, but the God damn Navy has done something to you—like nothing else matters."

"Nothing else does."

"Wise up. Pose for those pictures and let some reporters interview you once in awhile."

"Not as long as I am wearing this uniform."

"Next thing you'll want is for me to call you Lieutenant!"

"Would you believe I like that title better than Heart Throb of the Nation?"

"If you gave as much of yourself to being a good actor as you do to being a good soldier—or whatever they call you—you'd be number one around here instead of number two."

"See ya, L.B."

"Yeah, so long, Lieutenant!"

Taylor told Tom Purvis he hadn't been happier since he left Nebraska. "It seems everything I do is corny. Mayer thinks it's cute that I'm quite content in the Navy. So does Barbara. Sometimes I feel as though they are letting their little boy have his fun."

Purvis, 6 feet 3 inches tall and weighing 240 pounds, was Bob's constant buddy while he was in the Navy. Many times when Taylor was recognized, people thought Purvis was Bob's security man or bodyguard.

He was still unable to get through a meal in public without someone approaching his table. While his food went cold, he signed autographs.

One night a girl walked up to him in the lobby of a hotel and asked for his autograph. While his attention was diverted for a moment, another girl ran up to him, took out a pair of scissors and cut off his Navy regulation tie, leaving just a stub.

Taylor's face turned blazing red! He started after her. "That kid is going to get her face slapped!"

116

Tom held him back. "C'mon Bob, you must be used to that by now."

"Not in a Navy uniform, for Christ's sake! I can't walk around like this!"

He was burning and returned to his room for another tie. The phone rang. It was a man's voice. "Is this Robert Taylor?"

"Yes, it is."

"I just saw that display in the lobby. That girl had some nerve!"

"Who is this?"

"Just a man like yourself. Know what I mean?"

"Don't getcha, Mac."

"C'mon, you Hollywood men are all the same . . . always expected to be seen with a dame when it's really a man you want. Well, I'm the same as you, Bobby. We talk the same language!"

Taylor didn't hang up the phone—he threw it!—"God damn fags. We're going after him, Tom."

"Forget it, Bob. Relax, have a drink, calm down."

"Sure, how easy it sounds. You don't know how lucky you are, old buddy. Hollywood is not at all what it's cracked up to be. You've had a happier life than I've had. I envy you."

"Don't know what you're talking about, Bob, but I'll take your word for it. How about dinner now."

"Not hungry. Let's knock it off for tonight. I'm too aggravated to eat. How about taking off tomorrow for Dallas!"

The following day, Taylor was still annoyed about the tie and the telephone call. He and Tom flew to Texas in a Navy plane, but his mind was still seething over the night before.

Returning to New Orleans, Tom was getting a little annoyed with Bob's irritating mood. "I'll do the flyin' and you do the navigating, Bob."

Purvis said it was a cloudy day and he decided to snap Taylor out of his depression. "Bob and I would usually manage our flight plan by placing towns, rivers, railroads etc. In those days the planes the Navy gave us for student training were not well equipped for navigation.

"Taylor had a boring scowl on his face and was looking at the familiar landmarks. When we went into a cloud, he glanced automatically at the instrument panel, but when we broke through I'd tip the plane to one side, and Bob couldn't see a damn thing on the ground.

"I could tell he had lost his bearings completely. Being a perfectionist, he got very upset. In his silent confusion I watched him getting entangled in the shambles he had already created, so I called him Dilly, the name for a 'goof' in the Navy.

"He threw up his arms and managed a smile, but the name stuck and he always called himself Dilly on the phone or in letters long after we had left the Navy."

For the last time Taylor requested active duty "of any kind," but was told firmly that he was needed badly as an instructor. He was never really satisfied with any of the reasons for his not getting into action and blamed these denials on the fact that he was Robert Taylor, movie star.

He would never have accepted the job of narrator for the movie *The Fighting Lady,* if the United States Navy had not produced it in conjunction with Twentieth Century Fox. This 1944 documentary, the story of fourteen months in the life of a United States warship, won an Academy Award—the closest Taylor came to winning an Oscar.

Ironically the most humiliating experience in his life happened while he was in the Navy. When asked what embarrassed him most during his early years as a motion picture actor, he said it was when a beauty queen fainted on stage just as he was about to shake her hand, leaving him standing there alone with his arm outstretched. But that was mild compared to a mishap that occurred to him one day in Iowa.

He wouldn't talk about it for a long time, but he never forgot it—as much as he would have liked to.

He was flown to a Naval Air Station in Ottumwa, Iowa, to be the master of ceremonies at a celebration. It had rained in Ottumwa and patches of ice were here and there on the landing field. There had been a lot of publicity about Taylor's arrival and not only did the Navy represent itself at the airport but hundreds of civilians as well.

When the Navy's twin-engine Beechcraft landed, the air cadets took their place behind the Admiral and the crowds of people cheered as the plane slowly glided up to its designated parking area.

As the door to the Beechcraft opened, rather than wait for the step ladder, Taylor jumped to the ground as he was used to doing.

The throng of observers who had waited hours in the rain gathered around the plane. The Air Cadets lined up at attention and the Admiral stood waiting to return Taylor's salute.

The band began to play "Stars and Stripes Forever" . . .

As Taylor made his leap, he hit the ice and landed on his back, feet up in the air. He slid a few feet and every attempt to get up only made it more difficult for him. His cap flew off and it rolled underneath the plane where he couldn't get it.

He was like a turtle on its back. Some chuckled while others tried to contain themselves. The Navy Air Cadets looked straight ahead still at attention and many could barely maintain their military expressions while the Admiral waited . . .

Taylor finally got to his feet but couldn't salute because it is against Navy regulations to do so without a cap on. He had no choice but to stand there while someone retrieved it. By this time the band was on its third chorus of "Stars and Stripes Forever," and the Admiral was still waiting, biting his tongue to keep from laughing.

Taylor said, "I was never so humiliated in all my life!"

In January, 1945, Taylor went to New York City on a war bond drive and to promote the Navy film, *The Fighting Lady*. Barbara joined him and made it clear to the press that her being in the East was to see her husband and not for any professional reasons.

However one very well known columnist telephoned Barbara and she agreed to an interview. When he arrived at the Taylors' hotel suite he found himself alone with Bob who said Barbara would be back shortly.

When she finally did appear, she rushed into the room, said "hello," and fled into the bedroom muttering something about needing a shower.

Meanwhile the columnist carried on a lengthy conversation with Taylor. Bob was impatient because he was bored with small talk, and the columnist was impatient because he had expected an exclusive interview with Barbara Stanwyck.

An hour passed. Taylor occasionally banged on the bedroom door but got no response. He was annoyed but spoke about the Navy and his return to film-making when the war ended.

Taylor was trim and unusually handsome in his uniform, but he mentioned that if his fans were fickle he would get out of acting and find something else to do. The Navy had changed him, true. Hollywood wasn't that important if he had to start all over again.

The strained 'interview' continued and Taylor knocked on the locked bedroom door again.

The reporter left, annoyed and disappointed. His column the following day was devoted to Lt. Taylor, and how rude Barbara had been. Did she need a shower that badly?

When Barbara read the newspaper it apparently didn't bother her, because several nights later she ran into the columnist at a night club. She approached him graciously and explained her reasons for avoiding the interview. She explained she never should have agreed to it because Bob was on an official visit to promote *The Fighting Lady* and to sell war bonds. Being at his side was her wifely duty, and she did not want to take anything away from his attention. Furthermore it was up to her as a loyal American Citizen during wartime to back Bob and not to overshadow him in any way.

The columnist was so impressed by Barbara's humble explanation that he wrote a retraction applauding her.

Taylor was sent to Illinois to await his discharge papers, and he was still instructing.

One afternoon during class a young student looked up from his desk and finally realized who his teacher was. Taylor noticed the kid's mouth drop wide open, but ignored it. The boy continued to stare at him, not taking notes or listening to the lecture. He seemed to be in a daze.

After class he walked up to Taylor and said, "Lieutenant, I wonder if you would do me a big favor."

120

"You'd be doing me a big favor by paying attention tomorrow," Taylor barked.

"Yes, sir, but you see, my mother is a switchboard operator here on base and I know it would be the biggest thrill of her life if you would say a few words to her."

"Sure," Taylor said, and had a brief conversation with the boy's mother.

The young student was Roy Fitzgerald, better known today as Rock Hudson.

And ironically, ten years later the son of that switchboard operator would replace Robert Taylor as Doctor Robert Merrick in *Magnificent Obsession* and become the idol of a new generation . . .

On November 5, 1945, Taylor was discharged from the Navy as a Senior Grade Lieutenant. He hit the low point in his life when he tried to resume his career: good pictures were hard to find and even harder to get.

He tried to regain his position at MGM and in the public eye. But while he was in the service, a quick turnover in leading men had taken place: Cornel Wilde, Van Johnson, Frank Sinatra and Peter Lawford were given the choice roles, and these male stars were very much in demand.

Tyrone Power was given Twentieth Century's best when he returned—*Razor's Edge*—followed up immediately with *Captain from Castile,* and he was re-established as a top star.

In May, 1943, Taylor had been given a new twenty-year contract with MGM for $4,000 a week. It was the first Hollywood contract to carry a protective clause in the event of dollar-inflation.

When he returned to MGM in 1945, Taylor didn't ask for a raise because of taxes. Instead, the studio gave him a brand new twin-engine Beechcraft. He and MGM made a deal involving the aircraft, which was worth $75,000.

Taylor rented it back to MGM on occasion and it was written into his contract that the plane was to be returned to the manufacturer every 120 hours for check-up and if any of the instruments needed correcting, they were not to be repaired. They were to be replaced.

One of his Navy buddies, Ralph Couser, was hired by

MGM and assigned as Taylor's co-pilot. Couser was undoubtedly one of Taylor's best friends beside Tom Purvis, who lived in Illinois. He and Tom often met halfway in each other's planes.

Though MGM gave Taylor more than they had showered on any of their other stars, a good script, which he needed more than ever, was unavailable to him.

"You've changed, Bob," Mayer said.

"Is that good or bad?" Taylor asked.

"I don't know. Can't figure it. What do you want that we haven't already given you?"

"You might give me something great to make a comeback. Tyrone Power says it's like he never left."

"I have always told you, Bob, you are an individual and shouldn't compare yourself with anyone. What the hell do you care what happens to Power?"

"Just an example . . ."

"What do you think of Katie Hepburn?"

"Don't know her."

"I didn't ask you if you'd gone to bed with her. What do you think of her as an actress?"

"The best!"

"You've got her for your next movie!"

"I don't think I want to work with Miss Hepburn. I'm still recuperating from Garbo."

"Would the fact that you're going to be a louse in this picture persuade you?"

"Have I ever turned you down, L.B.?"

The script was *Undercurrent* and it was a disappointment to Taylor. However, it was the best offered to him, and the fact that Katherine Hepburn had accepted it gave him a little faith but made him sceptical about working with the unpredictable actress.

The first day on the set he saw her going over the script looking very cold and content. He walked over to her thinking how Garbo had turned her back on him without saying anything except hello.

Miss Hepburn shook his hand and said, "By the way, I see here that you are going to be wearing a raincoat most of the time. But the one the wardrobe department hung up over there doesn't suit me. What do you think?"

"Well, I . . ."

"Put it on. Let's see how you look in it!"

Taylor buttoned up the coat. "That's ridiculous!" she said. "Go down to Wardrobe and find some others."

He came back with a rack of assorted raincoats, trying on each one while Miss Hepburn looked him over very carefully. "Turn around, walk a bit, now sit down. No, no. Try another."

He modeled ten coats, but Miss Hepburn was not pleased.

She was ribbing him, but he respected her and took it.

"You'd better go back to the first one. You look too good in the others—no one will look at me!"

He plopped in a chair roaring with laughter.

When the movie was completed Katherine Hepburn was one of the many who said, "I never got to know him very well, but I considered Bob one of the most underated actors in the business."

Although *Undercurrent* was not a good comeback picture for Taylor, critics were unusually kind to him, welcoming him back and commenting he was surprisingly relaxed for an actor who had just returned to the screen after a three-year absence.

Taylor said he really didn't know what depression was until 1946. MGM had nothing scheduled for him and he spent most of his time hunting with Gable, who was also suffering from the same post-war slump. Gable hated the first movie offered to him when he returned from the service (*Adventure* with Greer Garson) and the critics agreed. Unlike Taylor, Gable hit the bottle heavily, drove too fast (resulting in one accident), and dated any socialite he met.

The studio did not comment on Taylor's buying a motorcycle and hitting the road with Gary Cooper and Keenan Wynn, but when Gable joined the group and was seen cycling at top speed, MGM disapproved. He was too reckless, they said, and was taking his frustrations out by tearing up the roads and anything else in his way.

Gable gave up his motorcycle, saying to Taylor, "Let's go huntin' up Oregon way, Baby!"

Barbara was concerned about Bob's cycling and asked

him to give it up, but it seemed to please him so much, she bought him an expensive new one.

His $75,000 Beechcraft, called "Missy" after Barbara, which could carry eight people comfortably, was Taylor's pride and joy and the only thing he really cared about. He was up early in the morning to drive out to the airport, even if it was just to polish the plane until it shined like silver, or take it up for a short spin.

Through "Coop," he met Ernest Hemingway and the three of them went off tracking down mountain lions in Mexico. Or he might join Bob Stack in some serious skeet shooting.

Stack admired Taylor all the way around. "We were close buddies even though sometimes we didn't see each other more than two or three times a year. He was that way. To Bob a friend wasn't someone you *had* to see all the time. If you had a common interest—especially where sports were concerned—you were a buddy!"

There was little publicity about Taylor's ability as a sportsman. He didn't want it because he considered this a personal part of his life and he felt he did not have to impress anyone with his outdoor skills. He refused to have MGM's publicity hounds following him on the trail. It interfered with his aim, scared the fish away, and in general made a circus out of a serious hobby.

Barbara was too busy with her career at this point to let Bob's fetish for the outdoors bother her too much anymore. Her name headed the Treasury Department's list of highest salaried women in the U.S. in 1944.

Taylor's fishing gear, sleeping bags and camping equipment were always ready to go, packed neatly on the back porch. Then Barbara would announce she had time off, and Bob, feeling obligated to stay home, cleaned his guns and stared longingly out the window. He admitted he would have been better off if he *had* packed up early and left, doing as he pleased rather than try to pacify Barbara—and holding back his resentment.

His hunting buddies were actually afraid to call him about a jaunt and were reluctant to bring up the subject when Barbara was in the room. She didn't especially like their conversations, which excluded her, and it annoyed

124

her to see Bob's face light up when he was engrossed in a gab session about sports.

Tom Purvis came out from Illinois for a visit, but stayed at a hotel. Barbara often said, "Don't ever want to be a house guest and I don't ever want a house guest!"

Taylor was embarrassed that Tom *had* to stay at a hotel, but he reserved him a room at the Beverly Wilshire, picking up the bill. The two checked in and Bob said, "Gotcha a suite, Old Buddy, so you'd have lots of room."

They had a few drinks and after looking the place over, Tom said he thought he'd unpack.

He opened his small suitcase, took out one sock, threw it in one closet, took out another sock, threw it in another closet, took out a suit jacket and hung that up in another, put his trousers in still another until he had managed to put almost everything he had brought—one by one—in a different closet.

"Never saw Bob laugh so hard in all my life!" Tom said. "But God Almighty, the darn place was big enough for ten people and then they wouldn't run into each other for a week!"

When Tom poured himself another Scotch, Taylor quipped, "Hey, you have one empty closet. Aren't you goin' to hang up your undershorts?"

Other friends of Taylor's came out to Los Angeles to visit him, but did not spend much time at the three-bedroom house in Beverly Hills that Barbara had bought when Bob was in the service. He had to sleep in the sewing room until they were able to build another bedroom.

No one seemed to mind not being invited to the Taylors' home. One friend said, "When I did go there I had to listen to Barbara yelling at Bob and watch him taking it. He never fought back."

In an interview Barbara gave regarding her marriage to Taylor she said, "He's a great sleeper. *I* sit up and read a book. He naps in the afternoon—naps he calls 'resting his eyes.' He never broke away from Nebraska. He still has a sense of belonging back there.

"He's likely to stay up in his plane and never come

125

down. He can do anything a bird does but sit on a barbed-wire fence!

"He's neat, but in the bathroom he's a mess. He leaves towels everywhere and is careless about cigarettes. His shoes are always shined but are all over the house. Can't tell you which he shines more—his plane, his shoes or his guns.

"He buys watches—dozens of them. I don't know whether he has more cookbooks or watches around here. He's always making popcorn and takes a bowl with him wherever he goes in the house.

"Bob is a fatalist and is not superstitious. He always remembers anniversaries—even trivial ones.

"I think he's changed since he's been in the Navy ... "

Taylor was interviewed too, but he didn't say much about Barbara. "I don't know what happened to my career. Maybe I'm not that good an actor. In fact I really don't think I am, and I admit I have a lot to learn. And yet I don't think an established actor loses his public appeal just because he is not a polished actor. I can name several top name stars who make no pretensions at being Barrymores.

"Barbara said to me, when I had made the top of the popularity polls, 'You'll take a fall, young man, and it will frighten and depress you, but it will pass.' What she was trying to tell me was that it happens to all of us sometime. The public is fickle.

"I never thought my looks would be a problem. I was concerned about my movies, my parts and how well I acted out my lines. If I ever gave any thought to my looks it was whether or not I should have my nose straightened or get rid of my widow's peak.

"People believe what they want to and they accept Gable and Tracy in any role. And I think that maybe my fans believed all that nonsense written about me when I left for England to make *Yank*. I will never get over that experience for as long as I live because I was innocent of everything.

"As for an actor's personal life, I just cannot believe that it has anything to do with his popularity . . . not these days.

"Writers criticize me for being too dignified, too reserved. I'm told that I never let go—that I have no emotions, but that's me.

"It's not the money that scares a star if his career appears to be fading—it's pride! When a salesman gets fired, only his friends and family know about it. But when a star is fired, the whole world knows it.

"Ya know, one of the most popular sayings around this town is that a dead star is the deadest thing on earth and the least liable to resurrection."

One evening he went to Mayer's house for dinner. Though Taylor and L.B. had many heart-to-heart talks and a few disagreements, they were undisputedly in tune with one another. But on this particular night Mayer did not know how much he helped Taylor when he needed it most.

In the middle of dinner someone brought up the subject of *Waterloo Bridge*. Taylor said it was his favorite movie.

Mayer said, "You were great in that one, Bob!" to which Taylor replied, "Don't know. Never saw it!"

Instantly Mayer instructed that his screening room be set up for the showing of the movie immediately after dinner.

Taylor sat watching *Waterloo Bridge* as if he were seeing himself for the first time. He admitted to himself and to others that he thought he gave a polished performance. "I never thought I could act until I saw that screening. It was a shocking revelation to me. I had it! There it was in black and white. It didn't matter to me that evening what the hell the public thought of me. I knew I could do it again if Mayer gave me the right script."

After that night he knew he would play the waiting game again. He called Ralph Couser and planned a flight to Scott's Bluff, Nebraska, for some duck hunting. Wallace Beery went along. This trip almost cost them their lives.

Returning home, flying at 15,000 feet, one of the props stalled because of heavy icing conditions. The plane began spinning to the right. They recovered from that one just as the other prop stalled and "Missy" spun to the left. They continued to spin while losing altitude.

Beery, who was asleep in the back, fell to the floor while the plane weaved and bumped around in the sky. Suddenly they dropped several thousand feet—Taylor and Couser doing what they could at the controls while Beery was rolling around on the floor.

At 10,000 feet, the Beechcraft leveled off. Couser looked over at Taylor . . . Taylor looked at Couser: "That was a real gut buster!"

They made an emergency landing at the nearest airport in the snow. Beery was sick and bruised. Taylor said they had better stay the night and have the plane checked over.

"Shit!" Beery yelled. "I'm not going up there with you again. I'm takin' a bus home!"

Returning to Los Angeles, Taylor got some clean clothes, called Tom Purvis, who was in New Orleans, and said he'd pick him up. "We're goin' to New York!"

Purvis said, "When Bob said he'd be someplace at a certain time, he was there. He never changed his plans and he was never a minute off!"

They ended up at The Waldorf Towers in New York, and though Taylor did not like night clubs, he *insisted* they go on the town.

When they entered the club he said he wanted to talk to his "favorite" waiter. Tom assumed he was planning a special dish. ("Bob was a food hound!")

Sitting over drinks at the table, Tom was hit in the head by a waiter's tray. It was a light tap and ignored.

The next time the same waiter almost dropped a meal in Tom's lap with an elbow dug into an ear. This time Tom felt it. He was annoyed but continued his conversation.

Five minutes passed when the same waiter approached. Six-foot three-inch, 240 pound Tom Purvis stood up this time and was ready.

Taylor waved the waiter off. "Just wanted to see how much you could take, old Buddy!"

"I was ready to flatten him, Dilly."

"C'mon, let's go for some food!"

"I'm with you. Let's get a menu."

"Not here. Ol Missy's waitin'! How about Washington?"

Magnificent Obsession (1935) with Irene Dunne
firmly established Taylor as the Pretty Boy of America

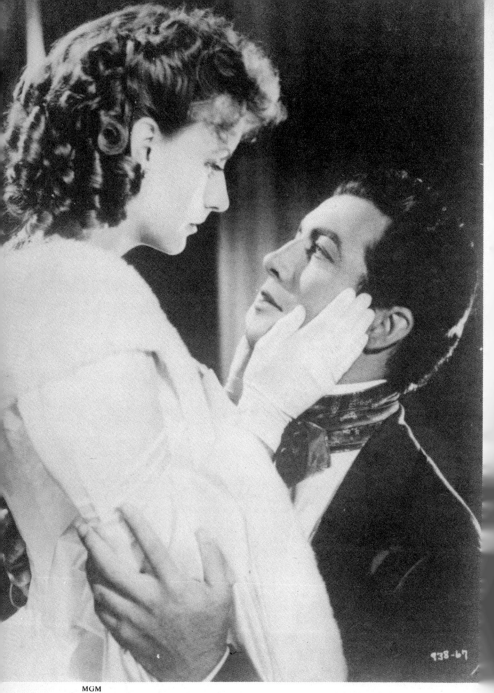

Robert Taylor plays Armand to Greta Garbo's Camille (1936)

M-G-M'S STUDIO BOSS MAYER AND HIS TOP TALENT. *Left to right, first row:* Captain James Stewart (on leave), Margaret Sullavan, Lucille Ball, Hedy Lamarr, Katharine Hepburn, Louis B. Mayer, Greer Garson, Irene Dunne, Susan Peters, Ginny Simms, Lionel Barrymore. *Second row:* Harry James (Betty Grable's new husband), Brian Donlevy, Red Skelton, Mickey Rooney, William Powell, Wallace Beery, Spencer Tracy, Walter Pidgeon (with beard for *Madame Curie* role), Robert Taylor (with G. I. haircut for real-life Navy role), Pierre Aumont, Lewis Stone, Gene Kelly, Jackie Jenkins. *Third row:* Tommy Dorsey, George Murphy, Jean Rogers, James Craig, Donna Reed, Van Johnson, Fay Bainter, Marsha Hunt, Ruth Hussey,
Marjorie Main, Robert Benchley. *Fourth row:* Dame May Whitty (in costume for *White Cliffs*), Reginald Owen, Keenan Wynn, Diana Lewis (Bill Powell's wife), Marilyn Maxwell, Esther Williams, Ann Richards, Martha Linden, Lee Bowman, Richard Carlson, Mary Astor. *Fifth row:* Blanche Ring, Sara Haden, Fay Holden, Bert Lahr, Frances Gifford, June Allyson, Richard Whorf, Frances Rafferty, Spring Byington, Connie Gilchrist, Gladys Cooper. *Sixth row:* Ben Blue, Chill Wills (in uniform for *See Here, Private Hargrove*), Keye Luke, Barry Nelson, Pfc. Desi Arnaz, Henry O'Neill, Bob Crosby, Rags Ragland.

With Hedy Lamarr in *Lady of the Tropics* (1939)

The tragic love story of *Waterloo Bridge* (1940), which paired
Taylor with Vivien Leigh, was always his favourite picture

"Yeah, yeah, yeah."

Taylor kept a wild schedule with "Missy," his haven. He would rather fly than eat and he often flew JUST to eat.

From Los Anegles he would wing to Palm Springs for lunch, to San Francisco for dinner or to New Orleans for some exotic food at Antoine's. Or to Oregon to fish for steelhead trout or to Texas to hunt quail or to California to hunt duck.

Otherwise his personal life had little to offer. He had found himself with two mothers—Ruth and Barbara—and solved this by flying off anywhere to escape.

Ruth began to show signs of senility. Her mind was deteriorating, although she was still praying and preaching the evils of sex. She was in her own world, and though she still referred to her famous son as Arly, now *she was Robert Taylor's mother.*

She urged Bob to take a more active interest in religion and it became impossible for them to discuss this intelligently. Bob believed in God and prayer, but was not a churchgoer. He considered people who only went to church on Christmas and Easter hypocritical.

"But Arly, you have to prove to God that you love him—go out of your way to worship. Hollywood is a wicked town."

Bob listened and would never argue about God or not attending church with his mother. His friends said that she *did* have an effect on him religiously, though he kept his feelings to himself.

Chapter VIII

Barbara and Bob each knew that their marriage was in serious trouble, although neither admitted it to the other. They tried to remedy it with a vacation in Europe. Barbara's amazing career kept her stimulated, and though there had never been an ounce of jealousy on Bob's part, he was eaten up inside because he had not been offered a good movie part since *Undercurrent*.

Their European visit was widely publicized. In London they were mobbed and the police had to hoist the couple on their shoulders. In the confusion Bob got a black eye. The morning papers printed: MOB SHINES ROBERT TAYLOR, and there were snickers in Hollywood: "Since when is Barbara a mob?"

Helen Ferguson, who handled public relations for the Taylors, met the couple when they arrived back in New York. Barbara was eager to get to work, and Bob was happy just to be home, but Helen said she had tickets to the theatre. Maurice Chevalier was appearing and the three attended.

When the curtain went down, an usher came up to them and said that they had been invited backstage.

Barbara and Bob were very sensitive about such things and would never go backstage unless specifically asked. Helen said surely the usher had asked the right party: "Let's not insult Mr. Chevalier."

When they arrived backstage no one seemed to pay much attention to them and they had to search for the dressing room, where they sat and waited for some time. Barbara wanted to leave, Bob started for the door, but Helen urged them to stay just a few more minutes.

Chevalier walked in and completely ignored them! Barbara turned purple and sat almost in tears. Bob took her by the arm and led her out into the street.

"Barbara was hurt and shocked," Helen said. "Bob didn't stop talking about the rudeness of Maurice Chevalier all the way to the hotel. He went on and on and on. Barbara never said a word—just sat there trembling!"

This incident infuriated Taylor!

He had had a boring vacation anyway and to end it like this upset him.

They returned to Hollywood, but home to Bob was just another place to hang his hat until he could get to the airport and take off.

Barbara hurried back to work in *Sorry, Wrong Number* and was nominated again for an Academy Award. She shrugged it off: "Not that I wouldn't like to have an Oscar, but I've lost three times before and it's hard to get your expectations up and not win. It's bad luck to discuss it. Besides," she said graciously, "I feel Olivia De Havilland really deserves it for *The Snake Pit.*"

Barbara was wrong and Jane Wyman got it for *Johnny Belinda.*

Taylor wasn't being hounded for interviews these days, but during one of the few he did not sound very happy: "I was better off financially when I was drawing a Lieutenant's pay than before or after the war. We were left with $5,000 a year more between us when I was earning comparatively nothing. Barbara was able to divide her income between us for taxation but I guess she'd rather have me home and pay more income tax."

To pacify him, MGM threw him a crumb—*The High Wall* with Audrey Totter. Taylor played the role of a war veteran accused of killing his wife and Miss Totter portrayed the psychiatrist who helps him prove himself innocent.

He did a worthy job in the movie, but in general *The High Wall* went unnoticed until he made headlines because of his testimony before a visiting subcommittee of the House Un-American Activities Committee inquiring into Communist activity in Hollywood.

His testimony not only brought the public to see *The High Wall,* but also brought him to the forefront as an outstanding American. He volunteered to testify in Washington.

REDS DISRUPT FILMS, SAYS TAYLOR —
ASKS DEPORTATION

"Film star Robert Taylor testified today that some of his fellow players 'act an awful lot like Communists' and are a 'disrupting influence' in the movie industry. Naming names, he took the stand in the investigation of Communism in Hollywood and testified that Howard Da Silva and Karen Morley are followers of the party line.

However, he stressed, Communists in Hollywood are the 'rotten apple in the barrel.' He said 99.99 percent of the film colony were of the same opinion.

He drew applause from the packed room by declaring, 'If I had my way, they would all be sent back to Russia or some other unpleasant place!' "

Taylor's appearance drew such a crowd that wooden barricades were put down in the corridors. Giggles were heard when Robert Stripling, chief committee investigator, asked, "How long have you been employed as an actor?" Laughter almost drowned the reply of "since 1934."

Question—Have you found considerable Communists or fellow travelers asserting influence over the movies?
Answer—I have been looking for Communists for a long time! I have seen more indications recently, especially in the preparations of scripts. I've seen things that appear on the pink side.
Question—Does any element in the Screen Actor's Guild follow the Communists' line?
Answer—Yes, sir. I must admit I have seen this. I am a member of the Board of Directors and it seems that at general membership meetings, certain people, if not Communists, seem to be working awfully hard to be one.
Question—Do they have a disrupting influence?
Answer—On issues in which there is considerable agreement, certain persons "stare"—not seeming to understand. Howard Da Silva and actress Karen Morley are among those who disrupt things at the meetings. They, among

132

others, ask questions and keep the sessions running to one or two o'clock in the morning.

Taylor went on to say he had rejected several scripts recently—something that was not common for him—because he felt they promoted the Communist line.

When asked to identify any Communist scenario writers, he named Lester Cole. Cole, author of *None Shall Escape* and *Objective Burma,* was one of nineteen suspected Reds who were subpoenaed to testify.

Taylor corrected his testimony, given on the West Coast, before a committee executive session to the effect that he had been "forced" to work in the film *Song of Russia,* and that the Government had put pressure on him.

He told about the head of OWI's film division, who came to Hollywood to discuss the movie with Mayer, and how he explained that Washington wanted the picture to be made in order to influence the American people in favor of Russia.

"Many pictures were being made then to strengthen the feeling toward Russia, but I don't think this picture should have been made," Taylor said.

He told the committee he would never act or work in any capacity with a Hollywood Communist, even if it meant the end of his career!

Representative Richard Nixon (R-Calif.) congratulated Taylor on his patriotism and fearlessness in testifying. He predicted Taylor would face ridicule and the smear tactics of the Communists as a result of his appearance that day.

"It doesn't bother me," Taylor said. "Anytime the left wing groups ridicule me, I take it as a compliment!"

The hearing room was jammed to capacity. A sixty-five-year-old woman scrambled up onto a radiator for a better look at the screen star, fell to the floor and struck her head. Several people, in the mad rush to the door when Taylor was preparing to leave, stepped on her. Many had their clothes torn and ripped as half of the audience left their seats to follow their hero.

Hundreds of women formed a pied-piper-like proces-

133

sion behind him for more than a block down the street to his car.

The hearing was halted temporarily because of the commotion and mad exodus. The court ordered more policemen on duty for the following day's hearing when Robert Montgomery, Gary Cooper, George Murphy and Ronald Reagan were scheduled to testify.

The pictures that appeared in the papers the following day revealed a stern and serious Robert Taylor. It was reported that he was annoyed by the feminine commotion, giggles and cheers and felt that this was a very solemn thing and should not have been treated like a circus by the public.

The Hungarian Ministry of Interior immediately banned all Taylor films. This was the first open Hungarian action against Hollywood productions since the wartime expulsion of all Allied films.

Russia's government organ, *Isvestia*, unmercifully panned Taylor, as predicted by Nixon: "There was a time when in America it was the vogue to sympathize with the Soviet Union.

"Quite a big business was done on this and Robert Taylor did it also. But other times set in, and under the influence of definite laws, it becomes fashionable to renounce one's sympathies 'to expose.' One may think that on this as well, Robert Taylor has done quite a job."

"Mr. Taylor is without bravery or stable views!"

Isvestia went on to praise Charlie Chaplin, calling him a good example of talent.

Taylor said little about all the thunder caused by his voluntary testimony except that he would not argue with anyone about allegiance to the United States. It was a waste of valuable time, but if anyone sympathized with Communism, he would gladly buy him a one-way ticket to Russia—"As long as they don't come back!"

He loved to dicuss politics, however. He was active during election campaigns and once said when his candidate lost, "Maybe if I had stayed out of it the guy would have won!"

As a result of the enormous publicity he was getting, Taylor was mobbed wherever he went. People wanted

134

to touch him, punch him like an old buddy, reach out to shake his hand.

He was constantly interrupted in public. Drinks were sent over to his table in restaurants and the senders always followed up with a visit to his table. "I didn't mind this type of adoration, if that's what you could call it. Folks would come over and talk to me about how they felt concerning world problems or about a relative who had been killed in the war. I sat over many a cold steak, but being admired for just standing up for what I believed was right, seemed normal to me—but a big thing to them."

Taylor probably signed as many autographs during 1947 and 1948 than he had ten years earlier. Tom Purvis said "Dilly" seemed to be enjoying the fact that so many people were coming forth to express their views on Communism. "However," Tom said, "I never noticed before that Bob carefully checked every piece of paper shoved in his face for an autograph. Seems he was stung once by someone who put a carbon underneath the sheet he was signing and his signature was on something else. Bob didn't elaborate, but not only did he make sure there was nothing underhanded going on, he also refused to sign "With Love," not wanting to seem phony either.

One evening when a group of high school girls rushed into a restaurant and surrounded Cary Grant's table, Grant played a little joke on Taylor. They explained they were on a scavenger hunt and had to get a star's autograph.

Grant, with a straight face, looked up and said, "But you girls don't want my autograph when Bob Taylor's sitting right over there in the corner."

It worked. They left Grant and scurried over to Taylor's table, much to his disappointment. One of the girls said, "I don't know too much about you, Mr. Taylor, except one night I brought my boy friend home to meet the family. When he left I asked my mother what she thought of him and she said, 'Well, he's no Robert Taylor!' and then I saw you on the front page of all those newspapers. I'm kinda a Frank Sinatra fan, but even if you can't sing, I'd still like your autograph."

Taylor laughed. "Better think it over, little girl. I don't wear red socks like Van Johnson, either."

"That's okay, he hasn't got a pointed forehead! What is that thing?"

"They call it a widow's peak."

"You're cute, anyway. Thanks for the autograph. Now my mom won't get mad if I'm late getting home tonight!"

"Yes, give my best to Mother."

Taylor said, after that episode, he hadn't known that there were little girls who were not aware of "Pretty Boy!" It must have been a shock to realize that their mothers were probably the ones who had torn his clothes off.

Being in the Navy and having made only two movies in four years made a big difference in Taylor's following.

Mayer met with him shortly after his testimony in Washington. "I think, son, that your making headlines the way you did was better than any script I could have given you."

"Maybe so, L.B. . . ."

"You'll always be remembered for that. Fine thing you did."

"Yeah, I suppose when the whole damn thing dies down, *Song of Russia* will be the top film in Moscow!"

Mayer pretended not to hear. "Say, Bob, what's all this about women all over the country knitting sweaters for you. We must have fifty in the mail room. Some dame in Albany made seven. Louella Parsons wrote that subway riders are menaced by knitting needles in New York."

"That's nice of Louella," Bob said sarcastically.

"She rules this town, son. Why, Louella is so powerful, all she has to do is make a phone call and a star is made or ruined. She likes you."

"Can she knit?"

"Doubt it."

"Good, that's one less sweater. God damn, L. B., I didn't come here to talk to you about sweaters!"

"Bob, do you still trust me? Don't answer that one just yet. I'll have a picture for you in a few weeks, but I don't want a squawk outta you. I have plans for you, boy. Sit tight!"

136

"I'd like to have another with Lana."

"What about Ava Gardner?"

"She'll do!"

Taylor's forty-first movie was *The Bribe* with Ava Gardner, Charles Laughton, Vincent Price and John Hodiak. His role of a Federal Agent who investigates a smuggling ring in the Caribbean was a serious one. The critics said he was "very good indeed when violence moves into the movie with tremendous crescendo."

The best result of Taylor's doing *The Bribe* was meeting Ava Gardner . . .

Barbara was taking a good solid look at her marriage. The trip with Bob to Europe had been a failure. If she complained about his being away from home with his guns and fishing gear in the past, that was nothing compared to his absences now.

"He flew from Los Angeles to New Orleans and back by way of Detroit just to test a new plane radio," she said. When he got home he shouted, "It works!"

"God, for a moment I thought he meant the plane!"

Barbara referred to "Missy" as *the crate* and had yet to go near it. Friends told her it might be very wise to take an interest in Bob's flying. He had 2,500 hours to his credit now and was aiming for more.

One morning she shocked Bob by volunteering to go up with him on a short flight. "It looks like a clear day and you probably won't hit any mountains, right?"

Bob was so excited he didn't believe it until she actually boarded the plane.

But there was no doubt that Barbara was terrified. She grabbed the seat with both hands and hung on for dear life. She closed her eyes and remained silent.

When they landed in Palm Springs an hour later, she was pale and sick . . . and surprised that she was still alive.

The fact that she flew with Bob was a miracle and the greatest gift she had ever given him. He talked about it for weeks and called everyone: "Hey, The Queen thinks I'm a helluva pilot!"

He called Ralph Couser, who said it was unusual to hear Bob excited about anything because of his amazing

137

control. But anyone who doubted his elation that day in Palm Springs didn't know Robert Taylor.

Barbara went further. She even attempted to ride a motorcycle, and the reporters were there to take pictures. However, she looked as if she were going to the moon instead of just down the block. Whether she ever got the motor started is not known, but it was apparent that she was doing whatever she could to please Bob.

She went on one camping trip with him and her only comment was, "Never again." Barbara was hardly the outdoor type and not the least bit athletic.

One close friend said, "It was obvious to everyone she was trying to salvage her marriage. But the traits that Bob had once admired in her were now annoying. Her aggressiveness, rough language, frankness and telling Bob what to do and how to do it, was getting on his nerves and he was embarrassed.

"When Bob returned from the Navy he found himself with two mothers. He loved Barbara but not the way a man loves a wife. He began to compare her to his real mother, who was at least a lady regardless of whatever else she was."

Taylor's friends all said she didn't like them and they didn't like her. She especially resented Ralph Couser, who was Bob's constant companion. Couser was not only a friend, but also had been hired by MGM to go along with Bob as his co-pilot when he was on location.

Though Taylor went out of his way to pacify Barbara —including carrying several St. Christopher medals with him at all times and keeping quiet during arguments— he was confused and terrified at this stage of his life. He told Barbara he had a prostate problem and it was difficult for him to be an attentive husband until the condition could be corrected.

Barbara didn't accept this excuse. If a man was not getting satisfaction at home, he was getting it elsewhere.

Bob began to believe he wasn't normal. Perhaps all that "pretty boy" nonsense was true after all and finally catching up with him. Maybe he did have desires in other directions and didn't realize it. The whole world had accused him of being a homosexual and now Barbara

133

was intimating the same just because he spent so much time with his friend Ralph Couser.

When Couser telephoned Taylor at home, Barbara yelled, "Hey, Bob, your wife wants to talk to you!"

He took it and much more.

Since Barbara could find no evidence of other women, though she accused him of sleeping with everyone, she enjoyed rubbing his "affair" with Couser down his throat.

Convinced he was losing his manhood, Taylor went to a psychologist. The doctor had known Bob for many years on a social basis, and was well acquainted with Ruth and Barbara.

"Taylor was extremely upset. He told me everything. It wasn't a professional call really, but there was no doubt in my mind he needed help. I asked him directly whether he had had any urge to be with a man."

"Christ, that makes me sick! Never! Never! I go for women period! Homos have pestered me for years . . . God damn queers!"

"Have you been attracted to any women lately?"

"I can look at a sexy girl walking down the street and get a God damn hot sensation in my insides!"

Taylor went on to explain that he "thought the world of Barbara" and would be the first one to admit he needed her, but perhaps not as much since he had been in the Navy. They annoyed each other and he didn't appreciate being told what to do anymore. "Maybe I grew up in the Navy, how do I know? We are both trying like hell right now, and Barbara does things for me she never would have done five years ago, but I see so many things I didn't see before. I don't want to lose her as a friend and for that matter, as a wife, but things are sure not working out. It's my fault . . ."

The discussion continued, but the important factor was Taylor's fear he was a homosexual. The doctor assured Bob he was not, but that only he and he alone would have to find *that* out for himself.

Though Bob found it difficult to see another woman, he did strike up a "friendship" with Ava Gardner, his co-star in *The Bribe*. She was also close to Clark Gable and a "good Joe"—understanding, witty, direct and sexy.

Bob enjoyed her company and they met occasionally—
sometimes at Ruth's house, much to her distress. More
than ever she was convinced that actors were sinners and
that Hollywood was evil. She tried again to get Bob
interested in religion and though he did not refuse her
pamphlets and listened intently to her philosophies on
Christ's coming soon to pick those he wanted to "live
with him in his house," Bob flatly declined any offers
to attend her prayer meetings. He told her she had not
failed to bring him up with the proper beliefs and this
was something he would never forget, but he wasn't the
type to prove it to anybody.

He also tried not to say "God damn" in her presence,
but somehow it always came out. It was part of his vocabulary. "Try to overlook it, Mother."

"I have been overlooking a lot these days, son."

On July 1, 1948, Dore Schary signed a contract with
MGM as vice-president in charge of production. He
brought new ideas that did not exactly agree with
Mayer's, though it was Mayer who had urged Schary to
come with his studio. But Schary's appointment affected
many contract players. Gable was one. He told Schary
that movies should be made to entertain rather than to
make people think. Taylor agreed with Gable, but was
not yet feeling the drastic changes that were taking place.

Gable was being given roles that he considered insult-
ing and spoke his piece. He told Taylor, "Just you wait,
Baby, Mayer's in trouble. Not that I care particularly—
he's your father, not mine—but I don't like the smell of
dead fish around here."

Schary's first disagreement with Mayer was over the
film *Battleground*. Schary bought it from Howard Hughes
(RKO), along with *Ivanhoe*, and he went even further
and arranged for *Quo Vadis* to be rewritten for MGM's
release.

Articles began appearing in the newspapers about
Schary's "taking over MGM" and the problems con-
fronting Mayer.

Taylor had been assigned to do *The Conspirator* in
England. He neither liked nor disliked the script, but was
not too keen on portraying a Communist Agent—"Ex-

cept that I get it in the end." He met with Mayer before leaving for Europe.

"Have a good trip, Bob. You like England, don't you?"

"Yeah, I always said the English people are swingers but they don't go around bragging about it."

"Bob, there are going to be some changes around here —maybe when you're gone, I don't know. I can't talk about it right now, but I want you to know I'll do my best where you're concerned. As a matter of fact, I was going through some old things here in my desk and came across a fan letter to you. Let me read it to you—for old times:

"Who makes the Co-eds shout with glee
Forget about Fraternity
As movie bound they rush to see
        ROBERT TAYLOR

Who makes old ladies shelve their canes
Forget about their aches and pains
And think of moonlit summer lanes
        ROBERT TAYLOR

Who makes the housewife shiver and shrill
with ecstasy they rave and thrill
til husbands want to kill
        ROBERT TAYLOR

What makes these women act so dumb
and movies go til kingdom come
and think their old men so much scum
        ROBERT TAYLOR

"How about that one, Bob?"

"Those were the days, L.B., but I don't think about them anymore."

On November 2, 1949, a beautiful seventeen-year-old actress said, "This is the day I grew up. I started work-

141

ing on *The Conspirator* and no one can say I am a child in this picture because I am playing Robert Taylor's wife!

"He is just as wonderful as everyone in Hollywood told me he was. I have to admit I did get nervous when he took me in his arms and made love to me, but the director said I shouldn't be upset."

The young lady speaking was Elizabeth Taylor and before her first romantic scene with Robert Taylor she was studying her algebra lesson in the little studio schoolroom near the set. When class was dismissed, she rushed out the door, stood for a moment while she dabbed her nose with a powder puff and put some perfume behind her ears.

When the scene was completed, she walked in a daze to her dressing room, flopped in a chair and with childish ecstasy said to her hairdresser, "I've just been kissed by Robert Taylor!"

She picked up her English textbook, looked at it for a minute and threw it on the floor. "I'll never be ready for class. I'm so excited! Why, do you know he is thirty-eight years old? And he said I was talented, but he did have to teach me one thing—how to powder down my lips."

Before Bob left for England to make *The Conspirator,* he wrote to Tom Purvis, "I'm headin' for Europe to do a picture with a little girl I think might be something one day! Think her first name is Elizabeth but I know we have Taylor in common."

He gave Elizabeth Taylor her first screen kiss, and there was quite a commotion on the set when it took place. She was trembling and he thought it was cute, but when the scene was over, he called his press agent in Hollywood: "I think this 'first kiss' business is going a little too far. Try to keep the publicity to a minimum. I don't need it and why tease a little girl like that?"

He was too late. The news was out almost before it happened. Taylor sent telegrams, made phone calls and pleaded with MGM to stop building up such a simple thing like a kiss.

As shooting of the movie progressed, Taylor began to take notice that "the little girl" wasn't so little after all. "She was stacked! But I didn't realize it until she appeared on the set in a negligee. Good God, she was just a child, but I couldn't help myself."

It was one of the few times in his life he found it possible to control his attraction to a woman, but unfortunately not "from the waist down!" "It wouldn't have been so bad if the scene were being shot sitting down, but standing up it would have been obvious to everyone if I didn't do something about it."

He spoke to the cameramen and explained his "physical situation," and they said they would try to focus the camera on him above the waist. "Doggone, I spent the entire day in that condition and I couldn't understand it. She was only seventeen years old and I certainly wasn't going to try to seduce her. I might have tried a few years later when we did another movie together, but she was in love with Michael Wilding and wasn't lookin' at anyone else!"

The Conspirator sold itself with the names of the two Taylors on theatre marquees. The critics said, "Robert Taylor and Elizabeth Taylor are the two most beautiful people on the screen."

Another: "Taylor, as a British Army Major spying for Soviet Russia, and Elizabeth Taylor as his American wife, were working under a considerable handicap because of the script."

Bob read the reviews and laughed. "Yeah, the script wasn't the only handicap!"

While he was in England he was seen at The Claridge Hotel bar having a drink, signing autographs and . . . waiting for someone. After his fourth Scotch a blonde woman stood in the doorway and looked at him. When he spotted her he smiled and she sat down beside him.

As she leaned forward, one healthy breast popped out for a moment but disappeared when she pressed against him and their lips met. There was quite a bit of petting for a few minutes until Taylor realized he was being watched. Wiping the lipstick from his face, he called for a check.

They strolled through the lobby. He said, "Pull up the front of your dress!"

With that she took his arm and placed his hand on her bosom. "You fix it, darling!"

Taylor, red in the face, grabbed her around the waist and pushed her out the door. One of the bellboys said, "Those were the pinkest nipples I ever saw!"

There was an item in the newspaper about the incident. Mayer telephoned Taylor: "Whenya coming home, boy?"

"In a few days . . ."

"Who's the broad?"

"What broad?"

"The one who couldn't stand up straight."

"Don't know what you're talking about!"

Mayer howled with laughter. Taylor hung up in a huff. His personal life was nobody's business. One brief night in London had taught him a good lesson. No women in public from now on!

He had a clean image, and he'd keep it that way. This was the beginning of the Robert Taylor mystique—never seen anywhere, no scandal, and if possible, no publicity about his private life.

When he returned to Hollywood he filmed *Ambush,* a Western, with Arlene Dahl, a new arrival in Glamour City. She said, "A year earlier I had written Robert Taylor from Minnesota for an autographed photo and here I am, making love to him on the screen!"

Immediately following *Ambush,* MGM gave him the role of a Shoshone Indian who wins the Congressional Medal of Honor at Gettysburg in *Devil's Doorway.* Many said Taylor was a peculiar choice to play a full-blooded Indian, but the make-up people had no problem. He looked every bit the part. However, the script was weak and the entire cast had little with which to work.

Ambush and *Devil's Doorway* were rated "Good." Taylor still considered himself in a professional slump and repeated himself in all his interviews: "I'm the luckiest guy in the world," or "I don't miss not having my clothes torn off my back," or "I'm goin' fishin'," and "I'm still a punk kid from Nebraska!"

Barbara was suffering from a slump also. Her movies were going from bad to worse. She laughed off the critics

144

and said they didn't have the control everyone thought they had. "If they did, we would all have been out of work a long time ago."

She asked for a comedy, but said she would take anything as long as the story was good: "I'll murder—and have done so—or take falls and have done so. But I thrive on work. I get more tired trying to find something to do when I'm not working."

She still maintained her independence and was not under contract to any one studio.

In 1950 Taylor was going into his sixteenth year under contract with MGM. Though he had not done a good movie since his successes in the early forties—*Waterloo Bridge, Johnny Eager* and *Bataan*—he was given new contracts and more money.

MGM had been working on *Quo Vadis* for over two years and though Mayer disapproved of the script, Dore Schary won again and was supported by other executives at the studio.

Whoever it was who chose Robert Taylor for the lead in this $7 million production—at that time the biggest in movie history—is not known, but when he was told he would play Marcus Vinicius, he said in his usual self-deprecating way, "Guess everyone else turned it down and they gave it to me!" But he gave the credit to Mayer because of the promise the latter had made to him in 1946—"Have I ever let you down, son?"

Chapter IX

Twelve years of planning preceded the shooting of *Quo Vadis*. It consumed a year's actual camera work; a production of a Circus of Nero large enough to seat 30,000 people, a whole section of ancient Rome and Nero's palace, were constructed according to careful historic research.

The Italian government lent MGM the treasured Forma Urbis, a model of the city of Rome as it appeared 2,000 years ago.

The huge Cinecitta Studios, eight miles outside Rome, covered 148 acres and nine big sound stages. Mussolini had built this when he thought Rome would be the film capitol of the world. It was bombed during the war and had no roof. For the filming of *Quo Vadis* a mammoth canvas was used to cover the interior.

Quo Vadis was the most expensive picture ever produced at that time and MGM added another $500,000 for its ad-publicity campaign, making a total budget of almost $7 million. (*Gone With the Wind* carried a cost of $4 million.)

Taylor lived better than ever in Rome. He occupied the entire upper floor of a new apartment house—he had eight rooms, five servants and a chef who was the former cook for the King of Italy. He was given the use of two cars, one of which was a limousine with chauffeur.

He was granted an audience with the Pope, and after viewing the Vatican he immediately wrote a letter to "Auntie Neuhauser" in Beatrice, Nebraska. He told her he had had an audience with the Holy Father, was in admiration of the monuments that he came to know at close range and in the midst of all the Roman beauty he had not forgotten her pancakes and the kindness with which she served them to him as a schoolboy. He sent his best to Lucille Lang, his childhood friend, and said "Auntie" must be very proud of Lucille, who was now known as Mother Lang and living in a convent in Brazil.

When Taylor was being fitted for his toga outfits, someone asked him if he remembered a screen test he had made for Samuel Goldwyn in 1933.

"How could I forget it?" he laughed. "I was forced to dress in a Roman toga with a wide-ribbon effect around my head. When they put me in front of the camera the director said, 'His ribs are sticking out!'

"I weighed 135 pounds and the costume just didn't fit. They told me to drinks lots of malted milk shakes. Actually, all I needed in those days was some money to pay for a square meal once in a while."

As Marcus Vinicius his ribs did not stick out. He said he was prone to overweight but learned to eat properly in Rome, even though he ate pasta twice a day.

Tom Purvis flew over to Italy to spend a few weeks with Bob. "My God, I didn't know what the hell I was eating when that chef prepared dinner for us at the apartment. Taylor and I would just sit there at the table while plates of food were served. I don't know how many times we asked each other what we were eating. We both loved to eat, but that was ridiculous! I didn't want to offend Bob and he didn't want to offend the chef. When I got back home my wife asked me what kinda food I had and she coulda kicked me when I answered, 'Don't know.' "

Taylor kept his word about not being seen in public and even though there were women, he was more than discreet. He even took Purvis to out-of-the-way restaurants.

He was up at 5 A.M. every day and in bed by 10. The filming of *Quo Vadis* was tedious. Deborah Kerr, who portrayed the Christian slave girl, Lygia, said, "The movie was made under terribly difficult conditions, enormous heat and many irritations, but at all times Bob was good-natured and un-fussy.

"When one thinks of his extraordinary good looks, he had every right to be a bit spoiled, but not Bob. He was unassuming, good natured and had a wonderful sense of humor.

147

"I only made the one movie with him—*Quo Vadis*—but it was almost like making three movies, it went on so long.

"I felt that Bob was a much better actor than he was given credit for. His outstanding handsomeness inevitably channeled him into 'hero' roles, but will anyone forget how excellent he was playing a heavy in *Johnny Eager*. I certainly won't, nor shall I ever forget Bob."

Taylor was not known to forget or muff his lines, but working underneath the mammoth canvas at Cinecitta Studios, proved to be a problem. The winds were strong and the noisy flapping of the canvas interfered with the sound.

Taylor and Miss Kerr had attempted a scene together but were stopped several times because of the wind. When things quieted down, the director wanted to do the scene quickly, but Bob muffed his lines three times. They tried it again and again until finally it went smoothly.

Bob walked over to Purvis. "God damn, this has never happened to me. Well it's over."

Except it wasn't. The director came over to Taylor and told him the dialogue was fine, but the microphone had picked up some noise caused by the winds.

"When you goof as many times as I did," Taylor moaned, "nothing comes out right. Thought I'd never get through with that one particular scene."

News reached Barbara that Bob was "playing around" in Rome. The gossip columns hinted he was seen with a number of women. Rumors persisted until finally one woman in particular was revealed—Lia DiLeo, a bit player.

The *Quo Vadis* cast laughed it off and everyone said it was a lot of nonsense—probably publicity. Purvis was convinced there was nothing going on. He said Lia had called Bob from the lobby. "He asked me to stay in the apartment while she was there. He told me she was an aspiring actress and it might make the wrong impression if he were alone with her.

"At that time I was sure there was nothing going on between them. Seemed to me it was the usual 'crush on a movie star' or 'maybe you can get me into the movies' angle."

Taylor might have fooled Purvis, but Barbara's telephone bills amounted to over $3,000 as a result of her calls to Rome. She didn't like the tone of his voice or his answers. Her motherly instinct was to find out for herself what was going on in romantic Italy.

It *had* to have been a very difficult decision for her when she made up her mind to join Bob. Neither had ever intruded on the other while working, and of course, Barbara was deathly afraid of airplanes. But she called Helen Ferguson and said, "I'm going to Rome and you're going with me!"

MGM said she was taking a vacation to be with Taylor and "eagerly awaited the chance to sightsee in such a beautiful country." The press covered her six-week visit to Rome in August, 1950. There were pictures of Bob pointing out places of interest and Barbara looking interested.

Helen, trying to cover up the tension, said, "Bob was so thoughtful. He knew that it was difficult to obtain various brands of makeup, tissues and so forth, but he made sure when we arrived we were well-equipped with everything we needed."

But the inevitable happened. Barbara and Bob had a violent quarrel. The subject of Lia DiLeo was most assuredly the cause of the argument. Taylor remained silent, which he usually did in a situation like this one. Barbara threatened divorce and admitted later this was only an attempt to frighten him.

It was rumored that Taylor confided to Gable six months later that Barbara had accused him of having affairs with several women in Rome and she ripped into his relationship with Lia to the point where he had to break his silence.

His one statement that "the pretty Italian girl excited him" infuriated Barbara so that she threatened Bob with divorce.

She left Rome immediately.

Quo Vadis opened simultaneously at the Astor and Capitol Theatres in New York City on November 8,

1951. (The silent version had been a huge moneymaker in 1913.)

It grossed over $12 million and in the early fifties was the fourth biggest grosser in movie history.

The critics concentrated on the film itself—the arena scenes, the gladiatorial combats, the lions eating the Christians, the burning of Rome and the photography, sets and costumes.

Little was mentioned about the acting. Peter Ustinov as Nero was excellent, but the performances of Robert Taylor and Deborah Kerr "appeared anything but inspired."

The cast of players listed Lia DiLeo as the pedicurist, and extras Sophia Loren and Elizabeth Taylor, who were in Rome at the time and mingled in the crowd scenes just for fun.

Taylor completed *Quo Vadis* in December, 1950, and was preparing to leave his apartment for the airport. He had heard little from Barbara since her departure three months before, and though he tried to keep his name out of the papers to avoid annoying her further, he knew his marriage was over. However, he did not want to hurt her any more than he had already. Their marriage had lasted over ten years—a long time by Hollywood standards. And this, after all, was a very important element of his clean and wholesome image.

When he appeared in the lobby of his apartment house with his baggage, Lia was waiting for him! He was taken by surprise when she flung herself into his arms!

He held her as she covered his face with loving kisses . . . and the press cameras clicked.

Taylor had been neatly framed! He smiled, but pushed her away very gently and hurried to his limousine. Lia did not follow him, but she was ready to make a statement to the reporters whom she had cleverly brought with her.

She said she was the former wife of the king's attorney, but now she was "Robert Taylor's big love," and had been throughout the filming of *Quo Vadis*: "He is tired of her [Barbara] and he told me so!"

Taylor refused comment at the airport and returned to Hollywood, where the pictures of him and Lia were front-page news. He completely ignored the press and went home.

The newspapers announced that the Taylors had separated, but within a few days after Bob's arrival in Hollywood, they announced they were going to San Francisco. It was revealed Taylor was admitted to a hospital there.

He was operated on for the removal of a double hernia and Barbara remained at his bedside every minute.

"Those hours he was on the operating table were the worst I have ever spent in my life," she told Louella Parsons.

When asked what plans they had, Barbara said they were going on a three-month vacation together, but instead went to Palm Springs alone and Barbara remained incommunicado at the home of friends in Hollywood.

In a matter of days the divorce announcement was made, on December 16, 1950, through their press agent, Helen Ferguson.

She called Louella Parson, but was unable to read the formal statement and broke down in tears. She handed the paper, to Howard Strickling, head of publicity at MGM, who had been asked by Bob to "be very gentle with Helen at this time."

In a joint statement, the Taylors said,

"In the past few years, because of professional requirements, we have been separated just too often and too long. Our sincere and continued efforts to maintain our marriage have failed.

"We are deeply disappointed that we could not solve our problems. We really tried. We unhappily and reluctantly admit what we have denied to even our closest friends, because we wanted to work things out together in as much privacy as possible. There will be a California divorce. Neither of us has any other romantic interest whatsoever."

The Stanwyck-Taylor marriage was often pointed out as the one perfect example that two famous film stars could have separate careers and a happy marriage, too.

"That was the trouble," Barbara said. "Separate careers! We have been separated just too often and too long.

"I have said many times I was a long-distance-telephone wife. Bob and I never could get together. When I was in a picture, he was on vacation. When I was off for a few weeks, he was sent someplace halfway around the world.

"The best we could do, usually, was shake hands at the door as we came in and out."

Louella Parsons wrote, "It is almost certain that this Italian girl had nothing to do with the Taylors' decision to part. Trouble started long before Bob went to Rome.

"I spoke to Barbara and I am inclined to think when they decided to end their marriage it came suddenly.

"It was Bob who asked for his freedom!"

On February 21, 1951, Barbara Stanwyck, looking chic in a slim, toast-colored suit with a matching hat topping her gray curls, told the court in a three-minute hearing (one of the shortest movie divorces on record) that her husband, Robert Taylor, was tired of being married and wanted to be a bachelor again.

"He said he had enjoyed his freedom during the months he was making a movie in Italy. He wanted to be able to continue his life without restrictions.

"I was very shocked and very grieved over it and I was quite ill. For several weeks I was under the care of my physician."

Barbara's friend and press agent testified in her behalf. "I went to Barbara's house and found her in a tragic emotional state. She said, 'I am going to give Bob the freedom he wants!' "

Superior Judge Thurmond Clarke interrupted her with a terse, "That will be enough. Divorce granted!"

Barbara asked the court for permission to drop the surname Taylor, and she was awarded their $100,000 mansion, all furnishings, and 15 per cent of Taylor's earnings until she remarried or either party died.

As she left court she refused to comment on rumors that her "matinée idol" husband wanted his freedom because he had fallen in love with an Italian beauty. "I don't know," she said with a crooked smile, "you'll have to ask Mr. Taylor about that!"

When she was asked if she had a new boy friend, Barbara widened her eyes and shuddered. "Oh, no! I've had enough. I don't want any more of that!!"

The divorce hearing made headlines, but the following day, February 22, 1951, the shapely Italian bit actress Lia DiLeo also had her day:

"BOB'S 'BIG LOVE' SEES NO HITCH IN HER PLANS"

Rome: Redheaded Lia DiLeo, for whose love Robert Taylor ostensibly broke up with Barbara Stanwyck, today was so little impressed with the "great lover" of American films that she indicated she would rather remain "good friends" with Taylor than marry him.

She admitted she was truly Bob's true love when he was in Rome, but she said marriage with Taylor didn't seem to be in the cards, though, "If it depended on him alone I am sure we would marry."

She said the break-up between the Taylors was inevitable. "I knew this would happen ever since he was here. He was tired of her and told me so!

She added coldly, "It was evident that after meeting me a divorce was the only possible solution."

The divorced Lia said she was reluctant to marry again, having had one previous disheartening experience along these lines. "Yet I might yield to his persistence, though after my first marital experience I have become convinced it is better to be good friends than to be hampered by marriage ties.

"I think I shall be very good friends with Robert instead of being his wife," she concluded frankly.

Miss DiLeo posed for photographers in a striped bathing suit that showed off every one of her curves to their best advantage.

Taylor called Tom Purvis in Illinois: "Got to get out of here to hide out. Can you put up with me?"

He flew his Beechcraft to Champagne, Illinois, where

Tom drove his car out to the plane on the runway. Taylor hopped in and dropped to the floor.

Purvis had gotten him a small apartment and Bob locked himself up, only going out at night to Tom's house, donning sunglasses and always squatting on the floor of the car. But after three days he was recognized by someone. "It's no use, Tom, I'm goin' back!"

In Los Angeles he alternated living with Ralph Couser and his wife, and with Ruth in Brentwood.

Ruth had mixed emotions about her son's divorce, but she told him to stay as long as he wanted. He slept in the maid's room.

"Just one thing bothers me, son—all that money you are going to have to pay Barbara, and you gave her that house, too—everything gone!"

"Not everything. I kept my coffee table."

Ruth sadly remarked that his coffee table wouldn't keep them out of the poorhouse. And was he going to bring any women to her house? Bob assured her at the present time the last thing on his mind was running around with women, to which Ruth exclaimed, "Thank God!"

Then she rambled on that she had read somewhere the big Hollywood studios were going to release many of their stars. "Will this affect you, son?"

Taylor hadn't read it in the papers, but the rumors at the studio confirmed what Ruth was saying. Schary's new regime was taking over and although MGM had pulled itself out of debt, he knew there were going to be cut-backs, and if many of the contract players were not fired, they would undoubtedly quit. Gable had mentioned it to him and asked Bob what he was going to do. Taylor said he'd go along until they booted him out!

Barbara was so emotionally upset over the divorce that she immediately moved out of their mansion and auctioned off the majority of the furniture.

The newspapers reported that one of the first items to be offered would be Taylor's bed. Included in the more than 600 articles to go on the block were 65 paintings, among them a Renoir and a series of ten studies of a pioneer woman of the West by Fredric Remington.

Barbara's bed went for $360, but Bob's laced leather headboard and end table built into it—including a carved wooden horse supporting a lamp—sold for $630.

Two days after the auction, Barbara and Bob were seen dining at Ciro's in Hollywood. She told reporters, "There's no use trying to keep it a secret. I'm carrying a torch for Bob, but it is too early to say whether or not we will be reconciled."

She said it was her second date with Taylor since the divorce decree, which would not become final until a year from the date it was granted. Taylor wouldn't comment, but Barbara said firmly, "There will be no other man in my life!"

Bob was trying to recapture what he and Barbara had when they were courting in the late thirties. Though he kept quiet in public, he did confide to close friends that he hoped seeing Barbara occasionally would bring them closer together, and he was adamant about trying to keep what he thought was an "unusual" marriage together.

Taylor did not want divorce, but Barbara had threatened him in Rome and to her surprise, he took her up on it. She wanted to frighten him, to bring him to his senses. Though she was not one to forgive and forget, she might have "just this once."

The night referred to by Helen Ferguson in her testimony at the divorce trial, when she ran to Barbara's side, was the night Taylor asked Barbara for his freedom—legally—and in a rage she promised that he would get his divorce but that she would bleed him for the rest of his life.

Those who knew the Taylors remarked that Bob did lean on Barbara too much during their marriage. He wasn't weak, but he was rather innocent about life and women when he met her.

Someone said she always told Bob what to do and how to go about it. "Could anyone forget when she gave him that new convertible? Why, she even told him how to drive it!"

Another observer said, "They could find nothing mutual to do in their spare time. If Barbara had learned to fly or at least forced herself to suffer through a few flights with him occasionally, they might have made a go of it."

Another: "They got tired of each other and their way of life. Barbara was and always will be a dedicated actress and I think her career came first even though she will never love anyone but Bob."

Another: "They should have adopted children. Bob loves kids and was devoted to Dion. But Barbara didn't have time to devote to them. She and Bob had one thing in common—the movie industry—period!"

Another: "As Bob matured he wanted a wife, not a sparring partner or counselor and certainly not a mother . . . he has one of those!"

Taylor would not talk about Barbara. He was hounded for awhile about Miss DiLeo, but he remarked, "What about her? I'm here, aren't I? Is she with me?

"I'm not going to carry on a transcontinental argument [New York to Rome], but I do not plan to marry anyone at present. It's wonderful to be foot-loose and fancy-free!"

He was sipping champagne with Rex Harrison and a group of friends but came to the restaurant alone. He was never linked with women during 1951 except for Barbara, but in his usual discreet manner he was getting around . . .

Though he denied everything that was supposed to have occurred in Italy—especially Miss DiLeo—he had gone out with many girls of all types in Rome. They were not actresses or well known in any sense of the word. He always took them to small places outside of town.

When his divorce was announced he was asked about his love life and he replied, "Well, what about it? I've got nothing to hide. My social life's an open book these days. In fact everybody's getting into the act. I've read so many different things about myself that half the time even I can't keep up with what I'm doing—or rather what I am supposed to be doing."

One of Taylor's secret dates was the well-known honey-blonde actress Virginia Grey. She had been Clark Gable's "favorite" for seven years until he eloped with Lady Ashley. Several days after his marriage was announced

Virginia received a call from a friend who asked if it was all right to give Robert Taylor her telephone number and she agreed.

He called her and said he would bring over some steaks, wine and records. It was obvious to her he did not want to be seen in public, so they spent their evenings at her place.

Virginia Grey said, "He would never talk about Barbara, but his divorce wasn't final yet and I just took it for granted he didn't want to be seen in public with another woman. Barbara was still in love with him—everybody knew that—and I found out the hard way that she resented any woman Bob dated. When I met her accidentally a few years later, what she had to say to me I cannot quote, but I had done the unpardonable . . . I had gone out with Bob Taylor."

She explained that he was a complete mystery to her. After spending their first evening together she left the room for a minute and when she returned he had disappeared.

Taylor had simply decided it was time to go home, and that's exactly what he did. When he telephoned her a week later he never mentioned the incident, but he would do this often.

She said Bob had a helplessness about himself—always wanting or starting to say something, but could put words on paper better than speak them because of his shyness. He feared rejection, one of the reasons he had someone else call for her telephone number, rather than just introducing himself.

"But Bob was warm and wonderful," Miss Grey said. "When we were toegther I forgot he was Robert Taylor. He made me interested because he was so unpredictable. Also, I don't think Bob liked himself very much and was not a happy man when I knew him. He was a real introvert when it came to a man and woman relationship."

She compared him to Gable: "You could get to know them so far and then—the wall!"

When Gable returned from his honeymoon he tried to resume his relationship with Virginia and she was forced to change her telephone number. Taylor was in Utah at the time doing a movie and when he flew back for a few days he tried to call her but was told by the operator he could not have the new number. He thought she was trying to avoid him and dropped her a note saying, "Being the kind of guy who doesn't need a building to fall on me to get the idea, I gave up!"

Another woman actress remembers Taylor as a frustrating man to date. Always writing letters, he would correspond with her when he was out of town, including such teasing messages as "Was in town Saturday night but didn't call. Thought you'd be busy!" (She wasn't!) Or "It's lonely here. Don't know why you didn't come along!" (She would have!) Or "Read in the papers you might get married. How come I can't get that lucky?" (He never asked!)

In his fashion, Taylor was being kind of complimentary and did it with such simplicity that he was labeled a mystery.

MGM allowed him all the privacy he wanted and kept his personal life out of the papers, but it wasn't Mayer who was protecting him any more. L.B. had lost control of his empire and stepped down to Dore Schary on August 31, 1951, when he resigned from Metro. When he spoke to Taylor in late 1949 and read the silly poem he had found among his papers, Mayer was setting the scene.

His leaving MGM frightened Taylor. Yet, regardless of how many items were written about this change affecting his career, Schary carried on in Taylor's behalf. Perhaps his tactics were different from Mayer's, but Mayer's "son" was one of the few contract players at MGM who did not suffer during this drastic transition.

The studio *was* slowly getting rid of their long-time contract stars and Gable suspected he would be next, but he beat them to it by getting his attorneys to break the contract. The King said at his farewell luncheon— "I wish to pay tribute to my friends and associates who no longer are alive!" Later when they offered him half of the profits if he would do a film for them, he told his agent to rub it in. "And when you get their best offer,

158

tell them to take their money, their studio, their cameras and lighting equipment and shove it up their ass!" [6]

Taylor, however, continued to sign new contracts with better money but said he didn't get that lump in his throat when he put his signature on the dotted line without Mayer standing beside him—both men grinning ear to ear.

He flew his plane to his favorite spots, where there was always a cowpoke somewhere in the Midwest waiting for him to pop in for some hunting or fishing, or he caught up with some of his cronies in the Northwest. North Dakota was another haunt where pheasant hunting was especially good.

Taylor was the jumpy type, and he loved to drive as long as he had gallons of black coffee with him. Once he drove from Illinois to Los Angeles in three and a half days—a usual five-day trip. Sometimes he even carried his own gasoline.

He liked rugged men—Gary Cooper, John Wayne, Keenan Wynn and of course his old buddies, Couser and Purvis. He even liked and kept in touch with "Redhorse" Meyes, his former instructor in the Navy, because "Redhorse" was wilder than a marsh hare—always picking fights and taking too many chances.

Purvis said, "Bob kept in touch with everyone—if he liked you. But if you threw him a curve, he was 'off you forever.' He became a fanatic about privacy after his divorce, but I don't think it had anything to do with the break-up of his marriage—he had been kicked around so much and never had any time to himself."

Taylor was now forty years old. It had taken him a long time to reach maturity, but he was taking advantage of it. Many of his friends said he was running away, but actually he was always running TO something. Taylor was not known to roam about aimlessly. He had a purpose to anything he did.

On one of his frequent plane trips trom Los Angeles to New York, he got hungry and landed in Palm Springs to see what a friend was cooking for breakfast, liked

6. Chester Williams, GABLE, (New York: Fleet Press, 1968), pp. 116 & 117.

159

what he tasted, ate, and flew to New Orleans to renew an old friendship with a restauranteur who had a set of diamond-encrusted teeth.

He picked up several friends along the way to New York, and one night invited the entire Copacabana chorus line out for dinner.

But he was still very sensitive about his good looks and any reference to his appearance cracked his aplomb.

Having dinner one night with friends, he was approached by a girl who took one good long look at him and said, with unbelievable gaucherie, "Gee, you're the most beautiful man in the world!"

Taylor quite literally paled, got up from a half-finished meal and left the premises alone.

His friends, expecting him to return after he cooled off, said that Bob hopped into a cab and took off for the airport. He flew off in his plane—for somewhere.

In Hollywood he was seen with several cute blondes—usually at a hamburger joint, anywhere that he wasn't expected. When he did date any woman who was well-known, he did not go out in public. Because of this his press agents had to make up stories about him—usually about a picture he was going to do or a house he was going to build or his kindness toward Barbara.

The reporters admitted they couldn't find him, but as usual he did come forth and speak up when he was angry or fed up with articles that were being printed about him.

"I keep reading that I'm the loneliest guy in Hollywood. If I read it five more times maybe I'll begin to believe it. Then I could have a hell of a time wallowing around in self-pity, except for one thing—I'm not given to self-pity!

"I get the picture through articles written about me that I'm slumped in a cell-like room, night after night, surrounded by bats.

"That's interesting, but inaccurate.

"In fact, I lead what I consider a very happy life— I mean a life that suits Robert Taylor just fine. The 'weepers' insist I'm just keeping a stiff upper lip or whistling past the graveyard.

"It seems almost impossible for a naturally solitary person like myself to convince the 'joiners' that I'm pretty

160

happy the way I am! Anyone like me—and I'll bet there are plenty—knows just what I'm talking about. We don't feel sorry for ourselves. We like it.

"I don't go to Hollywood parties because I'm not invited to any. I have exactly two friends in Hollywood and that might be stretching it.

"Let me tell you something—in Hollywood a party is not a party unless it is one of those 'Everybody who was anybody was there.'

"What a God damn crushing blow it must be to 159,890,000 Americans to find out that they're not anybody!

"I read about them like everyone else and I don't lose any sleep over it. Besides, you can't have the social whirl without losing your freedom."

He carried his typewriter wherever he went and wrote to everyone. Sometimes his letters were informative, if he were writing to a close buddy, but more often he would type for something to do—almost as if he were talking, which he didn't like to do.

He didn't go out of his way to make friends, but he would go out of his way for a friend.

On one fishing trip to Wyoming with Tom Purvis, they decided to camp out in sleeping bags. They were deep enough in the wilds to have to carry water and canned food for several days. Temperatures were in the low twenties and Tom, at 6 feet 3 inches, was half out of his sleeping bag. During the night he got thirsty ("We put too much salt on the fish we cooked for dinner and I was swallowing cotton!) He shivered over to the car when he heard something. It sounded to him like a lot of empty tin cans were being thrown around.

Purvis took one look and saw a bear snooping around their garbage. He ran back to his sleeping bag and this time it hit him! "Bob, are you awake?"

"Yeah."

"There's a bear over there."

"Yeah?"

"Tell ya one thing, Dilly, this damn sleeping bag fits okay *now!*"

"Yeah, well mine's too big. I'm at the bottom of mine right now and I'm not movin'!"

Next morning one could see two sleeping bags and four eyes.

"Think he's gone, Dilly?"

"How the hell would I know. My eyes are open, but I'm afraid to look!"

"You get up first."

"I'm gonna have to—gotta go over the hill to take a leak!"

Taylor moved slowly out of his sleeping bag, looked around and started up the hill. "Hey, Old Bud, if I see anything over there I'm gonna have some soiled underwear!"

The two fished all day looking over their shoulders and said nothing. When they were driving home, Tom made a crack about the fact that his sleeping bag just didn't keep him warm—bear or no bear.

Taylor kidded Tom about the whole incident and said he liked the cold weather.

"Any guy who plays golf in the snow has to," Tom said. "Why it was cold enough last night to freeze a fire!"

"Why didn't you shoot the damn thing and make yourself a rug!"

"I didn't see you runnin' for your gun, Dilly!"

"You kidding? Me leave my nice warm sleeping accommodations to save you?"

"If you like the cold weather so much, how come your sleeping bag was shakin' all night?"

"Having a nightmare that I was watchin' *Song of Russia* on TV."

Purvis had only been home a week when he received a seven-foot custom-made sleeping bag with built-in blanket, inflatable mattress, snap-in sheets and pillows. The gift card read, "Don't wake me up next time you see a harmless bear. Dilly."

Westward the Women was regarded with particular esteem, not so much because of Taylor, but because of the story itself—and the women, which included busty Denise Darcel and broad-beamed Hope Emerson.

Taylor took the part of a dirty and tough wagonmaster chaperoning a group of "tobacco-chewing ladies" from Chicago to California. With the pictures of their husbands-to-be tucked in their bosoms, the women face rape, death,

Indians, an accidental killing of a child, and the birth of a baby in a tilted covered wagon.

For exceptional realism, the women's clothing was not washed for twelve days, only sprayed with deodorizers.

Director William Wellman, worked the cast hard and when he suggested a seven-day filming schedule, Taylor intervened by offering to fly Wellman home every weekend—much to the director's delight and to everyone else's satisfaction.

It also gave Taylor a chance to get the cast and crew together to film his own home movie. He made his own posters, ribbing his friends back home, and everyone including Denise Darcel, took part. Tom Purvis was one of the recipients and has the reel to this day.

Taylor arranged every detail of the film and thought it was better than most of the movies he had made for MGM!

Westward the Women was classified as a "picturesque novelty," but it did bring Taylor back to the screen while *Quo Vadis* was making the successful rounds of neighborhood theatres.

MGM wanted Taylor in costume epics and assigned him to *Ivanhoe* with Elizabeth Taylor and Joan Fontaine. This movie was Dore Schary's pride and joy, but when Taylor read the script he didn't like it. "I'm not refusing but I'd rather not do it. I kinda like Westerns these days."

Within weeks, however, Taylor was in England portraying the sturdy and forthright Ivanhoe. The jousting scenes were most authentic and the movie maintained Taylor's popularity and established him as the public's Knight in Shining Armor.

Male audiences liked *Ivanhoe* . . . and Robert Taylor. The women, of course, were always waiting for their own knight charging on a white horse and again found a substitute for The Sheik and the everlasting Valentino.

Taylor was not displeased with the results of his medieval roles, but considered it extra-duty having to wear the heavy equipment required, saying he felt naked in a business suit. He wrote to Purvis, "I'm gettin' mighty tired of those iron jockstraps!"

163

Ruth said he reminded her of the hero Arlington in the novel she was reading before he was born. She raved over *Ivanhoe*. Bob said he really preferred Western britches because they were more comfortable.

"But those cowboy hats, son, why do you always pull them down over your face. Wear them on top of your head where they belong . . ."

Bob smiled. His mother had always adjusted his hat, even as a little boy, and he liked to pull it back over his forehead just to tease her, but now it was a habit and it amused him when Ruth threw up her hands before reaching out to show more of his face.

Chapter X

Though never involved in a public scandal, Taylor did receive some rather unusual publicity in the early fifties. A story circulated that he almost fell victim to a well-planned blackmail scheme in 1952.

He was in New York at the time and went out to dinner with a business associate. They were seated at a table next to a group of people who recognized him, but appeared nonchalant about having Robert Taylor in the same restaurant and sitting so close to them. However, one of the young ladies, a tall stunning blonde, couldn't take her eyes off him and he noticed she was deliberately flirting . . . which didn't bother Taylor in the least. She didn't smile, but kept her eyes on him. He continued to finish dinner, but between bites, he looked her over thoroughly.

Her companion leaned over and asked Taylor if he'd like to join the group. He declined, but suggested having a nightcap together later in the evening. When they met for drinks, the lovely blonde introduced herself as Rachael.

She asked him how long he would be in New York and he said just for a few days. She said it was a pity because she would love to take him to some fine restaurants in the Village. He accepted her invitation, but preferred they enjoy a gourmet dinner at his hotel. She understood that such a famous star would not want to be bothered with autographs and such. He told her to call him the next morning and they would set up a date.

Taylor left the group and retired for the evening. He was busy and actually forgot Rachael until she called two days later. Did he remember her?

Rachael arrived in a lovely pink silk dress that clung

to every curve. "You look beautiful," he said, "how about a drink?"

They had cocktails and a delicious dinner sent up to Taylor's suite. Over brandy, he put his arms around her and she responded.

The pink dress hung in the closet, and when Rachael revealed her matching pink undies, she asked Taylor if she could use the phone to call her mother. "It looks like I'll be here awhile and I wouldn't want Mommy to worry . . ."

Mother wasn't home. Could she wait just a few more minutes before they "retired" to the bedroom? This was a very important phone call. Rachael tried again and again, but no answer.

Actually she was not trying to call her mother, rather her accomplice who was waiting in a telephone booth downstairs. He was posing as her husband and the plan was for him to make a fuss outside Taylor's suite until he was allowed in, at which time the three would talk about how much it was worth to keep the incident quiet.

But Rachael's so-called husband had been picked up by the police for loitering in the hotel lobby and was told to get off the premises immediately.

Rachael found herself with Robert Taylor, almost in the nude, and "Mother wasn't home." She had no choice but to "go through with it." Apparently the evening was a success because she became one of Taylor's frequent dates when he was in New York. It wasn't until three years later that he saw her picture in the paper for attempted blackmail. One of the detectives told a reporter who some of her vicitims had been or, in Taylor's case, "almost was." And though the papers did not print the entire story, it got around.

Taylor ignored it and denied it ever happened, but there were those who knew the truth and jokingly said, "He must have been pretty good in the sack for Rachael to go back for more and not try to hustle a few bucks. She was a real pro . . ."

One of Taylor's favorite leading ladies—on and off the screen—was Eleanor Parker. They were to make three good movies together, and the first was *Above and*

166

Beyond, the story of Colonel Tibbets, who pressed the trigger that fired the atom bomb over Hiroshima in 1945.

This story had been sought by several film companies in Hollywood for five years following the war, but an absolute refusal met their efforts. Finally it was indicated in Washington that if Beirne Lay, Jr., co-author of *Twelve O'Clock High* and himself a former B-29 pilot, submitted an acceptable treatment, the project might be considered. Lay wanted to write the "story behind the story" as seen through the eyes of the wife of a man charged with one of the most gruelling responsibilities of the war.

Taylor was given the part of Colonel Tibbets in *Above and Beyond* and his performance was the closest he came to being considered Oscar material. The critics gave him the benefit and said he might have achieved it at another time. His type of acting wasn't appreciated then, despite his perfection in a role that was made for him.

Eleanor Parker, who portrayed Mrs. Tibbets, was an established actress who had been nominated for an Oscar as best actress in 1951 for her talent in *Detective Story.*

When she met Taylor in 1952, she was in the process of separating from her second husband, producer Bert Friedlob.

She and Taylor were seen lunching together occasionally in New York while on a promotion tour for *Above and Beyond.* Their "friendship," the press said, was "mutual admiration and professional devotion."

She told reporters she would very much like to do another picture with Bob, but to set them straight, that her relationship with him was platonic, she took out pictures of her three children and mentioned her husband.

The fact that Eleanor and Bob were seeing each other privately was a well-known fact at MGM and to their close friends, but their closeness was never revealed to the public.

They might have married, but Eleanor was in many ways like Barbara Stanwyck, and she was eleven years younger than Bob. Friends said it was difficult to put into words exactly why Eleanor and Bob did not reach the altar, but the general consensus was that she was an independent woman, a little flighty and somewhat domineering—all the elements Bob had faced in his first marriage.

His only comment was, "She makes me nervous."

Nevertheless, they were in love and their acting together was always close to perfection. One MGM official said, "There was no doubt that they were very much attracted to one another and it showed up on the screen vividly."

Bob continued to see Eleanor as well as other women, but he always managed to carry on his affairs so that none were aware that any others existed.

The only mention of his involvement with anyone was with Barbara. They were seen together more often after their break-up than during their marriage. She was eager to reconcile, but he had to be sure and made every attempt possible. Although he could not rekindle the sparks, he desperately wanted her friendship.

Taylor was a "first" in another important phase of show business. In the early fifties the movie industry was taking a terrible beating from television. Film stars damned the little square box and for years refused to comment on it. Joan Crawford, for example, said that any movie star who appeared on television was unfaithful to Hollywood.

But Robert Taylor appeared on the Ed Sullivan Show in what the newspapers said "was an unprecedented move."

"The first time a major Hollywood film studio is allowing one of its contract stars to appear on television will take place on Ed Sullivan's *Toast of the Town* show on CBS-TV when Robert Taylor makes a guest appearance along with film clips of his latest movie, *Above and Beyond*.

"With a giant studio such as MGM finally granting permission for a top-name star to do a video show, the opening may finally have effect whereby a flood of other contract players, not only from MGM, but from other studios, will now pour into the medium.

"Up until now Hollywood held to the steadfast rule not to let any name personality under contract take part on a live TV show.

"The engagement of Taylor for the Sullivan Show, according to a Vice-President of MGM, is regarded as an experiment to see the value of television in the promotion of pictures." (Note: MGM was the *last* major studio to release their feature films in full for public showing on television.)

"Taylor's appearance also points up the growing cooperation between Hollywood and television. MGM breaking down might make it easier for *every* studio to leap into TV with name personalities they have at their command."

The film clips of *Above and Beyond* shown on the Ed Sullivan Show added to its promotion very effectively. Taylor as Colonel Tibbets assisted Air Force recruiting and publicized the movie in key cities throughout the United States.

Taylor was awarded with fine reviews: "A good, strong performance is registered by Robert Taylor. To the best of our recollection, it's the finest acting he has ever done.

"Equally splendid is Eleanor Parker's portrayal of Lucey Tibbets. She lives the role before your eyes!

"A surpassing film; all should see it!"

Because of the nature of *Above and Beyond,* Taylor went out of his way to promote it. He hated public appearances and MGM rarely forced him to "go on the road." It was he who volunteered for his rare appearances.

Actually at this time in his life, he had little to do in Hollywood because he had no real home.

He was still hanging his clothes at Ruth's and sleeping in the maid's little room on occasion, but he preferred to keep moving.

On one trip, he drove to Texas to buy a couple of horses. Helen Ferguson, whom Bob still kept on his payroll as press agent because she was Barbara's friend, called him and asked what his schedule was. He had made out his timetable and read it to Helen as if he were giving someone a detailed account of an auto race: time he was leaving Los Angeles, where and what time he would stop to eat, where and what time he would spend the night, the exact time he would be checking out the horses and the hour of his return back home.

Helen said, "I wish just once you'd break one of your iron-clad schedules!"

169

The minute he returned he picked up the phone and called her. "Well I busted the schedule. Got back two hours early."

Taylor bought his horses and boarded them in the country. When he wasn't going over a script or preparing for a movie, he was checking over his plane or grooming his horses.

He looked for a house or preferably a ranch, though he did not know exactly what he wanted to do at this time; but like everything else he undertook, he did not overlook anything.

He had been shown a small ranch in the valley and was considering buying it. Just to be sure, he looked it over. One morning after a quarrel with Ruth, he decided to have a place of his own, but he wanted to make sure how much it would cost to re-do the kitchen and carpet the floors, among other things. The real-estate agent had given him the measurements of the rooms, but he took his own tape-rule and got down on his hands and knees, carefully jotting down everything to the 1/100 of an inch.

As Taylor went about his measuring, another couple entered the door to inspect the ranch. They assumed he was the renting agent and carried on quite a conversation with him, only seeing his rear view.

"God damn! I had to stay in that position. I was afraid they would recognize me. Then my pants split. I could feel it happening slowly and I tried to ease up a little without showing my face. Then it happened—the whole damn seam went.

"I sat up, face to the wall, and told them I was busy —to come back later. The woman was laughing and she said she would gladly sew my pants up.

"All I could think of was her finding out who I was and telling everyone what color undershorts Robert Taylor wore. I finally got rid of them when I said the floors weren't level and I was bustin' my pants trying to figure out how to rectify the situation.

"Never did buy the place, but I also decided I had a big ass! Told my tailor not to put in any more back pockets . . ."

Such stories were related to friends, but never to reporters. Underneath his somber exterior, Taylor had an

170

unusual sense of humor and could have made himself a more colorful person if he had opened up publicly.

Like Tracy, Gable and Rock Hudson, Taylor was not good at personality interviews. They talked about everything but themselves. In Taylor's case he would get on the subject of hunting and fishing without realizing it. He found it almost impossible to talk about himself.

He has been called a bore; but actually it was *he* who was bored: Idle chatter bored him, party talk bored him, movie talk bored him. Sports and politics were his favorite subjects, and occasionally he liked to talk about actresses he worked with, comparing their beauty and talent.

His fellow actors admired him for his promptness, professional abilities and his being just one of the boys.

During the temporary downfall of movies in the early fifties, MGM sent their efficiency experts around to the sets. Budgets had to be slashed. One of the first luxuries that was eliminated was free coffee for the cast and crew. The stars, however, were allowed to have as much as they wanted free of charge.

This announcement was a genuine shock to Taylor. It infuriated him! First of all, if everyone did not have the privilege of free coffee, he wouldn't either. Secondly, he loved his coffee—gallons of it. Third, maybe, just maybe, he wouldn't report for work if an adjustment wasn't made. "The very idea of my being allowed free coffee while the less important people, as they are referred to, are not, burns my insides! They work harder than I do. It's a God damn shame. No coffee, compliments of MGM, no leading man, compliments of Taylor!"

The next day everything was back to normal. Coffee was served as usual. One of the cameramen said, "I really doubt if Taylor would ever not show up for work. He probably would have made some kind of deal whereby he would have had the coffee bill for everyone sent to him. There was no doubt that it was the principle involved, but he could never find it in his heart to hold up production for anything—even coffee."

After Taylor's divorce from Barbara he became more outgoing. He had to be. There were too many people who removed themselves from his list of friends when the divorce was announced because they sided with Barbara.

It was a good lesson, in a way, because he *had* to make a new life for himself, which meant going out of his way to show strangers he needed them as much as they wanted to know him.

Taylor met a young lady with money who was trying to make it in the movies. He liked her friends, who were a group of musicians, movie-extras, college students, nurses and doctors.

Janice was not romantically involved with Taylor. He knew her parents and they suggested he might enjoy some of her "off-beat" parties. She and her groups, they said, were outgoing and down-to-earth.

He had stayed pretty much to himself when he joined her and seemed to be getting a kick out of watching everyone laughingly engrossed in a game of charades at a rustic house at Malibu, decorated with posters and filled with large Oriental pillows scattered about on the floor.

Janice suggested Taylor meet everyone personally, but no one said more than, "How do you do?"

"Ya know, Jan, I don't think your friends like me!"

"Of course they do, but you have to realize who you are."

"Who am I?"

"Robert Taylor, big-time movie big-shot, silly! It's hard for them to treat you like an equal!"

"God damn, why don't they try?"

"God damn, yourself. Why don't YOU try? YOU go over to them—start up a conversation . . . go on."

He did, but a few minutes later he had disappeared. Janice called his house and Ruth said he was asleep.

What people did not know about Bob Taylor was that during all those years under all that Hollywood glamour, he was nursing a chronic inferiority complex. To him Gary Cooper and Clark Gable were big stars, while he was just Robert Taylor.

He could always see why a Mickey Rooney was so popular, but his own popularity was a mystery to him. He acted like the only man in the world who never heard of Robert Taylor.

172

After a brief guest appearance in *I Love Melvin,* Taylor agreed to make *Ride Vaquero!* It was a letdown, and one critic wrote amusingly, "Nothing could have been as static as the dusty shenanigans of such urban buckaroos as Robert Taylor, Ava Gardner and Howard Keel. In short, it rated not Tiffany's window, but the old cat bin!"

Although Ava Gardner was now married to Frank Sinatra, she remained a friend to Bob.

All the Brothers Were Valiant with Stewart Granger and Ann Blyth was not one of Taylor's favorite movies. But it was full of action and the mutiny scene at the end was exciting. Granger was not Taylor's kind of guy— "Too stuffy!" Fortunately Keenan Wynn and James Whitmore were also in the cast of players and both were Bob's pals.

In a letter to a friend he wrote, "Me? I ain't been out with anyone, ain't even seen anyone to go out with in a helluva long time. Gettin' now so I don't even miss 'it.' I'm just anxious to finish this friggin picture and get a-goin' somewhere.

"The studio sent two scripts for my perusal, but they both stunk and I turned them down. I naturally won't know until I get home whether or not they will accept my 'no' as final, but I'm hoping. In any case, unless I find something more to my liking and assuming they won't force me to do one of these, I'm still plannin' on goin' back to Paris as soon as they give me the 'no retake' sign.

"I love Paris—my favorite city in the world! So . . . I'll probably stay there until something worthwhile comes up. I'd like to do another picture during the summer months so that I'll be free for some huntin' and fishin' this fall, but it seldom works out that way. Maybe I'll be lucky this year . . ."

Whatever scripts Taylor was referring to are unknown, but a very good guess would be *Knights of the Round Table,* another costume epic.

MGM was still determined to make Taylor America's Knight in Shining Armor. Schary cleverly took up where Mayer left off.

Taylor "accepted" *Knights of the Round Table*: "One

of the good things about this picture was my starring with Ava again. When I was told to do *Ivanhoe* much against my wishes, it wasn't as boring as I had expected. I had Elizabeth Taylor in that one, and when I knew she was going to be my leading lady I kinda hoped this time I might get 'somewhere' with her. She was in full bloom then, but to my disappointment she was head over heels in love with Michael Wilding, and if it hadn't been for that, I would have tried my luck with her."

Once again Taylor gave in to the studio and went to England to film *Knights of the Round Table*, in which he played a trim, military Lancelot. Before he left he asked for some steaks to be sent to him from New York. He was very particular about how they were cooked and explained to the chef in his European hotel exactly how he wanted them broiled.

Apparently the chef overcooked them and when they were served, Taylor was furious. One of his friends said, I've never seen Bob so mad! He actually couldn't talk. He just stared at the meat and didn't even have to cut into one of them to know they were ruined.

"Everyone dug into theirs, but he just sat and fumed. He got up and stormed out of the room slamming the door—and I mean slammed the door! He wouldn't come back until the table had been cleared off and refused to mention the incident again. The chef stayed out of his way, too.

"A few days later Bob was invited to dinner and he snapped, 'A good party is only as good as the food—otherwise, it's nothin!' "

On May 23, 1951, twenty-seven-year-old Ursula Schmidt-Hut Thiess arrived in the United States from Germany.

She was born in Hamburg, the only child of an importer. During the years of World War II her home was bombed, her father lost his business and she was forced into farm-labor. She lived in unheated barracks, worked long hours and too often faced starvation.

After brief training as an actress with a repertory company, she married actor-producer George Thiess. It was an unfortunate wartime union, but she bore him two

174

children—first a daughter, Manuela, then a son, Michael.

In 1947 she divorced Thiess and appeared in Little Theatre productions, modeled for photographers, wrote stories for motion picture short subjects earning on an average of $35 a month.

Both beautiful and broke, she was one of the most ambitious models discovered in Germany since the war.

Her modeling career began in the fall of 1950 when she was looking for a job as an actress in Munich. Lore Wolff, fashion editor for the U.S.-sponsored magazine *Heute,* caught a glance of her in a passing car and ran after the automobile.

She was asked if she would like to pose for an article on artificial pearls, and Ursula said she would.

Lore Wolff claimed what most impressed her about Ursula was her look of "sweet irony," and kept her on as a model. The job paid very little, however, and Ursula accepted a small role in a German production of *The Women.*

She was living with her children in one furnished room when Howard Hughes spotted her picture in a magazine. In February, 1951, she received a cable from RKO-Radio Pictures Corporation. Mr. Hughes wanted to know if she would be interested in a Hollywood screen test.

Ursula ignored the offer ("It was too good to be true!"), but when the second cable from Hughes arrived, she wired an acceptance. She left her two children with her mother in Hamburg and twelve days after she arrived in the United States, her picture appeared on the cover of *Life* magazine.

Ursula signed a seven-year contract with RKO but could only speak German. She was placed in the hands of their drama coach, Florence Enright, and four months later the studio executives were advised Ursula was ready to be cast in English-speaking roles.

They sent her to India for the lead in *Monsoon,* an independent production for RKO release. On her return trip to Hollywood she stopped off in London and the press proclaimed her "The Most Beautiful Girl in the World."

Things were happening quickly for Ursula, who had

come to the United States with only the clothes on her back.

She appeared in *Kiss and the Sword* with Robert Stack and *Bengal Brigade* with Rock Hudson.

On April 24, 1952, her agent invited her out to dinner at the Coconut Grove with him, his wife and a blind date —Robert Taylor.

Bob called her the next day and many dates followed. They were seen in public often, making the usual night club scene, mainly for Ursula's benefit as an up-and-coming Hollywood actress.

Just as suddenly as they entered it, they were no longer part of the social whirl.

Ursula surprised Taylor one night by suggesting they dine in her tiny apartment. She had prepared German pancakes, and from then on their evenings were spent at her home.

Taylor was captivated by Ursula's ability in the kitchen. He said she didn't strike him as the "homey" type and it took a while to be convinced she was "for real."

He told reporters many months later that while they were scouting the night clubs for him and "the beautiful German girl," he was enjoying Ursula's home-cooking.

When asked about marriage Taylor said, "Of course I want to get married again. I don't know when or to whom, but it would be a dismal prospect to be a bachelor for the rest of my life!"

One of the newsmen casually mentioned the euphonic name of Urusla Thiess: "Are you betrothed?"

"NO, definitely not!" Taylor replied, but he talked about her anyway. "Ursula is truly lovely. She has the most' beautiful eyes I have ever seen. They're brown with specks of gold. And her lashes are at least a half inch long—I'm not exaggerating!"

"How do you feel, Bob, being seen with a girl who is prettier than you are?"

"You boys must be new in the business. Don't you know you're not supposed to say anything about my being pretty?"

The reporters pressed for news about the long-lashed Ursula and Taylor interrupted. "By the way, fellas, you pronounce her name T-e-e-c-e, ok? Yeah, she's somethin'

176

alright." Then detouring to the equally alluring topic of beauties he had cinematically eyed, he said, "I've known the best of 'em, I guess."

"Who is the greatest beauty of them all, Bob?"

"Well, Elizabeth Taylor, I guess. Her eyes are really violet, you know! Then there's Garbo—what a sensational woman. What a dame! Her style was sheer perfection, why, she was unbelievable. Yeah, guess you'd have to say Garbo has it over all of them."

Taylor blew a smoke ring in the air. "Women? They're wonderful . . ."

After eighteen months of steady dating, Ursula told Bob she was bringing her nine-year-old daughter, Manuela, over from Germany to live with her. She said this would mean a change in their relationship. "I can see you afternoons, but how can I explain your being here all the time?"

Bob went back to his mother's to live and saw very little of Ursula.

She admitted that she made a point of avoiding him. He had never mentioned marriage and seemed quite content with their "arrangement."

Ursula, on the other hand, was not overly interested in her career except for the money which she needed to support herself and the children. Michael, her seven-year-old son, was staying in Germany, but she still felt obligated to send money to her mother for his living expenses.

She was a woman who needed little since she had been brought up with few clothes and no luxuries. However she was going to make a better life for her children and preferred marriage to a career.

Under her seven-year RKO contract she was earning $2,300 a month, and though this financial state afforded her whatever she required, it did not offer stability or security.

Ursula was sophisticated enough to know that Hollywood was fickle. She was not impressed. More important, she was in love with Taylor, but decided if he would not marry her, she would find someone who would.

Bob, though seeing other women occasionally, including Barbara, was satisfied with Ursula as a woman. He

177

admitted he could not ask for more, but "getting hitched" was something else.

Ruth, of course, did not like Ursula. Her excuse this time was the two children. "I hope you realize, son, that you are still paying Barbara 15 per cent of everything you earn. Are you still seeing her?"

Bob said he did see Barbara once in a while because he liked her but there was no chance of his going back to her.

Ruth commented, over her knitting, that she had overheard him calling "that German woman," but that she never returned his calls and why was he chasing her?

Taylor replied that to chase a woman properly was expensive: money for flowers, jewelry and nightclubs. If he spent too much money, he would probably go broke, and if he went broke . . . "Well, you know where we'd end up?"

Ruth asked, "Where, son, back in Nebraska?"

Taylor laughed, kissed her forehead and said teasingly, "No, Mother, your favorite place—the poorhouse!"

Before Taylor left for Egypt to make *Valley of the Kings,* he called Ursula to tell her he was leaving. She said, "That's nice. Good bye!" and hung up.

Eleanor Parker was Bob's co-star in *Valley of the Kings* and still very much infatuated with him. She was obvious about her strong feelings for Taylor, and though he had Ursula in his blood, he returned Miss Parker's affection.

All of his letters to Ursula went unanswered.

While in Egypt there was an article about him in the newspapers there that was also was printed in the United States:

CAIRO JANUARY 2, 1954 EGYPTIAN EDITOR TUT-TUTS GALS FOR DROOLING OVER BOB TAYLOR

"Columnist Mamoud Abdel Moneim in the newspaper *Al Misri* complained Saturday that Egyptian women have been acting strangely since American actor Robert Taylor arrived here.

"They have found excuses to knock at his door. They reserve restaurant tables next to his, they pretend they are journalists to attend his news conferences. They have been observed making provocative gestures with cigarettes, dropping them from their lips, trying by any means to attract his attention.

"WHAT WILL ROBERT TAYLOR THINK?"

"WILL HE THINK THERE ARE ONLY FLIGHTY WOMEN IN EGYPT?"

"Are there no men to keep them in check?" [7]

When the film was completed, Taylor left Egypt, his romance with Eleanor Parker in limbo. The day he arrived back in Hollywood he called Ursula, but she refused to see him.

He was so frustrated, he went out and purchased a star-studded engagement ring, but was afraid to give it to her. He wrote to Tom Purvis—what should he do? Tom replied, "I'm the last guy to tell you what to do, Dilly."

Taylor held on to the ring and applied himself to his role in *Rogue Cop* with Janet Leigh. He handled the tough-guy role with ease and never sneered more broadly or hit harder than necessary. Perhaps his cold determination as the crooked cop was a result of his dissatisfaction arising from unresolved problems in his personal life.

On the set he was approached by a reporter who had seen Taylor at a party with Barbara Stanwyck and wanted to know if there was a chance of a reconciliation.

Taylor hissed. "I wasn't with her. I just dropped by for a few minutes and she happened to be there. That's all. Why don't you bug off, for Christ's sake?"

However, the reporter wasn't so easily dismissed. "Whatever happened to Ursula whatever her name is?"

"I don't give a good God damn, really. She's a nice girl . . ."

"Man to man, Taylor, she's a beautiful woman—and available. Is she seeing anyone else?"

"How the hell should I know?"

Taylor walked back to his place on the set of *Rogue Cop* with a scowl on his face. It never occurred to him that Ursula might be going out with other men.

7. *New York Daily Mirror,* January 3, 1954.

179

He went home and looked at the engagement ring again, but put it back in the drawer. At this point he feared rejection and if Ursula refused him he could only blame himself. He picked up the phone and dialed her number.

"Can I see you tonight?"

"I'm afraid not."

"Just for a few minutes. I have something I'd like to show you."

"Sorry, I have guests for dinner."

"A man?"

"No, a couple of friends."

"It will only take a minute."

Ursula agreed, but insisted he was to stay for just a little while. Later Ursula said, "You might say I played a little trick on Bob. I took a big chance, I know, but since he didn't appear to have serious intentions, I had made up my mind to ignore his calls until he proposed. I can assure you, this was the only trick I ever played on him!"

Taylor arrived at her house but refused dinner. He sat and pouted, tapping his shoe nervously. Ursula was a charming hostess to her friends and took her time serving dinner, ignoring Bob in general.

He fiddled with a cup of coffee, smoked a pack of cigarettes and chewed on his bottom lip. Just about the time he began to turn green, the other guests took the hint and said they had to leave. By the time they reached home, their telephone was ringing.

It was Ursula. "I've accepted a ring from Bob. We're engaged!"

The announcement was made on April 30, 1954. Taylor told the press again to pronounce Ursula's last name correctly and said they had no marriage plans.

His close friends laughed. "Who does he think he's kidding? He's building a house in Pacific Palisades big enough for a family and he says the place will be his bachelor quarters. Taylor never could tell a convincing lie."

Ruth was overwrought. "You can't marry a woman with two children. You'll be ruined for sure this time and you'll drag us all down with you. What am I going to do?"

As with Barbara when he married her, Bob assured his mother that he would continue to support her and nothing would change, but Ruth told him this was different and that Ursula's two children would be a heavy burden on him financially.

"Maybe I'll marry John," she said.

John was a man Ruth had been seeing for several months, but Bob had been paying for their dates—dinners, the theatre, cab fare, etc. When she announced her plans, Taylor said he thought it was a fine idea, but made it clear if she married John, he would not support *him, too.*

Ruth was positive her son would go bankrupt and assured him that John had proposed many times but now she had no choice but to accept. It was her last chance, and if Bob would not be able to take care of her, then John would!

However, when she approached John about it—telling him that Bob was apparently going to get married and would not be able to support her anymore—he left her and she never saw him again!

Ruth continued to brag about the many marriage proposals she had gotten from John, but she could never explain his sudden disappearance.

Taylor wrote to Tom again asking for advice about whether or not he should "go all the way" with Ursula. And again Tom said he'd rather stay out of it.

But Tom said he wasn't surprised when Bob called him one evening. "I'm gettin' married, ol bud. Headin' out in the morning. Keep it under yer hat till you hear from me!"

On May 24, 1954, just three weeks following their engagement, Ursula and Bob boarded his plane at 4:00 A.M.—giving their friends Ralph Couser and Ivy Mooring, only twenty-four hours' notice. They flew to Jackson Lake, Wyoming, where a cabin cruiser and minister were waiting.

The group sailed out to the middle of the lake and they were married. No one except Tom knew about their

181

elopement and Taylor made sure he would have complete privacy by planning the wedding as he did.

It was very casual, though Taylor and Couser wore business suits. Ursula and her close friend, Ivy, exchanged clothing—each ending up with the other's shoes and slips. The informal wedding pictures show Ursula with polka-dotted shoes and Ivy with the underskirt that matched the wedding slippers.

After they drank a bottle of champagne in the middle of the lake, the cruiser docked for the night and around twelve o'clock Taylor called his press agent in Hollywood—too late for the morning edition.

The next day the newlyweds flew to Cloverdale, California, where Bob was scheduled to film *Many Rivers to Cross.*

They found a small cabin three miles from location and when Taylor's MGM publicity man, Jim Merrick, showed up with a photographer from the studio, Bob said, "No pictures, Jim. Sorry."

"Bob, there are reporters everywhere. You're going to have to give them something to keep them quiet for awhile."

"Ursula and I are making out our grocery list right now. If you want to wait until we're finished, okay."

It took the Taylors some time to jot down what they needed at the market. When they finished re-checking it several times, they posed for only six pictures.

Hundreds of newsmen lingered in Cloverdale, but didn't get a glimpse of Bob and Ursula for ten days.

The cast and crew working on *Many Rivers to Cross* got together and planned a party for the couple after leaving them alone for over a week in their honeymoon cabin.

MGM personnel had one problem—Eleanor Parker. She was to appear in the movie with Taylor and had just arrived in Cloverdale, apparently unaware that Bob had gotten married. No one knew for sure, however, and there was a serious discussion as to who should invite Eleanor to the party. Some brave soul volunteered and approached her about attending the "wedding celebration" for Bob and Ursula Taylor.

Miss Parker's pleasant expression faded and she remained in a state of shock during the festivities, looking pale and close to tears for several days.

Bob told a friend years later just how close Eleanor came to breaking up his marriage that was only a few weeks old. Exactly what he meant is not known.

Under the circumstances it is surprising that *Many Rivers to Cross* was successful: Eleanor Parker was with Bob daily while he was honeymooning with Ursula.

But this picture also proved Taylor's flair for comedy.

His tramping around like a Kentucky trapper, who could care less about his shotgun bride trailing him through the backwoods, was quite funny.

Many Rivers to Cross was "slapstick in buckskin" and everyone had to chuckle during the last scene when "Bushrod" Taylor struggled with an Indian and "Mary Stuart" Parker kept getting in the way.

Unfortunately for the public this was the last movie Taylor made with Eleanor Parker. Of all his leading ladies, everyone agreed that she complimented him the most on the screen.

Chapter XI

Not only did Eleanor Parker show her disappointment, but the Taylor-Thiess marriage was quite a blow to Barbara Stanwyck also. She said publicly that she had been carrying a torch for Bob all along. She repeated once again, "There will be no other man in my life!"

Many people said they thought Bob had been confused for some time as to whether he should reconcile with Barbara or marry Ursula.

Taylor's unusual concern about his image as a motion picture personality was astounding. This was the strongest force in his life. He wanted to make the public think of him as a clean-living guy and not the typical Hollywood gadabout. There would be no scandal, no stories of his getting drunk and cursing waiters, no indication that he was running around with women, no elaborate houses that made good publicity photos in *Modern Screen,* no speeding automobiles and traffic tickets, no expensive cars that could be recognized as belonging to a movie star—and never any derogatory reference to anyone.

But divorce *was* a mark against him—a sign of weakness and failure. He had been accused of adultery and his wife had wept on the witness stand that he wanted to be free with no restrictions. His so-called mistress had made her statement to the world-wide press that "Bob was tired of Barbara"—a cruel thing to do to someone as admired as Miss Barbara Stanwyck.

He wanted the world to see that he respected her, and in no way wished to hurt her. She glowed with happiness when they were together after the divorce and if it meant he could have erased the bitterness he would have gone back to Barbara to prove he was a decent human being who had not been touched by the usual temptations of Hollywood.

For five sour years before Barbara divorced him, he tried to hold on, and when she made it apparent that for once in her life she was willing to forget an injustice, Taylor brought forth every emotion he could muster—moonlight and roses, wine and music, but all were ineffective.

The fact that he met and fell in love with Ursula had nothing to do with his situation involving Barbara. He had almost married Eleanor Parker but was able to walk away from it. She had remarried, but Barbara was alone now that Dion was in school and she had not dated anyone.

His guilt was the strongest threat to his happiness during his courtship with Ursula. He refused to give in to the fact that he was human after all. Being a perfectionist, he worked for perfection and expected everyone else to do likewise. He had no pity for those who gave up easily. "If you find at the beginning of any undertaking that you cannot be one of the best, then don't get involved!" He loved golf, but was never good at it, so he gave it up.

Taylor's impulse to marry Ursula three weeks after their engagement was not unusual for him. The decision to give her the ring after keeping it for such a long time was. Asking Tom for advice was only his way of getting assurance to do something he knew he was going to do anyway. Why wait for the inevitable?

There were a few similarities between Ursula and Barbara—lonely and emotional childhoods, poverty during their early lives, strength, and divorce, but their differences were innumerable.

Ursula was undeniably Taylor's type of woman. She was above all a wife, and believed that her man was the head of the household who made all the decisions. At least that is what she allowed him to believe in the beginning. She learned to hunt and fish, loved the outdoors and enjoyed flying with Bob. Because of him she became accustomed to horses and rode well.

She did her own marketing and preferred to keep house herself.

She will tell you that it was her European influence that made her what she was to Taylor—the contentment to spend time alone together rather than with other people, the outdoors and casual living, the homemade cooking. Bob was the only important thing in her life. He came first.

When they returned to Hollywood following Bob's work in *Many Rivers to Cross,* they settled in Ursula's tiny house with her ten-year-old daughter, Manuela. Bob hung his clothes in the dining room.

The movie industry was suffering from the effects of television and was at its peak of decline in 1954. Taylor would read at least a dozen scripts before accepting one. He said he would not make a movie that would offend even a child. "If MGM *demanded* I do a film, I did it even if it was a bad one . . . meaning a poor script. Temperament is not my cup of tea. It just doesn't come naturally to me.

"Sometimes I wish I could give the studio a pot-full of trouble, but the things that upset me are usually not worth raising hell about.

"Also I don't know enough about motion picture technique to consider directing—though it is written in my contract that I can.

"Acting is the only thing I know much about and I like it. I'm not dedicated to it, however, in the sense of 'living my *whole* life' as an actor."

Taylor was making $6,000 a week and his name on a marquee was still box office insurance for any movie. He signed another six-year contract with MGM in January, 1955. It included also a six-year extension so that the money could be paid off during a twelve-year period.

Ursula, still under contract to RKO, was still drawing $2,300 a month and obligated to do two more movies for them. Bob was opposed to her filming *Bandido* because he wasn't too fond of Robert Mitchum, her co-star. However, she went ahead because of her obligation to the studio and completed her career as an actress in *Americano.*

Taylor was assigned to portray *Quentin Durwood,* the film version of Sir Walter Scott's novel. Comments on this movie varied. "Mr. Taylor did much better by Sir

Walter when he did *Ivanhoe.*" And, "Mr. Robert Taylor is playing the heroic role of a high-minded champion of fair ladies and it is beginning to be a trifle dull!"

MGM finally agreed, and this was the end of The Knight in Shining Armor era for Taylor, which didn't bother him at all.

At once he was sent to South Dakota to make *The Last Hunt,* the story of buffalo hunters, with Stewart Granger, Lloyd Nolan and Debra Paget.

He wanted Ursula to go with him. Knowing he would be working on location most of the time, Taylor would not make the same mistake twice. He was not going to have a part-time marriage this time.

But Ursula announced she was pregnant!

Taylor called Tom. "Can't tell you, ol' Bud, how I feel right now. Ursula is going to have a baby and I'm speechless. God damn, I never knew a guy like me could get so excited over something that happens all the time. She's calm and I'm goin' out of my mind. Isn't that somethin'? Can't believe it . . ."

Tom couldn't get a word in. "Dilly just kept talkin' on and on. I'd start to say something and he'd interrupt— chattering like no one ever had a baby before!"

Before he hung up, Taylor said, "I'll tell ya somethin', Tom. The best thing I ever did was marry Ursula!"

He went to South Dakota and Ursula stayed with friends in Sheridan, Wyoming.

One Saturday morning he got up early and drove 500 miles just to see her for a few hours. He took his own food, coffee and gasoline. Sunday he was back in the Black Hills of South Dakota to continue filming *The Last Hunt,* a movie that was giving him a problem.

The director of the film was known as 'The Swearing King' and every other word out of his mouth was a four-letter one. He didn't just speak them in normal tones, but could be heard echoing throughout the location area.

There were many sightseers who were driving cross-country—women, children, grandmothers etc., and Taylor was very upset that these innocent people would be offended.

He spoke to the publicity director, George Nichols, about it one night. "If these people think enough of me

187

to stop their cars and watch me filming while the director uses such foul language, it is going to ruin 'the Taylor image.' It's taken me too long a time to keep it clean and I won't have this big mouth destroy everything. These people will go home and tell their friends what goes on when Bob Taylor does a movie! My pictures will go to hell. Not only that, but he comes out with words even I haven't heard, but anyone with half a brain knows what they mean."

The director was a talented man and Taylor didn't want to cause any friction, offend him, or "pull rank."

"George, got an idea. Tomorrow we'll take him to lunch but we'll go someplace about twenty-five miles from here. I'll drive and you get him to sit in the middle. Use all the dirtiest words you can think of and dream up some more!"

The three men started out the following day. Taylor and Nichols talked rapidly, not giving the director a chance to get a word in. He sat in the middle listening to the conversation between Taylor and Nichols, especially stunned at Bob's foul tongue. When they arrived at the restaurant, Taylor made unusually fresh remarks to the waitress, who appeared hurt and insulted.

Nichols followed, ignoring the director. Bob told some filthy jokes loud enough for everyone to hear. One man gave them a sour look and Taylor turned to him and said, "If you don't like it, move your ass to another table!" The man started to say something but was told what he could do.

Taylor kept his hat on and pulled it down far enough so that he was apparently not recognized.

He sent the food back and called the cook a God damn son of a bitch bastard. He pinched the waitress on her fanny and made a few jokes about that too.

Driving back to location the conversation continued. The director got the message. From then on, he said nothing more offensive.

Taylor said he would never make a movie that the whole family could not see, and he never did. ("Do your drinkin', screwin' and swearin' when the public isn't around!")

Ursula never used vulgar words—quite unlike Barbara—but accepted with ease the off-color jokes and man-talk when she was with Bob and his buddies.

Taylor's life with Ursula did not change him. She merely gave him back his original personality. Many of Taylor's friends said they admired him because of his unusual love for her and for not being afraid to show masculine sweetness and love openly.

She was the one person he complimented often, which intrigued his buddies. They said most men would not consider it manly to shower so much love and admiration on a woman, but Taylor was direct with his feelings. "I don't know what I would do without her. It is like a wonderful dream. She's simple in her wants, understanding, and raised in the tradition that the husband is the breadwinner and head of the house. I think this is important for a marriage to succeed.

"You mustn't allow dissatisfaction. When there's a first break in a marriage, it's like a hole in a dyke . . . keeps getting bigger and bigger . . ."

Terrance, known as Terry, was born on June 18, 1955. He was Bob's pride and joy. However, Manuela Thiess ran away from home because she resented the appearance of a new child in the house. Though she was found and returned, Manuela was never truly happy.

The day Terry was born, Barbara Stanwyck was making a movie. The announcement that Robert Taylor had become a father of a baby boy was made over a loudspeaker.

Barbara burst into tears. An observer said, "At first we thought she was overcome with joy, but I think she was genuinely hurt. Barbara was always good at covering up her emotions, but she had no control this time. Everybody was happy for Bob, but Barbara wasn't smiling. She was jealous, I think. Call it what you will, she wasn't herself."

Soon after the birth of Terry, Ursula and Bob moved into their new home in Pacific Palisades. Eleven-year-old Michael Thiess came over from Germany and joined the family.

Taylor appeared on the Ed Sullivan Show and accepted the first Winchester Award as Outdoorsman of the Year. A special symbol of the award was the presentation of

189

a milestone in Winchester history—the 1,500,000th Model-12 shotgun engraved in gold and fitted to Taylor's measurements.

Winchester reported that before Taylor was chosen, some of the best shooters at Winchester had hunted with him to find out exactly how good he was. "He's not only an excellent shot with a rifle but he is one of the finest wing shots we have ever seen. Taylor is also an excellent horseman, pilot, woodsman and dog handler."

A framed sheepskin certificate announcing the award stated:

"Winchester in recognition of his skills in the field and devotion to the outdoors herewith names Robert Taylor OUTDOORSMAN OF THE YEAR 1954 as the man who through his prominence and personal example has done most to increase interest in our American heritage of good marksmanship and sportsmanship in the field."

A few years ago he had been voted the most popular male star in all countries abroad by the Hollywood Press Association, representing 500 million moviegoers in the world, and in 1951 he was given Harvard's Lampoon Award for the worst acting that year in *Quo Vadis*. "By Golly," he said, "I finally won an award and I never worked harder in my life!"

He did not retire to his den and trophies, however. He hid them, which irritated Ursula. When a friend came to the house and asked to see a plaque he had gotten for something, Taylor would look dumbfounded. "Gee, I don't know where the hell I put that thing . . ."

There was one award he would not accept—Gable's throne. When The King left MGM, everyone said Taylor was the undisputed King, but Bob was adamant. "This business has given me everything I have today—except Gable's throne. Nobody can fill that!"

He was loaned to Twentieth Century Fox for *D-Day the Sixth of June* with Dana Wynter in which he played a U.S. Air Force captain in the same task force as the husband of the woman he loves. The two men become friends and the picture ends as Miss Wynter walks away from her love (Taylor), not telling him her husband had been killed in action.

"I was very impressed with *D-Day the Sixth of June* because it reminded me of *Waterloo Bridge* somehow. Trouble is, reading a script is like reading a book and then seeing the movie—never the same."

The Power and the Prize followed immediately. Elizabeth Mueller was introduced in the film, but though she gave a good performance, Miss Mueller dropped out of sight after her début.

Burl Ives and Charles Coburn supported Taylor in this movie about an ethical businessman pitted against unscrupulous giants of the industrial world. The reviews were very good. Taylor was described as "convincingly ardent and courageous as the temporarily diverted tycoon" and "earnest and likeable as the fair-haired boy."

These were the uneventful years in Taylor's life, though he was content as family man, father, and earning a top salary as one of America's biggest box office stars.

During one of his interviews in 1956 he said, "There are two types of stars in Hollywood—actors and personalities. Well, I'm a personality."

"What about Gable, Mr. Taylor? What do you consider him?"

"A friend who likes to hunt as much as I do."

"Professionally . . ."

Taylor was eating lunch at the MGM commissary and concentrating more on his food than on the interview. "Professionally, what?"

"Do you think Gable is an actor or a personality?"

"Both!"

"Is there any reason why you consider yourself a personality rather than an actor?"

"Hell, if you've seen any of my movies you'd know the answer to that. People come to the theatre to see Robert Taylor, not a good piece of acting. The critics still refer to me as pretty, handsome and beautiful—a freak. I learned a long time ago to accept myself for what I am. That doesn't mean I'm not tryin' to do better, but I'm also tryin' to catch a bigger fish."

The reporters followed him to the set of *The Tip on a Dead Jockey*. He proceeded to sit down and immediately fell asleep. When the director noticed this, he woke him up to prepare for the next scene. "You boys still here?"

"If you don't mind, Bob, we'd like to watch . . ."

"Dull as hell, this movie. Hey, haven't I met you somewhere before?"

One of the newsmen tipped his hat and said he had interviewed him when he was doing *Ride Vaquero!*

"God damn, that was another bad one!"

"All I can remember was trying to get a story out of you, and Ava Gardner walked over to the table. You put your hat over your face and went to sleep!"

"Who wants to talk to me when Ava's around?"

"Yes, true . . . but you can fall asleep pretty fast."

Taylor smiled. "Anytime, boys, anytime."

Tom Purvis called Bob. "Read an interview about your fallin' asleep. Can't you even stay awake in front of reporters?"

"I only fall asleep when I feel like it."

Purvis reminded Bob about the time he was in the back seat of his station wagon and Ralph Couser was in the front. "You were drivin' and all of a sudden we ended up in a ditch. Ralph took hold of the wheel and straightened out, but you grabbed it and gave him hell! Can't tell me you hadn't dozed off!"

"My eyes were tired, that's all," Taylor retorted.

"Yeah, sure—and how many times do you fall asleep with a lighted cigarette in your hand. Ursula swears the house will burn down one day!'

Taylor was like that. He rose early—usually at dawn—whether he was working or not. He could go to bed whenever he felt like it. He once said, "Funny thing, I'm never *really* tired . . . bored, maybe, but not tired!"

In 1955 Taylor and Ralph Couser had a falling out. It was a trivial thing that neither would discuss, but it had to do with money. Taylor would fight you for a dime because of the principle involved. They didn't say a word to each other and Couser's name was never mentioned in Bob's presence. Their dispute bothered both of them, but Ralph was like Taylor—stubborn! They had been close friends for over ten years, but when they parted, it was for good.

192

There is no evidence of any other incident involving a close friend where Taylor was concerned. He knew, of course, that his business manager was investing poorly for him—yet he refused to release him. He had several press agents he didn't need simply because he didn't want to put them out of work. Helen Ferguson remained on his payroll (out of obligation to Barbara) and he went out of his way to help her as he did when married to her best friend.

One Sunday morning Helen called Bob to find out if he knew of a carpenter who might be willing to work on the weekend. She said she wanted to cut a baseboard in one of the rooms of her house to fit a table into a desired location. Within the hour Bob arrived at Helen's home complete with tool kit. After four hours of precision-labor he finished a professional job of baseboard-slotting.

The following Sunday he presented Helen with her own elegant tool kit, fully equipped.

Tom Purvis retired at the young age of fifty and moved to Bradenton, Florida. Before he had time to get his furniture off the moving van, he received a very expensive backyard barbeque from Taylor. "A house is not a home without! Dilly."

Tom said Bob was very unpredictable when it came to gifts, but he was the kind of a guy who remembered a friend's request when he was in Europe. "I told Bob once when he was going to Switzerland to get me a watch. I made it clear that I would pay for it but not to go out of his way. It was apparent that he really shopped for the one he finally picked out for me—even had some alterations done. The damn thing did everything but talk. He handed it to me and said it was worth well over $600 but he got it for $250. I almost swallowed my cigar! I gave him the money, alright, but never expected him to pay more than $75. At the time I was a little peeved, but I have it to this day and it's never been off a minute!"

Tom and Bob never had a falling out. They invested in property and other ventures that usually made small profits. Bob tried to get Tom to go along with him on a film venture for Winchester and was very excited about the project, but Tom said there were two things he'd never get involved in—running a motel, and motion pictures. It was his way of saying "no." Bob was miffed, and never mentioned it again.

Taylor had an instinct about people and either liked someone at once or was polite and distant.

Men liked him each in a different way. Some admired him for "not mixing with the big shots"—some for his devotion to Ursula—others because of his knowledge of horses and his love for sports—few for his depth.

He rarely gave compliments, and whatever he said to anyone, good or bad, he never took back.

One Hollywood producer labeled Tayler as a Hamlet, and went on to say that there were few things interesting about the other top male stars whom the public worshiped, but only those very close to Taylor recognized these characteristics in him.

He was one star who did not get caught up with what was real and what was fake. It is common knowledge that most actors live their roles in real life—never leaving the camera, and truly believing that they should maintain their superficial script-like personality long after the studio had closed for the day. This was not Robert Taylor. He was' what the clock dictated—an actor on the set, and just another guy everywhere else.

Taylor was pestered by men as well as women. They pursued him for one of two reasons: a homosexual wanted to meet Bob, or a tough guy wanted to see if "Pretty Boy" could match him drink for drink or provoke a fight.

On most occasions Taylor ignored these proposals; when someone telephoned him at his hotel it was simple enough for Bob to hang up after a firm and polite decline.

In Wichita, Kansas, while on a hunting trip with a few cronies, he got a call from a man who had had too much to drink. "Heard you were in the motel, Taylor, and would like to buy you a drink."

"No, thanks, fella, I'm a little tired!"

"Well, then, Taylor, maybe I could come up to your room and we could relax."

"Maybe some other time, but not now!"

"Maybe I'm not quite good enough, is that it? I ain't got no fancy clothes like you, Taylor. Whatsa matter, pretty boy, pooped after a hard day of kissin'?"

Taylor got red in the face. "Look, friend, why don't you take a nice long walk . . ."

"No, Taylor, I don't want any of that Hollywood smooth talkin' shit!"

"OK, friend, why don't you come up to room 520—first door on the left. Make it about five tomorrow morning. I'm lookin' for a stunt man who can do a little fallin' off a horse. Ya see, I'm too pretty for that sort of thing and I can tell by your voice, you're REALLLLLLLLLLY tough. I'll guarantee you at least fifty dollars a fall, and by tomorrow night you'll walk away—that is, hopefully walk away—with a couple of hundred bucks! Now, you get lotsa rest, friend. I gotta get some sleep myself—ya know, all that huggin' and kissin' tuckers a guy out. See ya at five sharp—right here in room 520 . . ."

Taylor hung up the phone and said, "I've gotten these calls when I wanted to kill—especially from fags, but if this joker shows up, I'll give him that job!"

No one knocked on Bob's door early the next morning . . .

One of his hunting companions commented that when they packed up their guns and fishing gear, everyone in the group was serious. He said he could remember only one time that they didn't concentrate on how the fish were biting or how many quail were waiting for them.

It was in 1950, shortly after Bob and Barbara announced their divorce, that they set out for Oregon by car, Taylor and a buddy in the first car and several other men in the second. As the trip progressed, the two automobiles were several hours apart.

Taylor and his friend stopped in small towns along the way, taking their time over coffee or Scotch while meeting people in diners and roadhouses. They were dressed in old clothes, Taylor with his hat, as usual, covering his forehead and eyebrows. Whether or not women he met on this particular trip knew who he was, no one will say, but he flirted and took several of them home.

The second car stopped off in the same towns, and

the men were told by some of the local townsmen who answered their questions with a snicker that their friends had been and gone. When questioned further, they explained with a smile that there was little coffee left and the few girls who had been available weren't available anymore. When the second group finally caught up with Taylor, they kidded him about the trip, but he wouldn't talk. How he managed to do as much carousing as he did always amazed everyone. No matter what the situation, when it involved women he never volunteered any information.

When he was on business trips and obviously traveling as Robert Taylor, his conquests were always arranged by someone else; he never walked up to a pretty girl and made a pass. He simply didn't have the nerve. If they liked the idea of meeting Taylor somewhere for a drink, they accepted the invitation through a second party; the young lady would disappear without notice, Taylor either leaving before or after her departure.

For some reason women kept quiet, too. They were satisfied, and liked him, knowing that if they wanted a second go-around with Taylor, not to talk about their dates with him.

Taylor was not happy living this way no matter how many women were available to him and only in his letters would he express his loneliness and discontent:

Tucson, Arizona (excerpt—1951) ". . . and it all continues dull. Being single and alone is depressing though frankly I'm not looking for marriage or anything permanent at present. Seems to me I knew Tucson very well, but it has never been as dull as it is right now— maybe it's me! This hotel is turning into an old folks home—everyone is pushin' eighty! Gotta give 'em credit, but I'm considerin' opening a concession in the lobby to sell plasma and intravenous injections. Hell of a life!"

Psychologically his meeting and marrying Ursula only brought deeper fear into his already troubled mind. Loneliness stalked him again: "Will Ursula be faithful? Will she leave me? Will she be happy just being my wife? Can she put up with me? Does she know how much I need her?"

Had Ursula married "just a punk kid from Nebraska

196

who had an awful lot of the world's good things dumped into his lap," or did she marry Robert Taylor, movie star?

Ursula was as noncommital as he was, but those who knew Bob before he married her observed a couple who were deeply in love. Their eyes said more than any words could express. He had changed for the better, but didn't realize he was more outgoing, laughed without restraint and was aware of her presence—always.

In the beginning Bob was the master of the house, proving to himself that he WAS the boss. In later years this changed, and Ursula was the strength, though she gave Bob all the credit in every sense.

Hall Bartlett, who was married to Rhonda Fleming at the time, said, "Their's was the greatest love story. It happens to one in a million. We'd get together for a few drinks, and no matter what he was talking about, he was looking at her. They would not sit together holding hands, but if you sat back and took a good hard look, there would be Bob on one end of the room, Ursula on the other, and they would manage to catch each other's eyes at the same time. This continued throughout their marriage."

Bob never confided his fear of losing his position as one of the highest-paid movie actors to Ursula, but she would laugh when he wasn't around, "Why it wouldn't bother me to scrub floors if I had to. We will always make out."

They had no butlers, chauffeurs, maids, secretaries or stooges to run errands. Ruth did the baby-sitting on the few occasions that Ursula and Bob went out.

Ursula got along with Ruth much better than Barbara. The two women had no disagreements and Ursula took Ruth for who she was . . . Bob's mother, who was sinking deeper into her religion and speaking of the evils of Hollywood. She was treated with respect and she still made it clear to Bob he would never have any money now that he had three children.

Taylor did not invite Ruth to live with him but did pay her expenses at her little house at 1063 Selby Street in Los Angeles. She became one of the family on birthdays and holidays. Ursula always made sure Ruth was welcome. She knew, however, that Ruth was displeased, and accepted her role as Bob's wife as one that his mother resented.

Taylor's sixtieth movie was *Tip on a Dead Jockey*, in which he played a neurotic pilot who gets involved with a smuggling gang. The film was panned, but Robert Taylor was still powerful enough in 1957 to take the public away from their television sets for a few hours.

On October 29, 1957, L. B. Mayer died, broken-hearted. His last words were spoken to Howard Strickling, head of studio publicity at MGM. "Don't let them bother you. Nothing matters . . . nothing matters . . ."

Taylor said, "For seventeen years it was he who guided me, and I never turned down a picture that he personally asked me to do. Some were so God damn rotten I thought he was trying to ruin me, but when things got tough he'd come up with a real plum. As far as I was concerned, he knew exactly what he was doing.

"He was kind, fatherly, understanding and protective. He gave me picture assignments up to the level that my abilities could sustain at the time and was always there when I had problems.

"I just wish today's young actors had a studio and boss like I had. They groomed us carefully, kept us busy in pictures, thus giving us exposure, and made us stars. My memories of L.B. will always be pleasant and my days at MGM are my happiest—professionally."

Elizabeth Taylor thought L. B. Mayer a horrible beast and to this day she will say so publicly. "Every year the whole studio *had* to celebrate his birthday. We would all be assembled on Stage Thirty which would have a dais and then tables for peasants like me. The kids would HAVE to stand around him and sing 'Happy Birthday.'

"We were under contract and we were bloody well told to. Then he'd have a picture taken with a kid on each knee and he would say to the whole assembly including the peasants, 'You must think of me as your father. You must come to me—any of you—with any of your problems, no matter how slight they might seem to you because you are all my children.' Then he gave the full gesture—the open-arm embrace.

198

"But just try to get an appointment. And if you ever got behind those golden doors, you would just have to keep your mouth shut. My mother did once and they had an argument. He yelled, 'You're so God damned blankety-blank stupid you wouldn't even know what day of the week it is. Don't try to meddle into my affairs. Don't try to tell me how to make motion pictures. I took you out of the gutter.'

"I yelled back at him, 'You and your studio can both go to Hell!' I never did apologize and I wasn't fired. I swore I'd never go back into that office and I never did." [8]

Robert Taylor, on the other hand, was an exception as far as Mayer was concerned. Many of the top stars at MGM said they were treated badly and they could name only a few who were handled like kings and queens: Taylor's name was always mentioned.

He remembered, "Perhaps the only time I couldn't get in to see him was when he changed my name and I wanted Ramsey. Even then I can't say he refused to see me: he just wasn't in his office. I have to laugh when I think of Ramsey Taylor and how much I wanted that name. He knew better and I didn't—that's the way it always was with Mayer."

After Mayer resigned from MGM, Taylor was sent several scripts for his approval. There was no one to guide him and he knew nothing about being on his own. He judged his acceptance according to the script's caliber and how it would affect his image—simple as that. Schary did push him into doing *Ivanhoe*, but actually it was a compliment because Schary considered it the best script around and it turned out to be one of the top-ten grossing films in 1952 and a Taylor favorite.

When he showed his preference for Westerns, Schary gave him his choice.

There were observers who said that in 1951 not only did Taylor lose Mayer but also Barbara—two strong forces in his life. With Mayer out of the picture, Barbara *might* have helped him through this difficult period. Regardless of her personality drawbacks, she was smart in

8. Elizabeth Taylor, ELIZABETH TAYLOR (New York: Harper and Row, 1964), pp. 15–17.

her decisions about making movies and for whom. She might have advised Bob to get out then and there, but this is speculation. Her own career was in jeopardy, and in 1953 she made almost as many movies as she did in 1933, but only one—*Titanic*—was successful. She said as long as the customers wanted to see her, she would continue to make movies, and added, "After all, they SHOOT old horses."

However, after *Crime and Passion* in 1957 she was asked if she thought she was through as a film star. "Sure, why not admit it? I can't stay up there forever. It's a man's world and it's getting worse. I don't know, they aren't writing beautiful adult stories anymore. In the past three years I haven't been sent any scripts—period. Oh, I know stars who say they can't find anything they want to do in films, but I wouldn't lie like that.

"I just haven't had any offers!"

Barbara's frankness spoke for the majority of established motion picture stars of the Golden Era. One of the few who were hanging on was Taylor, because he was one of the few still under contract to a major studio. His movies never lost money, but then he had MGM behind him even without Mayer. His productions were not cheap by any means, regardless of the story content.

In 1958 three Taylor movies were released: *The Law and Jake Wade* with Richard Widmark ("Taylor, looking grim and mature, carries conviction as the lawman!"); *Saddle the Wind* with John Cassavetes and Julie London ("The three stars are consistently good in this intelligent Western drama. Taylor turned out a thoughtful performance."); and his last picture as an MGM contract player, *Party Girl* with Cyd Charisse. ("As the true blue legal spokesman for the mob, Robert Taylor makes the most of a fairly stereotyped series of situations. He is a grim, but stalwart operator who is as convincing as might be expected in a well-worn role.")

In *Party Girl,* the forty-seven-year-old Robert Taylor looked unusually good after sporting a "five-o'clock shadow" in two consecutive Westerns. His widow's peak was still noticeable and in his role as a crippled lawyer he wore a mustache; his outstanding features were now even more devastating than when his profile made women faint as he knelt at Garbo's feet.

Finally in 1958 Taylor and MGM parted, but his contract called for a three-year option committing him to make two more pictures for the studio. He was even given a pension.

He said, "I should have left them six years ago, but it's hard when you have been with a studio for twenty-four years." He broke Bing Crosby's record of twenty-three years with Paramount, and became the longest running contract player in the history of motion pictures.

He said it was impossible to save any money on straight salary and he was anxious to make enough money to retire. When asked how it felt to be able to pick his own pictures for the first time in his acting career, he remarked, "That remains to be seen. I've picked a few before. What I have done is establish a price—$200,000 per picture and a percentage of the gross. I'll make two or three pictures a year and the money, because of the percentage, will be spread over a long period of time.

"Maybe I'll have something to show for my life . . ."

One of the saddest days in Taylor's life was when he moved out of his dressing room on the MGM lot. It wasn't leaving the studio that had been his second home for almost twenty-five years that gave him an empty feeling in the pit of his stomach, but rather all the memories that spoke to him . . . Jean Harlow's bobbing breasts as she scurried past him . . . Clark Gable's "Hi, Baby!" that had greeted him every day . . . Wally Beery's cursing off a hangover in the morning . . . Garbo's limousine . . . Joan Crawford looking well-groomed in her carefully selected dress unwrinkled whenever she passed you on the lot . . . Lionel Barrymore grumbling about something . . . Lana Turner's sexy smile that always made him feel like following her to her dressing room . . . Katherine Hepburn looking like a freckled tomboy . . . and the invisible throne that only L. B. Mayer could fit into . . . and even those God damn reporters who were waiting to heckle "Pretty Boy" . . .

Chapter XII

Taylor's first attempt at making independent films was *The Hangman* at Paramount. Showing no emotion, he said it was a disaster. "I haven't seen it and have no intention of seeing it. In fact, I haven't seen any of my last three pictures. And come to think of it, I haven't been to a Hollywood première in ten years.

"Why the hell should I? Who wants to see me?"

The press did not agree with Taylor's opinion of *The Hangman:* "One of Robert Taylor's chief assets has always been his quality of conviction. He contributes a great deal of this to his role as the hangman."

Again Taylor proved his flair for comedy when he was accidentally handcuffed to Tina Louise and mounted a horse with her in pursuit of a killer.

Taylor chose *The Hangman* not only because it was a Western, but the character of Marshall MacKenzie Bovard was the type of role he preferred—a tough, determined, mean and ruthless man who was always on the side of law and order.

On January 13, 1959, he wrote to Tom Purvis:

Dear Couz—
By Golly, I've been plumb careless about my letter-writin' lately—but, again, you'll jest havta forgive and forget. I'se been real busy.
Sometimes, like durin' the past coupla weeks, I honestly get to thinkin' I must be livin' right. As you know I stuck my neck out a yard plunkin' down the money necessary to buy that ranch down in the Canyon—and still havin' this house we're livin' in on my hands.
Well sir—the first couple who came to look at it, after we put 'er on the market, went for it big. I had been

askin' $137,500, but I knew damned good'n well that I'd go for a lot less. They offered me $125,000 cost at close of Escrow and they jest by God bought themselves a house. They also want to buy several pieces of furniture and appliances which we will not need in the new place—round dining room table and chairs, kitchen stove and ice-box—washer and dryer, etc., etc. All in all I think we were damned lucky. We won't make any money on the deal, but we'll sure as hell break even and will have lived here very comfortably for four years.

The second reason I think I'm livin' right is that Ursuleeeeee went down to the "Doc" a few days ago and confirmed our suspicions! She's got another one "in the oven" and right about now, what with morning sickness and all, I guess she kinda feels like sluggin' me. However, we're really very happy about it. We wanted one more and waiting too much longer wouldn't have been good for either of us.

Ursula comin' up on 35 years now and I don't think it'd be good for her to have kids after that. And that is *assuming* that I'd be able to hold up my end of the function! Which is one helluva'n assumption!

In addition to the two pictures I'll be makin' in Europe another deal has come up which looks good to me and I think I'll go for it.

Four Star Productions, Dick Powell's and David Niven's outfit, have come up with a TV Series which they want me to headline. It's a pretty fair idea and will be done by the best producer-director-writer team in television. I'll do six shows in the series and appear briefly in the other 26 out of the 32-show series.

For the ones in which I appear full time I will draw $7,500 for three days work. For the ones which I simply "host" and appear in briefly I'll draw $4,500—i.e., for the one-year series of 32 shows I'll draw $150,000 in salary. I'll *also* own and this is the big money gimmick—*50% of the entire series!* This percentage, in the event we have a hit show and continue the series for three years, could be worth a coupla' million dollars, part of which would be Capital Gain.

The office is now setting up my own Corporation—Robert Taylor Productions—and everything I do from now on, either as a motion picture or in TV, will be done thru the corporation. I'll be under contract to my own corporation and will be paid for it.

Last week I flew down to Missouri and came home with a helluva new *Pointer*dog for pheasant and quail. He is really a dandy, but I took him out to my Vet to be thoroughly checked over and they discovered that he had just about every type of worm known to the canine world. They've just wormed him and the poor bastard is so "pooped" out that I wouldn't run him on pheasant if I never shot again. We plan on building a six-dog kennel at the new place.

Sorry that ya went and "split your girdle," Curley—but I have a hunch it was fun gettin' thataway. I have to stay away from that kind of silage or I'd never get a job. Get me up again' those nuts and I'm a gonner—no willpower atall!

Love to Vi and the deductions.

As ever, Dilly

In 1959 Taylor purchased a ranch from the owner of Phillips '66 which had 113 acres in Mandeville Canyon across the street from Dick Powell's home and just twenty minutes from the heart of Los Angeles. His deal with MGM made it possible for him to afford the property valued at $940,000.

The "Ursulor Rancho" was Taylor's first *real* home. He always referred to it as "the farm" and it came complete with a kidney-shaped swimming pool, corrals, stables and a little cottage for a handyman.

The ranch provided the Taylors with sixteen miles of bridle trail without leaving their property. A master light switch took care of the entire riding area. Taylor cut his own alfalfa hay that was neatly stacked near the barn. Joining the family were cattle, fourteen quarter horses, eight dogs, lots of cats, over sixty chickens and rabbits.

Taylor wanted to turn it into a working farm so that it would pay for its own upkeep. When the vegetable vendor came around, Bob would trade his eggs for vegetable peels for the chickens.

According to his rule, he installed an outdoor barbeque and loved to cook steaks, knowing within seconds when they were done. "Never gash a steak!" he'd scream and slap your hand.

Ursula managed the household, did her own marketing and was in the children's school car-pool. Bob did the shopping for groceries often, but was usually on the phone from the market with Ursula trying to figure out her writing. "When Ursula uses a pencil, her handwriting is a combination of German, English, RKO, and mishmosh. Even our checks bounce because the people at the bank think she's a counterfeiter!"

He was a happy guy now. MGM had held back a great deal of Bob's salary and what was left over was given to him over a period of time. He continued to pay Barbara 15 percent of his yearly income and supported Manuela and Michael Theiss, though the two children were not satisfied with Robert Taylor as a stepfather. He was unusually strict and old fashioned when it came to bringing up children, and although he tried not to interfere with Ursula's two children, their behavior irritated him.

Manuela and Michael managed to get themselves in trouble for various offenses involving the police, and the headlines always read: ROBERT TAYLOR'S STEPSON or DAUGHTER ARRESTED. Except for his name appearing in the papers with unfavorable publicity, Taylor remained in the background and let Ursula handle the situation. He paid their fines, bails, school tuition, hospitals and living expenses.

Taylor was obligated to do MGM's *The House of Seven Hawks* under his three-year option clause. He kept his mouth shut about this picture, obviously discontented with the results. However, the critics once again disagreed with him, and said that he was always competent in his role of a romantic adventurer. "The picture's one distinction is that Robert Taylor, with a minimum of material, is still showng his successors how a dull job can be well done!"

Joe Hyams, Hollywood correspondent of the *New York Herald Tribune,* wrote a series of articles on stars who had combined professional longevity with steady box office success. The eighth in the series was about Taylor:

"Robert Taylor is so normal he is almost a bore. He has never been involved in a scandal, never been awarded an Oscar and never been scalded by the critics. No one in Hollywood seems to have a word to say about him other than he's too damn nice.

Nice people rarely make interesting copy and try as hard as we could we were unable to find even one instance when Taylor displayed temperament or even mild irritation. Considering the fact that he is 47 years old and has been a motion picture star for twenty-five years, his record is remarkable!

Edwin Knopf, who produced *Tip on a Dead Jockey*, says he believes Taylor's 'normalcy' is what keeps him at the top. 'Those character traits which are so inbred communicate themselves to the audience,' he said. 'Audiences sense the fine qualities and like them. In addition, he's a fine artist, a no-nonsense guy who studies his script more thoroughly than any actor I know.'

Richard Thorpe, who directed Taylor in six films, agrees with Knopf and most of Hollywood about Taylor. 'He's a rarity,' he said. 'A lot of the big stars are really heels off screen and the public doesn't know it at first. It takes them awhile to discover it. But Bob is really a nice guy and it comes through on screen. Also, he's a rugged, handsome man and they're pretty few and far between these days.'"

Joe Hyams asked Taylor what he thought had kept him on top: "Damned if I know," he said. "I've been wondering myself for years. I guess the important thing is to get a good picture once in awhile.

"Acting is the easiest job in the world, and I'm the luckiest guy. All I have to do is be at the studio on time, and know my lines. The wardrobe department tells me what to wear, the assistant director tells me where to go, the director tells me what to do. What could be easier?"

Hyams concluded his article by saying, "The best summation of Taylor's character came from an old

206

farmer in Utah who talked with him for hours while on location recently. Asked what he thought of the star, the old timer replied simply, 'That's one man who never growed himself an ego!' " [9]

On one subject Taylor was adamant, and that was his privacy. No one other than friends was permitted on his property or inside his home.

Despite the pleas of the MGM publicity department, he never allowed photos taken of his son, Terry. Unless an interview was very informal, he refused publicity involving his personal life, and when the pressure was put on him he said, "The public should not be entitled to anything I do not feel they should have. I'm aware of the necessity of publicity, but I don't go out and look for it. Too much of it is worse than none at all. I should know!

"I want my son to grow up normally and not think there is anything different or special about his father.

"Besides, when I go home at night I want my life as an actor to end . . ."

Taylor had bought a section of land in Nebraska near his hometown of Beatrice, planning to make this his country home, but Ursula, who lived through endless winters in Germany without heat, had a phobia about cold weather.

Instead they settled for Buffalo, Wyoming. Their cabin there was Taylor's favorite hunting and fishing retreat. Except for a modern, well-equipped kitchen, the place was decorated in Hune wood and comfortable furnishings. Water was supplied by a mountain stream which also provided a series of ponds, and from the front door of the cabin, Bob had only 15 feet to walk and catch all the mountain trout he wanted.

In keeping with the rustic atmosphere he wanted the "plumbing" away from the house . . .

One of his favorite activities was to camp out for a week at Slide Lake in Teeton National Park near Jackson Hole, Wyoming, to fish for cutthroat trout.

He liked to invite Tom Purvis to go along, "now that you have that custom-made sleeping bag," and Purvis

9. Joe Hyams, *New York Herald Tribune*, April 8, 1957.

said, "Sometimes the temperatures would go below zero. It never bothered Taylor, but my blood was thinning out in Florida and I damn near froze—regardless of the sleeping bag that Dilly thought would lure me to go along with him.

"He'd get me up to go elk hunting at 3:00 in the morning. I'd drag my 240 pounds outta that thing just about the time I was warmin' up. One day around dawn we were stalkin' elk and out of the mist stood one big as an elephant—seemed to me.

"Bob and I froze—and it wasn't the weather. Neither of us said a word. Finally that big wild thing turned around and disappeared. 'Why the hell didn't you shoot, Dilly?'

"Bob was a little shaken, but he covered it up by saying, 'I wasn't worried about us, Curly. I was wonderin' what would happen to that poor elk if he charged a moose like you!' "

However, the relaxation of the wilds with his hunting buddies was put aside for awhile. Taylor was doing a pilot film for his television series, and was scheduled to leave for Africa to make *Killers of Kilimanjaro*.

In February, 1959, he arrived in Mombasa to play the role of an engineer building a railroad in South Africa. *Killers of Kilimanjaro* was both a travelogue and adventure picture, accepted for its splendor of authentic scenery and background alone. (This movie was a Columbia-Warwick Production owned by Taylor).

When he returned to Hollywood in the spring, Four Star Productions was well under way with Taylor's television series, *The Detectives*. Proctor and Gamble grabbed it right away with a budget of $50,000 per half-hour show.

ABC-TV publicists said, "If this series starts shaping up as a dud, the sponsors will be the first to hear about it—and the guy who'll tell 'em will be Robert Taylor."

They reported that the echelons at the network were as enthusiastic about *The Detectives* as was Taylor and would give it the full publicity treatment at the proper time. Proctor and Gamble did not have to be sold on their sponsorship. They speculated that Taylor would draw viewers of both sexes to their TV screens.

Taylor commented that it was impossible to fool the public: "I don't care what you say—they can spot cheap sets, casting and all the typical money-saving gimmicks. Try to cut corners and you wind up in the cellar with a seven-point rating. No, if we're going to do a series, it's got to be first-rate or I don't play ball. I've got too much at stake to begin with, but I'm betting we'll have a winner."

When he was asked why he didn't yield to television before, Taylor explained he was under exclusive contract to MGM and too busy making movies. But when he found himself on his own he turned to TV as the next logical step. "Besides," he said, "my picture price was $300,000 and nobody wanted me! A guy can't live on a weekly pension of $865."

As Police Captain Matt Holbrook, Taylor portrayed a mature, dedicated and friendly law-enforcement officer. Holbrook was a believable character and Taylor needed only to be himself in the role.

He had no illusions whatsoever of contributing anything "artistic" to television and emphasized the fact that he didn't like the television medium. In fact, he didn't even enjoy watching it. He made it clear he was doing it for money, and when the series was through, he would never do another. It was too time-consuming, and he had no time off to go hunting and fishing.

The Detectives premièred in September, 1959, but Robert Taylor didn't see it. "I don't own a television set!"

A month later Hy Gardner invited Bob to lunch. He took Mrs. Gardner along, and when she met Taylor she looked at her husband and asked, "Why is it that columnists age faster than movie actors?"

Hy asked Taylor if he felt any older than when they were together twenty years ago.

"Nooooo, not unless I see myself in those old TV movies, which is why I don't watch them."

"How come you succumbed to *The Detectives?*"

"Hy, it's as simple as A B C—a five-letter word pronounced M-O-N-E-Y. If you get the right vehicle, TV is a harmless and lucrative racket. You don't have to worry about rehearsals because there are none. If the

209

series catches on, the segments can run forever and you can sit back and deposit residuals without ever having to look at yourself on the screen."

"Bob, who do you think was the greatest actor on the MGM payroll when Leo the Lion did the loudest roaring in Hollywood? Gable?"

"No."

"Tracy?"

"No."

"You?"

"Helllll, no! The greatest actor at MGM was Louis B. Mayer. He could play all the parts, male leads, leading ladies, ingénues, everything but Rin Tin Tin. They don't make 'em like Uncle Louie any more."

"Joe Hyams said your life was so normal you even bore yourself. Haven't you gotten into any public controversy?"

"When I appeared before the House Committee on un-American Activities investigating communism in Hollywood in 1947. My beef was that I was prodded into doing a movie that I thought was pro-commie—a thing called *Song of Russia*. I think it's making the rounds of television again. I must remind myself to miss it!" [10]

It wasn't long after *The Detectives* appeared on TV that Taylor gave in and bought a set. He claimed it was for his family's pleasure rather than for his own amusement.

Though his show was a success, Taylor's biggest thrill was his new baby daughter, Tessa, born on August 16, 1959. He called her "Puss Puss," and nicknamed himself "Ol' Dad."

Taylor devoted his entire time to his television series and did not film a movie for over a year. He worked close to the ranch and was able to come home at night like any other normal working man.

He admitted he liked doing movies much more than television. When a friend of his from Beatrice asked him

10. Hy Gardner, *New York Herald Tribune*, October 13, 1959.

to help someone get into show business, he pointed out that the motion picture business in Hollywood was in bad trouble because it was cheaper to make movies in Europe. Taylor could not encourage anyone to get into "this dilemma" because television was the "breeding ground" and even in this medium it was "dog eat dog." He advised the young eager chap from his hometown to choose another career, adding, "Trying to get into the movies today is the same thing as diggin' your own grave. . . ."

The Detectives ran its course on ABC-TV for two years. In its third year NBC-TV expanded the series from a half hour to an hour and called it *Robert Taylor's Detectives.* In a letter to Purvis, Bob wrote about his situation at work and at home.

April 16, 1961

Dear Curly,

After a coupla weeks of real sweat over what was gonna happen with the TV show we finally got 'er ironed out. Our ratings were good, the show seemed to be popular, and I couldn't figure out just what was going on back East. Between agents, and sponsors, and networks, it was quite a hassle. But we finally came up smelling purty good.

We're switchin' over to NBC and will have an hour show this year instead of ½ hour. Our time will be on Friday nites, 8:30–9:30 Pacific Coast time which may be a help. Can't really tell yet.

It'll be a helluva lot more work for me—but the money will also double. My salary for the year will be $300,000 plus 40% of the ownership of the series. I had to give up another 5% to NBC and the other guys in the deal also had to give up their 5% so as it turns out I own 40, Four Star owns 20 and NBC owns 20 leaving the producers with 20.

Anyway, I guess we'll eat for *one* more year without you goin' back to work, so rest easy.

Lookin' forward to our trip down the Rogue River next October, so don't let me down!

As ever,
Dilly

Tom said Taylor was a "worrywart" about money and was so open about it because of his sincere concern. Even a "good deal" had its drawbacks. He was negotiating with MGM about buying a plane he had been using and they came to terms. He paid $15,000 for Old Betsy. He told Tom that was about half the price they could have gotten for her but he was going to put her up for charter and if at the end of six months he was not netting enough to let him fly her a little, he'd sell Old Betsy and take a Capital Gains on what profits there might be. "One thing I'm sure of—I won't lose anything at that price!"

Another time he said he had done some promotion work for *The Matson Line* and was given two round trip tickets to Honolulu. He sent Ursula and Terry to Hawaii, spent a few days with them and returned to work. "I think it will do Ursula a lot of good to get away from the house, the baby and especially me for a little while.

"And besides, I DON'T WANT *THE MATSON LINE* TO GET AWAY FOR FREE!"

Ursula agreed to appear on TV with Taylor on one of his weekly shows. If a love interest were going to be written into a script, he was going to do the show with his wife and not a young actress.

There was a good deal of publicity about Taylor's new role as the straightforward cop who is too busy with crime to get involved romantically and how the public had accepted him as just that. Having Ursula take the part of a police reporter was a strong indication that he was not going to change the concept of this image.

The press at times denounced Taylor for his outlook and said he had changed too much and it might be wise for him to give in to a little hand-holding. One reporter who observed him working on the set wrote that Taylor was like an old lady and wanted everything just so.

The entire article about Taylor was uncomplimentary and one of the writers on the show, Cal Clements, said, "When Bob came in the morning after he had apparently read it I told him I thought it was a damn shame and the others agreed. Bob said he was used to it and to forget it."

212

Someone else remarked, "Adversity is a challenge to Taylor."

And he was the first to admit he didn't like practical jokes when he was working. One story that Clements particularly remembered was the day Taylor found an old pair of shoes in his dressing room. They were huge with soles over an inch thick and resembled those worn by the Frankenstein monster. Beside the shoes was a note. "Bob, a friend of yours dropped by to see you and said he'd be back later to pick up his shoes."

Taylor looked at the note, then at the shoes, examining them very carefully and said, "Hmmmm. Don't think I know this guy. What did he look like and did he say when he would be back?"

Everyone was in on the joke and trying to control his laughter except Bob. Someone said, "Oh, he was a big fellow almost eight feet tall and he had a bolt through his neck!"

Taylor laughed about it later but at the time he didn't appear to be amused. His mind was always on more serious matters and even the time he was sitting with some men on the set looking over his script while a nude photo of a toothless girl was being passed around, he was nonchalant about the comments and whistles from the other boys. He looked at the picture minus her clothes, handed it to the next guy and said, "God, I wonder who her dentist is?"

Robert Taylor's Detectives faded from the television screen at the end of the 1961–62 season. The show was doing well, but it is not unusual for a good series to be cancelled. Taylor was distressed because of the loss of a steady income, but he said doing a weekly one-hour show was tiring.

"Hell, half the time I was workin' in places like the railroad yards where it's 100 degrees in the shade. Talk about 'lather' enough to bathe one buffalo? God damn, the meringue you could have scraped offa me woulda shampooed a whole herd! If I was back in the Navy they'd prescribe salt pills. However, I doubt that I could lift one. If I could find some of that old-fashioned remedy they used to call HADICOL it might have perked me up a shade!"

213

He did not have time for a vacation and little opportunity to go hunting or fishing. NBC asked him to do another television series with Robert Loggia based on the filed articles of the United States Department of Health, Education and Welfare, to be aired on Thursdays from 7:30 to 8:30. He accepted, but a conflict arose between the producers of the show and the Government, and the series was cancelled.

Taylor said, "Everything in the world that COULD go wrong HAS gone wrong!

Manuela had disobeyed Ursula by quitting high school for a short-lived marriage. She suffered a miscarriage, but decided she did not want to live on the Taylor ranch and moved in with a girl whom Taylor described as "some squirreley girl friend," who according to Taylor was "slinging hash in some joint near the beach."

Michael was expelled from the military academy he was attending. He returned to the Taylor household, but Bob couldn't handle him. Ursula was convinced her son should return to Germany where the school laws were not as strict. She also hoped that his real father might be able to do something with him, and Taylor offered Michael $100 a month until he was eighteen. "After that, you're on your own!"

Both children had joined a group of hippies, and Taylor refused to allow their friends on Ursulor property.

To add to his personal problems, Ruth was becoming more senile every day and wandered away from her home on Selby Street forgetting who she was. The only thing she could remember was, *"I am Robert Taylor's mother."*

She had given up calling him "Arly" and became completely engrossed in being the mother of a celebrity even though she thought the life of an actor was a wicked one. It had gotten to the point that if grace was not said before a meal, she was shocked.

One evening the family, including a few friends, sat down for dinner and during the first course, Ruth began to rant that actors were disrespectable and were too busy with their lives of sin, divorcing, drinking and cursing. She got up from the table and left the room.

214

Taylor smiled. "Guess we forgot to say grace again. Oh well, I'm just a heathen!"

Ruth embarrassed him in other ways, but he became used to her and the family played along. One habit Ruth had was handing Bob money, on his birthday or for Christmas, money that he, of course, had given her. She made quite a production over the fact that she was giving money to her famous and wealthy son, and made sure everyone, friends included, were gathered round when she made her generous gesture.

But more than anything else, her disappearances bothered Taylor. He would receive telephone calls from drugstores, cab drivers or strangers on the street informing him there was a woman who claimed to be his mother. Somehow she was always found and brought home. What Taylor did to hush up these numerous incidents, no one knows.

Michael was finally sent back to Germany with his grandmother under the guidance of his father, George Theiss, and Manuela was forbidden to bring her new boy friend into the Taylor house.

She was arrested, and pleaded guilty to being under the influence of drugs. Later she violated her parole only to be charged with drunkenness. Within two years the police booked her four times—twice for using drugs, once for forgery and once when they found her at 5:45 in the morning in a parked car with two men and a bottle of wine.

Ursula appeared in court and confessed tearfully, "Michael is having growing pains, too, but nothing like this. Manuela has always been a little rebel, but we never dared to think she would sink so low. I hate to see her hit bottom more and more, so I'll just leave it to the court now. She has been on probation, but this is her fourth offense and I think their action will be less lenient now. I hope they order a psychiatrist." That is exactly what the judge did.

In March, 1962, Taylor found time for a long overdue physical examination at Scripps Clinic. His x-rays showed a spot on his lung, but it turned out to be one he had had since he was two years old. He said, however, those

215

three days waiting for the results were the worst he had spent in his life.

"I'll never go through that again!"

Not long before, Clark Gable died of a heart attack and Taylor had been a pall-bearer. His grief was far more than the tragic loss of a buddy. Gary Cooper died six months later and Dick Powell was suffering from cancer of the throat.

The loss of his two close friends and the possibility that Powell might not make it, shocked Taylor deeply. He began to worry about everything—mostly money and health (but the latter was something over which he felt he had no control, since he was a fatalist). Gable was only fifty-nine years old and Cooper, sixty. Taylor was then fifty, and though growing old had little effect on him, he was aware that both friends were in his age bracket and had everything to live for. He also knew they worked harder than they should have—accepting roles that younger men would have had a difficult time undertaking.

Shortly after he got the good news about his check-up he wrote to Purvis that he was a "shade spooked" for a couple of days waiting for the results and it had cost him a "chunk of money" to find all this out, but worth the expense.

. . . and now that my problems are solved for the time being anyway, let me tell you somethin', Ol' Bud, you've got troubles comin' your way if you follow that map you whipped up for your next vacation! It's slowly beginning to dawn on me why we darned near got lost on that flight we made from New Orleans to Dallas when you started callin' me Dilly. It was YOUR lousy navigation!

When I looked at your map showing the Florida coast, the Dry Tortugas and Cuba, I ran like crazy to my Atlas and you sure didn't do Castro justice. If Cuba runs North and South then Castro's a Methodist Minister! Damned good thing the Rooskies didn't shoot you up into that rocket. You'd probably gotten up there around 200 miles, down to 180 and missed the whole damned earth! I just hope your navigation improves or Castro'll have one old

216

fat boy I know for dinner some nite! And I don't mean as a guest!

Taylor went on to say that ABC had offered him a half-hour show for next year but that he had already made a deal with Walt Disney for a picture in Europe starting June, 1962. "The money ain't the best—leastwise it ain't what I usedta get—but that figgers and I AIN'T PROUD NO MORE! I gotta keep workin'. My expenses seem to be goin' up and up and up but the Disney picture sounds like a good one and at least Ursula and the kids will be able to go with me to Vienna.

"The yarn, incidentally, is called *The Miracle of the White Stallions* and has to do with saving of the Lippizan horses by the American Army when Patton went into Austria.

"I do not play a white stallion OR Patton!

"Maybe when I return we can do some huntin'. Seems like too damn many of my old buddies are departin' me these days—'n I don't like it atall! Jest don't YOU get any fancy ideas of goin' back into the Navy, now willya? They ain't usin' Stearmans no mo! And we ain't checked out in them-thar Jets!"

Though Taylor had written to Tom, "I ain't proud no more," he actually had been turning down one script after another. Most were not to his liking; those that were good required him to play a younger man. His answer to that was always, "No!" Or the role called for him to make love to a younger woman and the answer again was, "No!"

He said he didn't want his photos retouched to make him look twenty-five years old again.

As Colonel Podhajsky in *The Miracle of the White Stallions* he was rewarded with excellent reviews. One newsman wrote, "Robert Taylor, weathering prettily with the years, seems more and more able to portray hard-bitten men. This, for an actor who used to be too beautiful for words, is high praise."

Taylor was so pleased with this movie that he made rare public appearances on television talk shows and gave out interviews generously.

217

Gay Pauley wrote an article in the *New York World Telegram* about meeting Taylor. "I flew at the opportunity of meeting the 'it boy' of my teen years. The trouble with meeting one of my girlhood idols several years later is the shocking realization that not only is he older, but so am I.

"When asked if I wanted to meet him, I said I sure would. After all, in my youth I had spent quite a bit of my weekly allowance on the man, sighing with mililons of other females as he made love on the screen. Why not see what my teen-age 'thrill' was like?"

"OK," Taylor said to her, "I'm used to people like you who remember me when they were 'little girls.' I don't mind at all. Teen-agers still have their idols, but now they worship Marlon Brando or Paul Newman or Tony Curtis . . . a different type of leading man.

"I don't mind that I'm not playing the great lover any more. Changes in roles are inevitable if you are going to progress as an actor. Just as age is inevitable. "At the time I was enjoying (?) that fan hysteria, when autograph seekers mobbed us at hotel entrances, I was young enough to appreciate it. I don't miss it today. Maturity has its rewards.

"Fans have changed, too. They're blasé. Television has brought personalities right into their homes."

Miss Pauley said Taylor laughed when she mentioned that he was neither gray nor balding. He said a crop of hair was inherited, and as for gray, well, he didn't consider himself "old enough for that yet."

She asked him how he had changed and he said, "Well, I don't run up the stairs any more. I still weigh the same, but the sands have shifted!"

He told Miss Pauley his only professional ambition was to make just one more good picture. [11]

Cattle King with Joan Caulfield was the second and last film Taylor was obligated to do for MGM. During his years as "Pretty Boy" in the late thirties he had read the script and wanted to do it. Finally twenty years later he got his wish.

11. Gay Pauley, *New York World Telegram,* 1963.

MGM said "farewell" to him in grand fashion. After the lion's roar, Robert Taylor's name colorfully appeared touching all four corners of the screen, and even he confessed he had never seen his name in such big letters.

In *Cattle King* he portrayed a rancher in this Western about the National Trial Act in the 1850's. One critic said, "There is no actor in Hollywood who sits a horse as well as Robert Taylor."

The picture was a real attention-getter, but unfortunately it was not that *one good picture* Taylor was looking for.

After he completed *Cattle King*, and was able to spend more time on the ranch, Taylor decided he needed a ranchhand. He interviewed several men, one of whom was Art Reeves, who had been employed by Wild Bill Elliot.

Art said the day Taylor had told him to come over for a chat, he found himself waiting with several other boys seeking employment on the Ursulor Rancho. "I saw this 'Dude' dressed up like a combination between Roy Rogers at a rodeo, and Liberace. He went in to talk to Taylor and I thought to myself, 'Who the hell would hire a guy dressed like that? Why, his wardrobe was more expensive than Taylor's!' "

"When Taylor got around to talking to me, I think he had already made up his mind on that 'Dude' and I was right. But a few weeks later he called and asked if I was interested in takin' the job. I wasn't going to make it too easy for him and said I would think it over. He was a little taken back and hung up the phone. Few days later he invited Wild Bill to dinner and Elliot said that Taylor wanted me to come along.

"This was his way of begging, though can't say that is a good word to use. I made some comment about that 'Dude' and Taylor said the guy just didn't work out. Then he offered me the job again and I accepted."

Reeves was known as "Uncle Art" to the children and would remain on Ursulor Rancho to the end. He was a close confidante to Bob, and though they had their minor differences, they never had an argument.

Art was devoted to Taylor but admitted, "Bob would drive me nuts when he'd get his gander up about something—like the tool shed, for instance. I knew where everything was, but the place was a mess!

"Bob was very neat and liked things in order. He'd come out of that tool shed when he couldn't find what he wanted, hollerin' like hell. One day I saw him looking over a broken fence and he walked over to me. 'Ya know, Art, that fence has been that way for days. If I don't get *someone'*—meaning me!—'to fix it, I'll have to do it myself.'

"Well, I was busy doing something more important, but he stood there waiting for me to take the hint. He made me so damn mad that I went into the tool shed and handed him a hammer. He looked at it—then at me —scowled—and fixed that fence himself. He was fussin' and mumblin' under his breath, giving those nails a good pounding, but he mended it better than I could have."

Taylor, being such a good correspondent, wrote many letters to Art when he and Ursula were away, but he never got a reply. "God damn it, Art, I'd like to know how things are on the farm when I'm not there. Just a note's OK."

Still no replies . . .

Taylor expressed his concern over the horses. Were the chickens laying eggs? Did the heavy rain in Los Angeles do any damage to the house? Any mail? Any calls? Still no answer.

Finally out of desperation, Taylor enclosed self-addressed cards with questions typed on them. All Art had to do was fill in yes or no.

Still no reply.

Taylor blew his stack! "All you have to do, for Christ's sake, is drop the damn card in the mail box!"

"What, with no stamps on them!" Art replied.

The next time Bob put stamps on the self-addressed cards and he got a response.

Reeves and his wife, Barbara, became part of the family, and lived in the little cottage near the stables. They were, in fact, married in Bob's house and given a reception at Taylor's invitation. Their cozy dwelling was off the dirt road entrance to the ranch, and one could get no further if he wasn't known to Art, who could hear a car turning off Mandeville Canyon Road whenever he

220

was in the house or corral. When *he* stepped into the driveway, you stopped! Softspoken, with little to say, he was a big muscular man with powerful hands that were usually buried in his hip pockets. He gave the right impression—no trespassing.

If you were a friend, he'd wave you on up the circular driveway to the rambling one-story house with kidney-shaped swimming pool on the left, a magnolia tree on the front lawn (a fifth-anniversary surprise from Bob to Ursula). A German Shepherd, Duchess, was always around if she heard anyone approaching. Her barking usually made the other animals on the grounds contribute to the conversation. These included horses, hunting dogs, and the wildlife somewhere in the surrounding mountains that engulfed the ranch closely on three sides.

If Ursula were home, a dusty station wagon was parked outside. She was often seen roaring up the dirt road around 4:30, when school was out, distributing dogs, cats and children from every door and window.

She had an appointment book, but it was not filled with social engagements; rather 3:00—bake cake, 3:30 —prepare the roast, 4:00—do some sewing, 4:30—pick up the children, etc.

"All the food we eat is homemade. That is a household law. I'm busy every minute making chicken soup, bread, and there's always fresh coffee on the stove. Bob and I usually had a cup in front of us and the first place he headed when he came home was the coffee pot!

"I've always felt uncomfortable with live-in help. Privacy is so important and somehow you lose this when there is someone else living with you. I like to cook and I don't mind in the slightest the duties involved in household chores or the children. I have to be a part of everything in my house."

When Ursula could not sleep or got angry or nervous, she got down on her knees and scrubbed the floors.

She was referred to by Bob as *Mutter* (German for *mother*) or "my little hamburger." In public it was "The bride" or "Mama."

Everyone's favorite spot in the house was in front of the hearthstone fireplace; they sat around the thick heavy coffee table that had once been a collection table Bob found in an old church. He had the legs cut down and George Montgomery sanded and polished it. The markings, carvings and scratches underneath the polish gave the table a look of antique distinction—Western-style. It was the only piece of furniture Bob kept from his first marriage. He loved it and said he wouldn't sell it for any price.

Every Christmas the house was decorated in a warm festive manner. There was a "healthy" wreath on the front door with a sign, THE TAYLORS WELCOME YOU.

Giant candles flickered near the fireplace and Christmas presents were scattered everywhere—on the mantle over the fireplace, on shelves, on chairs and bookcases.

Though Thanksgiving Day was for the family alone, which included Art and his wife, Christmas was open house to friends from 2:00 to 6:00. The Taylors celebrated their Christmas on the eve and the tree was trimmed by Ursula in the "tree room." After dinner the door was opened and presents were there for the taking.

So many gifts were sent to Tessa and Terry that Taylor insisted most of them be shelved until a later date or given away. The children didn't like this very much, but Ursula tried to pacify them by giving each a gift every day for two weeks before Christmas—a German custom.

"Daddy" played Santa Claus, sneaking off before Christmas dinner was finished. Ursula rang a tiny bell under the table announcing the arrival of Ol' Saint Nick, and over the intercom, "Santa," who was down in the stables, yelled, "Ho, Ho, Ho." This sent the children running to the front door, where they would find Santa's bag of little presents that Ursula had started buying during the previous summer.

When Terry got beyond the age of believing in Santa Claus, Bob let him assist in the "Ho, Ho, Ho" act for Tessa.

If it weren't for Ursula, no Christmas cards would be sent. As much as Bob loved to write letters, he hated the idea of addressing hundreds of cards and very often they were eliminated entirely. Ursula liked to buy stationery with a gold wreath or some other Christmas emblem and drop a note to old friends. Some said Taylor disliked the

222

"Christmas card bit" because he was afraid he would forget someone.

His presents to the children were inexpensive and practical. He loved to shop at Thrifty's, a discount store chain in Los Angeles, and was almost as bargain conscious as Ursula. In turn, he was embarrassed and angry when he received an expensive gift from a friend. For days he'd complain about it, threatening to send it back, and then Ursula would convince him that it would be discourteous.

But when it came to breeding horses, mortorcycles or a *very special* gift for a close friend, he was overly generous. Each member of the Taylor family owned a motorcycle, and when Terry showed little interest in horseback riding, Bob didn't force the issue. But even the toughest of Bob's buddies cringed when he took his son on motorcycle jumps. Terry would not admit his fear, but Art said, "When Bob got Terry on that 'bike' doin' those jumps, even I shuddered!"

Other extravagances of Taylor's were guns and camera equipment. Although he was a master with rifles, he could not get the hang of a camera. On special occasions he would spend hours setting up his very expensive equipment and get everyone to pose just so, but few pictures ever turned out. If it hadn't been for Ursula and her Brownie camera, there might never have been a family album.

Chapter XIII

Taylor invited Purvis and his wife to the ranch in the fall of 1962. They also planned on doing some hunting in Oregon or fishing in Mexico.

September 12, 1962

Dear Slufoot:

Sorry to hear that yer pedal extremities are still on the fritz. Guess that must be what comes from not puttin' on shoes early enuff in life. Anyhow, don't worry about the care you'll be able to get out here. We have a darned good blacksmith who comes over every month or so to take care of the horses and, if yer dogs start to give ya trouble, we can always take ya down to the barn and let him hammer out something kinda classy for ya!

In your letter you mention something about needing a "hat." You sure as hell won't need one, so ferget it—unless yer worried about your hair gettin' mussed up!

Your "digs" will be ready for ya on October 25th and we'll try to make ya comfortable. I'll bring in a few extra bales of bedding from the barn just in case the bed ain't big enuff for ya.

I also have my eyes on a few old milk cows which've been roamin' the hills around here and hope to knock one down with a car on Mandeville Canyon one of these mornin's. Gotta have somethin' to BarBQ and the horses are too expensive. In any case, please don't worry—we'll eat, even if I have to trap a sackfull of these quail which come down and feed outside my window every mornin'. Take good care ole Bud—love to all of y'all from all of us—and if ya have any trouble finding a pair of kicks big enuff to accommodate those new insoles, just wait until ya get here. I'm sure I could talk Universal Studios

Taylor was romantically linked with Lana Turner
for the first time in MGM's *Johnny Eager* (1942)

Lt. and Mrs. Robert Taylor (Barbara Stanwyck) posed for this
portrait shortly before Taylor went into active service in 1944

Lt. Robert Taylor and his buddy Lt. Tom Purvis
at a naval air station in New Orleans, 1944

MGM

The Bribe (1949), with Ava Gardner,
marked the low point in Taylor's career

Taylor gave the seventeen-year-old Elizabeth Taylor
her first screen kiss in *The Conspirator* (1950)

out of a pair of those dandy shoes they useda use on ole Frankenstein!

As ever,
Dilly

October 15, 1962

Dear Dismal—
Your duffle arrived in good shape day before yesterday and I unpacked 'er yesterday and put it down in your "digs" nexta the chicken coop! I had sent all my horse blankets out to be cleaned so I'm usin' yer "longies" on one of the animals until you get here. OK? He's a nice and clean horse tho, so I don't reckon you'll have to wash 'em until sometime next season.
Ole Dale "Wells Fargo" Robertson had a party out at his place last nite and Mama kept me up until 2 this AM. I guess I better stretch out on the floor and get a little extra sack time before I take Terry to Sunday School.
See y'all on the 27th—

Dilly

Taylor's referring to taking a nap on the floor was typical of him. Not only did he always stretch out on the floor, but he sat on the floor wherever he was. He was asked once if he had any Japanese blood in him because he liked to squat next to the coffee table and eat.

When Tom and his wife, Vi, arrived at the Ursulor Rancho, they slept in a large room in the stable area. It was furnished nicely, like a hotel room, complete with stereo.

They all packed their fishing equipment and flew to the Baja Peninsula in Mexico for a few days. They were guests of the son of former President Rodriguez of Mexico.

The Purvis family left for home and Taylor wrote that he wasn't much at being or having house guests, but, ". . . the horses enjoyed your company and the next time you come out I'm afraid you're gonna have to use that same stall again or hurt the hosses' feelings!

"You and Vi got out of here just in time, Curly. You

225

mighta gotten your toupée singed a little. It's really been a bitch!"

Taylor described the disastrous fire that swept through the canyon area vividly in his letter:

> On Monday morning we got Terry on the bus to school around 7:45. Art called around 8:30 to ask if we'd heard anything on the radio about a brush fire. I hot-footed it out front and you could already see the column of smoke rising hundreds of feet in the air in a northeasterly direction.
>
> The fire spread just like one of the old prairie fires back in the Midwest when I was a kid. By 11:00 Terry's school had been evacuated and a Public School near it had burned to the ground. By 3:00 a police car screamed up the drive here and said to get the hell out in a hurry—the fire was coming fast!
>
> I had already had Mutti [Ursula] pack a bag for the kids and herself and she took off down the canyon for Ronnie Reagan's place with the two small frys. Two guys from UCLA who had done odd jobs for us, plus another youngster from the Valley, showed up to help. I loaded two of the dogs in the station wagon, Art drove up on the hill to get the two mares down, and I sure as hell never figured he'd get them out. I drove to the Reagans to be with Mutti and the kids. While there we watched the progress of the thing on TV and through glasses, and by golly I wouldn't have given you 5¢ for our chances of saving a thing.
>
> However, Art, with the help of the guys, herded all the horses down the canyon, took the rest of the dogs and put them all up with about 100 other horses out of the canyon in that playing field at the school on the corner of Mandeville Road and Sunset Boulevard.
>
> At 11:00 that night the policeman at the foot of the canyon told me Ursula and I could make it back up if we wanted to come so we went back up in the station wagon. You never saw such a mess! I'll bet there were 150 fire engines in the canyon, all fighting blazes which were burning on both sides, and really having a helluva time. However, the fire had crossed the canyon below our place about ¼ mile and from there on up it wasn't

226

too bad. We stayed up all nite with the sprinklers on the roof going and other sprinklers going in places where they'd do the most good. Art stayed down with the horses at the school.

The fire almost completely encircled the old Dick Powell house, burned out some of their fences but they saved the place. For a while there it looked like it was coming right across the street but we were just lucky I guess.

'Around mid-morning on Tuesday, Ursula drove back down to the motel where we had put the kids and when she tried to come back up, they had closed the canyon. The fire was breaking out again all over the place. So . . . my "little hamburger," not to be stopped, went over to the playing field, saddled up "Old Bobby" and came riding in here around noon.

The police came roarin' in telling us to evacuate—that the fire wasn't five minutes below us and coming this way. However, this time we were mad and said, "the hell with it—we'll stay!" We had everything on, including the well, and things were fairly well wet down and we figured we could at least save the house and other buildings.

However, again we were lucky and the wind shifted back to the northeast. As a result I don't think we lost a blade of grass on the entire property and everything looks normal. The canyon below is a mess, though, and it isn't as bad as the area north of Bel Air Country Club. That really took a beating. At the present count 457 homes were completely burned out, to say nothing of those that were partially destroyed.

The fire companies and the guys flying the old B-17 bombers with borate solutions were really great. For a while things got so hot here in the canyon that it was like World War 2—those damned bombers'd come over here at treetop level, drop a wet load of that stuff and pull straight over the hills. It was exciting but just a shade scary too.

All the horses and dogs are back now and things are settling down again . . . except the private school Terry goes to was burned to the ground, with the exception of the little first-grade building. I guess he'll go back there next week and they'll have to start on a new building.

He seems to be enjoying the vacation. Puss-Puss [Tessa]

227

is just fine and thoroughly enjoyed her two day stay in the motel. I guess eating out in a restaurant pleased both of them."

Taylor's remark about his children "eating out" typifies his method of bringing them up. Tessa and Terry knew only the simple things of life and their father did everything he could to keep it that way.

Before they went to school in the mornings, they had to earn their allowances by cleaning out the dog pens and gathering eggs. Their rooms were always in order.

Taylor was a remote father. Neither child wanted to make him angry and often Taylor would play the game of being peeved to frighten them before they went too far. He was completely in awe of Tessa and loved to tickle her and romp with her. She had her mother's temperament—quiet and gentle. When she wasn't doing her homework, she liked to do needlework and sew. She also saved every penny of her allowance.

On the other hand, Terry was short-tempered like Taylor. He resembled his father when he was a boy— tall and lanky. And *he* spent every cent of *his* allowance and would hint to his dad that he was broke all the time. Old Dad, however, never loaned him any money. "If you need a few bucks, find something extra to do around the farm."

One evening Terry decided his sister needed a haircut because her curls were always getting into her eyes, so he took a pair of scissors and gave her a slight bob. The following day Taylor told Art, "Old Terr's sittin' a shade on the bias today. I warped his ass pretty good. In any case he still seems to think I'm a nice guy."

He said the toughest thing he had to do was tell Terry "the facts of life," and as usual he turned to Purvis. This time, rather than put his problem on paper, he sent Tom a tape. "How come your two kids are so God damn smart. I can't figure it out. Guess the human race doesn't run any more true to form in the breeding category than do horses or dogs. You're such a dismal bastard, Curly, and wind up with two bright kids! Me—with my absolutely brilliant mind, who could easily solve this whole

228

"space" problem if I wanted to get into it—and my two younguns can't now, and probably never will be able to, spell *pussy*. Not CAT—*PUSSY*. On second thought Terry might. He's gettin' that look in his eyes! How the devil did you tell Johnny about 'IT'?"

Tom responded but as usual rather than get seriously involved told Bob to "say it outright," but to wait for the right time: "When Terry says something sexy ask him what he's talkin' about. The kid probably won't know and then you explain it to him."

A few weeks later Taylor had that talk with his son but said it was "real rough" and that "Ol Terr knew more than I did!"

A House is Not a Home starred Shelley Winters as the famous madame, Polly Adler, and Taylor the racketeer who backs her. Though one critic said, "Robert Taylor gives a professional touch to an underworld character," another review was highly amusing:

"Something was missing in this picture and to be blunt about it, the missing ingredient is sex! There is hardly a suggestion of it. It may or may not discourage impressionable young girls from a life of sin, but it certainly is enough to keep anyone away from the movie!"

A House is Not a Home was degrading to both Taylor and Miss Winters. The book had been a best seller and the story a truthful and sensational one—until however it reached the motion picture screen. Taylor thought the role of gangster Frank Costigan would be as strong and heavy as *Johnny Eager,* but it wasn't. Of course it was 1964, before sex movies were readily accepted, and long before the film was released the public was waiting in line to see Polly Adler's life story.

Taylor might not have done the picture if it hadn't been for money and if the movie script had followed the revealing book accurately. He admitted *he wasn't proud any more* and would do almost anything to earn a living, but he stuck to his guns that his image was important.

Had he been asked to portray a "real" Frank Costigan and Miss Winters the "real" Polly Adler, he would have turned it down.

He appeared on *The Mike Douglas Show* as co-host, sang a few songs and even danced a little. Douglas surprised him by having two of Bob's old friends from Beatrice, Nebraska, who used to sing with him in high school, on the program. The whole show was a practical joke because Taylor could not carry a tune and hated to dance. Purvis taped the shows and sent them to Bob, who wasn't the slightest bit amused. He told Tom, "It might have made YOU laugh, but I was lowering myself. You have enjoyed your life much more than I have, Old Bud. These days I'm doin' things that I never thought I'd have to do."

Purvis said Taylor cried "poor mouth" too often and worried about everything. "Why, if Bob didn't have something to worry about, he'd go out and find something!"

Taylor also remained adamant against anything or anybody who was anti-American. He was quietly active in politics and supported his candidate. He usually was the first one in line at the polls, and believed in "my country, right or wrong."

When his hometown newspaper announced that he was going into politics he wrote to the editor:

Dear Bob,
The item which appeared in your UPPER ROOM column—the one speculating upon my intentions toward a political career—handed me a mighty pleasant chuckle. Many years ago I learned that it was professionally unwise to take issue with, or try to refute anything which Walter Winchell printed as fact. However, in this particular case, and since I'm the guy who should know, I feel safe in assuring you that I have NO ambitions, present or future, in that particular direction. Politics are something about which I know very little, other, of course, than that which is known by any citizen who takes his right to vote seriously.
Mind you, I see no reason why an actor shouldn't go

230

into politics. It seems to me that honesty, intelligence, a firm belief that America is one of the finest countries in the world and that our political philosophy is the best in the world should be all the requirements that anyone should need. I believe that we need fewer professional "politicians" and more just plain good people in politics. So much for that. Before I sound like I'm making a campaign pitch, perhaps I'd better sign off. If you happen to see any of my old Beatrice friends, please give 'em my best.

As ever,
Bob

One friend described Taylor as a guy who wanted to fight in active duty during the war but was too old; a guy who wanted to look like Humphrey Bogart because the public would concentrate on his wrinkles rather than the perfection of his face; a guy who would have been truly satisfied to be a rancher all his life and was amazed if a woman looked at him twice; a guy who would have carried the American flag in every parade in the country or downtown Moscow; a guy who really wanted to be Billy the Kid or the Sergeant in *Bataan;* a guy who lived *Waterloo Bridge* all of his life.

Judging from his other characteristics, it was no surprise that he remained loyal to Nebraska. In October, 1963, he and Ursula went to a fund-raising drive at Doane College in Crete. He made the front page of *The Beatrice Sun:* "DOC BRUGH VISITS ALMA MATER TO TOUCH OFF BIG DOANE DRIVE!"

Doane College conferred on Taylor an Honorary Doctor of Humane Letters. ("If I had to talk, I'd be a nervous wreck!")

Mrs. Mary Ellen Farries, his drama coach at Doane in 1933, helped him into his gown and said, "Spangler—oh!—should I call you Robert Taylor or Bob?"

"Just call me what comes naturally!"

He headlined a student gab session, took in a pair of one-act plays and attended a "those who knew him when" luncheon. A brief campus tour provoked a comment. "It looks wonderful—unlike California's government-sponsored schools with brick and glass all over the place!"

He attended the Nebraska-Colorado football game and was given a standing ovation. At a press conference afterward he cautioned that any dramatist Hollywood-bound today "better take along a lot of luck." He said it wasn't as easy to get a start as it was when he headed West and that many of today's movies go too far into controversial areas, forgetting that their purpose is to entertain. He concluded by saying, "Beatrice was and is my hometown!"

Taylor drove off alone for a few hours to Filley, twelve miles east of Beatrice; population 149; birthplace of Spangler Arlington Brugh fifty-two years ago.

He walked down one-block-long Main Street and looked in every shop window, smiling at anyone who passed. He wasn't recognized. Later he sat in his car to meditate.

When he received a copy of the Beatrice newspaper he wrote to the editor to thank him: "The things said therein really gave me a lump right where it's hardest to swallow. It may seem strange to a lot of people but what the 'people back home' think has always been very important to me—and many a time a decision on my part has been influenced largely by what I figured my old friends and associates back in Nebraska would think of it.

"This may be partly selfish, but primarily I think it's because I've always felt that the best people in the country either lived in or came from that part of the USA. The nice things you said meant more to me than a laudatory review in *Time* or *Life* or *Look*. (And that's good, I guess, on accounta those magazines have never been too complimentary anyhow!)

"The whole damned Nebraska trip this time was a real thrill right from the little luncheon in Crete plumb thru the game, dinner with Spiv and Abbie, coffee and cinnamon rolls with the Shirerdas in Wilbur on Sunday and the drive through the western part of the state on our way to Wyoming. I saw a lot of old friends and my only regret was that I had so little time to spend in getting reacquainted with most of them.

"When you have a spare minute, please enter me on your list of subscribers and have the *Sun* mailed to me here in California. It need not come via air—just regular mail—and leave me know the rate for everything so's I can send you a check, rubber or otherwise. Thanks again for everything."

On the way from Nebraska to Wyoming he told Ursula, "I should fly into Nebraska more often and spend time with my old buddies before it gets too late. It makes me feel awful old, but I might as well get used to that! It's a fact so why not face it, right?"

When they arrived in their cabin in Buffalo, Wyoming, the Taylors found out that the property on which it was located had been sold. They spent a week there packing and putting their furniture into storage, hoping to find another place close by.

It was depressing for Bob to close up his little cabin in Buffalo, but he had always known that as much as the children loved it there, Ursula preferred warm weather and had gone along with buying it in the first place to please him.

When they returned to Hollywood, more bad news was waiting for them. Michael Thiess had made headlines:

ROBERT TAYLOR STEPSON ARRESTED IN POISONING OF DAD IN GERMANY

December 23, 1963: Munich, Germany
Michael Thiess, stepson of Hollywood star Robert Taylor, has been arrested on suspicion of attempted murder. Police said the youth is suspected of having served poisoned tea to his father, Munich film producer George Thiess.
Formal charges have not yet been filed against the boy. Under German law, he can be held during investigation by the state prosecutor. Police said Michael had moved in with his father and the two had a series of arguments last February.
At this point, police said, Thiess advised them he suspected his son had attempted to kill him with insecticide in his tea.

233

Michael served a year in prison for attempted murder, was sent back to the United States and put under psychiatric care. Both he and Manuela spent time in sanitariums off and on, and Ursula always blamed their problems on the hardships they suffered during their childhoods in war-torn Germany.

Taylor paid the bills for all their additional care. His fixed overhead which was $3,000 a month was too high. Next Ruth had to be put into a nursing home because of her peculiar behavior. She was no longer able to function mentally, and except for the fact that she could only repeat, "I am Robert Taylor's mother" when she was found roaming the streets, she didn't know who she was or where she was most of the time.

Ruth was placed in a nursing home that cost Taylor $1,000 a month, but no matter how expensive, it was a relief for him to know she was safe. He had not failed to call her every day or have someone else do it when he was out of town. It upset him to see her affecting Terry and Tessa when she did not know who they were or who Grandma was.

A few months later Art resigned to take a better job elsewhere and Taylor said this was the last straw in his run of bad luck. The two men talked it over and decided the offer was too good for Reeves to turn down. "I love ya, Art, and the kids won't know what to do without their Uncle Art around. God damn, they spend almost as much time with you and Barbara as they do at home. Well, I'll tell ya one thing—maybe now I can find a guy who'll keep my tool shed the way I like it!"

Art asked Bob for a letter of recommendation, saying, "Just don't mention that gosh darn tool shed."

ROBERT TAYLOR
July 15
1964

To Whom It May Concern:
If you're interested in a brief, one-line recommendation, you may as well stop right now. If, on the other hand,

you're interested in what I have to say about Art Reeves (the Bearer) then draw up a chair!

Art Reeves has been in my employ for the past five years, heading up the breeding operation of my little Quarter Horse farm here in Los Angeles, California. In addition to taking care of horses (stallions, mares, colts and riding stock) he's also taken care of the chickens, the dogs, the rabbits, the pigeons, and, at times, our two small children. I point this out not because ALL of this was his responsibility but because it seems to me a kind of complimentary side-light on the man himself.

In the years Art has been with me I can't honestly say I have ever found anything which he couldn't and wouldn't do. This includes carpentry, plumbing, electrical work, animal husbandry, etc., etc. If there's anything he does *not* know something about, I've yet to find out what it is—and this may be due to the fact that he has the intelligence and integrity to *learn* whatever he doesn't already know.

Although our breeding operation is not a large one we have not lost a foal—or a mare—in all the time Art has been with us. Our horses have, without exception, been beautifully cared for at all times. The same goes for the entire farm.

Art has a great disposition—an admirable way with people with whom he has been obligated to come in contact—he's a hard worker and a willing worker—and, most importantly, he's honest to the "nth" degree and one of the most "sober" people I've ever known.

The only thing I have AGAINST Art Reeves is that he's decided to leave us to tackle another kind of work on his own! Mrs. Taylor, and I, all the children and horses and dogs, are gonna miss him. We wish him all the luck in the world in his new endeavors—and he can work for me again any time, anywhere. . . .

Sincerely but regretfully,
Robert Taylor

However, to the delight of all the Taylors, after a brief absence Art returned to the Ursulor Rancho. Taylor, trying to hide the fact that he was relieved and happy to see Art back in the little cottage near the stables, said, "What happened? Didn't they want a baby sitter with rough hands?" Then they all walked back up to the main house and sat down to dinner.

There surely was more action on the ranch than there was in Taylor's professional life. His letters centered on activities at the farm and no words about movie or TV offers. "We had another stud colt out of one of my mares by Audie Murphy's $45,000 horse. The stud fee was $500 so I'll have to sell him at a good price when he's a yearling." "I had 50 more baby chicks sent out from Iowa and they'll start laying in about five months. We will kill off all the old hens and 'surround 'em with dumplings! I'm also buyin' a couple of female rabbits and a buck to harpoon 'em." "Caught a litter of five baby skunks down by the barn yesterday. We hadda kill the mother and two of the babies, but the other three have been deodorized and we hope to make pets outa them."

He told Tom, "The mother woulda made a fine toupée for you, Curly!"

Taylor was getting restless and returned scripts by the dozen. He still refused to accept any roles that called for him to be anything but a guy in his fifties. He was turning down some good offers but repeatedly stated his image meant more to him than money.

He said, "People think I'm a millionaire, but I'm not. I've saved a little money, but every time a chance comes along to really strike it rich outside the movie business—like the real-estate deals some stars you hear about—I was always a dollar short or a day late."

Art said Bob had always wanted a lot of time to hunt and fish, but being out of work was becoming both a serious financial and emotional problem.

"He kept busy," Art recalled, "going on errands with me—the two of us looking like a couple of bums. Once we stopped in a diner for some coffee and a man walked up to Bob and asked him if he had ever been on the movie or television screen.

"Without looking up, Taylor took some change out of his pocket, threw it on the counter and said, 'MORE OFF THAN ON!', got up and walked out!"

When Taylor got a call that his agents had made an arrangement for him to do a picture for Universal produced and directed by William Castle, he was startled.

He asked why he hadn't been consulted and the answer was that the offer was too good for Bob to turn down, and that they had committed him to do *The Night Walker* with none other than Barbara Stanwyck.

"I'll have to give this one somè thought," he said. "Send over the script."

The script wasn't bad, because a William Castle production was always good, but it was really the money that made Taylor eager to do the picture. His friends said if he had been consulted before arrangements had been completed, he would have turned it down, but they got him in too deep, and he would embarrass too many people if he backed out.

When reporters asked him how he felt about co-starring with his ex-wife, Taylor replied, "Who could pass up the opportunity of working with such a wonderful, talented woman!"

He was dubious but said while working with Barbara it didn't seem as if they had ever been married. Ursula was on the set often and hoped to be friends with Barbara.

"Why don't we have her over for dinner one night, Bob?"

Without any further explanation he said, "You don't know her like I do."

He knew that Barbara had been through a great deal herself. She was very much alone now that many of her closest friends had died and her son, Dion, had been arrested for theft and several other crimes. He had gotten himself into trouble on a number of occasions until Barbara refused to talk to him again. She publicly disowned Dion Fay, who said in an interview, "I just worshiped Bob Taylor and he became a real father to me. I shall never forget him."

However Taylor kept his distance and had no intention of giving in to Ursula's suggestions that they meet Barbara socially. *The Night Walker* was completed without incident. Many photos, not for release to the public, showed them laughing together and apparently enjoying each other quite a bit on the set.

The reviews praised Stanwyck and Taylor. "William Castle has two old pros enriching his new eerie suspense

237

thriller, *The Night Walker*. Barbara Stanwyck and Robert Taylor, coming out of semi-retirement from films, are the invaluable assets in the Universal release."

Taylor commented he didn't know he was in semi-retirement.

Urusla always urged Bob to take up writing as a career. He loved to write letters and most of his friends have them to this day—not because they were from Robert Taylor but because of his humor and talent with words. But to him, writing a dozen letters a day was fun.

Ursula told him he should write a script. "The movies will kill you one day." But Bob didn't think he was talented enough as a writer and would stick to acting. "Besides," he said, "how can it kill me if I'm NOT working?"

During this inactive time for Bob it was Ursula who had the strength, and she used it wisely. Sitting around the house made Taylor nervous and he began to pick on Ursula about little things, but she ignored him. When he'd fall asleep, which could be any time or any place, she'd work off her frustrations by scrubbing floors, sometimes during the night when she couldn't sleep.

Once when they went out for dinner with a group of seventeen people in St. Louis there was no table service. Everyone sat waiting for his food for almost an hour. Bob was turning red and Ursula knew he was getting ready to take action. Rather than cause a scene which would have been embarrassing, she went into the kitchen, put the food on the plates and served everyone.

She and Bob hated restaurants, but when they did plan an evening out, he would ask Ursula to do "the dirty work" of making reservations. It was difficult for him to do. "I don't suppose you have a table for two for dinner tonight at nine?" he'd say.

Ursula said she asked him why he didn't give his name because surely the management would have set up a special table for him even if they *were* filled, but he didn't want that. "In fact, Bob just *couldn't* do it. At first I could not understand what frightened him about making a simple dinner reservation. Then I realized he didn't want to give his name because it might put someone out. I laughed, but Bob didn't think it was amusing at all. I

238

guess you might say our strengths and weaknesses balanced each other."

When they entertained at home, they limited their guests to no more than four or five. It would be a casual evening, with everyone sitting on the floor with a few drinks and a lot of good food. Once a year they felt obligated to have a big party, but they disliked it and felt uncomfortable. It just wasn't their way of life and they hated to feel they HAD to.

Their friends were business associates, Taylor's hunting buddies and only a few show business people, who included Dale Robertson, Ronald Reagan and Bob Stack, who was in awe of Taylor, Dick Powell, Rhonda Fleming and her producer husband, Hall Bartlett.

When *The Night Walker* was released in January, 1965, Taylor was interviewed briefly. He had little to say about himself except that he was never terribly ambitious and simply wanted to do a good job at whatever he did. He was just a guy from Nebraska who was once a punk kid from the Midwest who had an awful lot of good things dumped in his lap. His greatest accomplishment, he said, was Ursula.

After Taylor had been out of work for awhile, Tom Purvis noted discontent in Taylor's letters and tapes. He suggested that Bob spend a few days with him in Florida, but he made it sound as if he were needed. "My daughter, Nancy, has her own radio show in Orlando and she sure could use you right about now."

Taylor never turned down a personal favor. In the early fifties, when he was very busy making movies, Tom wrote that he was opening a new extension to his Ford Agency in Mattoon, Illinois, and was going to have a little celebration. Taylor said he had a few days off and would fly out.

"He didn't have time off," Tom said. "He MADE time! Bob arrived on the day of the opening and told me it was okay to publicize the fact that he was there. If he were promoting a picture and asked to make a public appearance he would turn it down. He showed up in Mattoon and signed autographs all afternoon and served coffee. The police had to block off the street and my little

239

opening turned out to be one of the biggest days the town ever had!"

Taylor flew to Orlando and was interviewed by Nancy Purvis on her radio show. He said he'd stay as long as she wanted him to . . . coincidentally, he mentioned that he might be doing a movie in Florida, something called *Johnny Tiger,* the story of a dedicated teacher of underprivileged Indian children in the Seminole section of Florida.

Taylor wanted to do this picture very much. It was one he thought would change his image at middle age because he was portraying a widower father who wore glasses and smoked a pipe. Chad Everett played the Indian, Johnny Tiger, and Geraldine Brooks came out of semi-retirement for the role of the white doctor of the Seminoles.

When the picture was completed, the Indians awarded Taylor with a fancy jug labeled MOOSE JUICE—complete with cups. They all had a round and though Bob kept a straight face, his insides were on fire. On his way home from Southwest Florida he stopped off to see Tom: "Here, Ol' Bud! Whatever is left in the jug will knock your head off!"

He was very excited about *Johnny Tiger*. This was a new beginning as far as he was concerned, and this was what he had been waiting for for such a long time. He put his heart and soul into the movie and would have paid for the entire production to get it on the screen.

Taylor was elated over Chad Everett's performance and proud that Geraldine Brooks had supported him. Unfortunately, Universal wasn't. They released *Johnny Tiger* on a double bill with *Munsters Go Home,* and there was little backing and publicity.

Taylor, however, attended the world première in Florida which was his first appearance at an opening in many years. He wanted Ursula to join him, but she said she had nothing to wear. This was in no way an exaggeration because she lived in jeans and multicolored slacks all the time. She owned one good outfit that she wore to weddings and christenings and a red dress that she put on *every* Christmas.

She told Bob it would be foolish to go out and spend

a lot of money for a dress to wear only once, but he told her it was very important to him and he wanted her to go shopping for a good evening gown *and* not to worry about the money.

Taylor said she went out and was gone all day, in the end coming back with nothing. She said she saw only one dress that she liked and it cost $400, an exorbitant amount! Bob said, "I told her not to be so chintzy and to go back and buy it. Next day she brought 'something' home but where she found it, I don't know, probably at the Salvation Army. She didn't mention the price, but it sure didn't fit so she got out her sewing kit, went to work and when she got through it looked fine on her. Now she'll have a long dress for the next twenty years!"

At the première of *Johnny Tiger* he said, "I *felt* that part—it was me. This nonsense about 'living the part' being taught today bores me! If you have to be out of breath, *getting* out of breath is crazy. You can be breathless without running around the studio several times. I've worked with 'method boys' and I've had to keep on guard from laughing in their faces!"

He went on to say he thought he had done a damn good job as the white schoolteacher in Seminole country and the critics agreed. "Taylor may be slightly obtuse as an educator but he handles his role naturally and with ease. It is a worthy piece of acting." Unfortunately, *Johnny Tiger* did not accomplish what Taylor had hoped. He was very, very disappointed. "I guess I wanted the impossible—to portray a mature man in his fifties who wears glasses when he reads and puffs on a pipe."

The general consensus was that Universal did not give *Johnny Tiger* enough publicity, and by putting it in neighborhood theatres with *Munsters Go Home,* lowered its prestige. The public liked Taylor's new image and the press backed them up. He was asked for interviews and gave them generously. Many of the cub reporters wanted him to talk about the old days in Hollywood.

"Mr. Taylor, a lot of people who saw *Johnny Tiger* can't help but refer to it as *Johnny Eager.*"

"There's a big difference, boys, even though the last name has a TI in front of it instead of an EA. Guess my generation has me pegged, but I was pleased with both movies and a lot has happened since I slapped Lana Turner in 1942."

"A lot of write-ups are stressing the return of Robert Taylor to the movies. How do you feel about the compliments that you look as good as ever and that moviegoers want more of what they saw in *Johnny Tiger?*"

"I was awful when I started in the business—just awful! The studio put up with me, though, and I got the breaks. I learned through experience and today I consider myself an average actor."

"You're a legend, Mr. Taylor. How can you sum up your life as a movie idol?"

"Do you know," Bob confided, "when they told me I had been chosen for *Camille*—and I guess you boys heard of that one—I was surprised and damn frightened. I can remember the first day on the set I went home and told my mother, 'This is incredible! I report for work the first day, they introduced me to Garbo and expected me to make love to her immediately.' Today it is hard to believe that at one stage I signed a seventeen-year contract with Metro with no options on either side. I had signed many contracts with them, but this one was seventeen years! Can you imagine? When I came off contract I even got a pension from them. I was never suspended once and now that it's over I find it hard to believe."

"You aren't thinking of retiring?"

"Hell, no. The acting profession is a good job."

Robert Taylor was a motion picture star and wanted more than anything to be an actor. With seventy-two movies behind him, he had been panned, stewed, cooked, degraded, criticized, embarrassed, deceived and humiliated. Yet now with the press on his side, he still could not forget that it was they who almost destroyed not only his career, but him as well. It was the press who had labeled him "Pretty Boy" and put him on the front page of every newspaper to prove that he wasn't a homosexual after all because he had some hair on his chest. It was the press who said he didn't look like a doctor in *Magnificent Obsession,* that he didn't look like the type who should be bitten by mosquitoes in *My Brother's Wife,* that he should have had a reservation in Arlington

242

Cemetery rather than assume the role of an officer in *This Is My Affair,* that he looked like a kid in a new cowboy suit in *Billy the Kid,* that his widow's peak gave him away as the gangster in *Johnny Eager,* that he got his wings during the war because he was a movie star, that he stunk in *Quo Vadis.* When he was given a good review, it was *despite* the fact he was beautiful, *despite* the fact he didn't look the part, or *despite* the fact the public liked him. *The New York Times* loved to hammer at him with statements like, "Though Robert Taylor is not one of our favorites, we have to give him credit, etc. . . ."

One female reporter reminisced by saying she thought that the male members of the press had always had a private war going on with Taylor, and though they apologized on several occasions, they would not make up for ripping him to shreds when he was doing his best. She added that the top columnists, Hedda Hopper, Louella Parsons, Earl Wilson, Hy Gardner and Joe Hyams, were always on Taylor's side because they took the time to sit down with him and find out how truly modest he was. They could make or break any Hollywood star, but they chose to defend the "punk kid from Nebraska."

The fact that *Johnny Tiger* did not launch Taylor into a new type of leading man upset him so that he said, "From now on, I'm a strictly for *money actor.* I couldn't care less without that green stuff!"

He made up his mind that the movie industry wasn't going to kill him like it did the others.

Cooper died of a broken heart; Gable collapsed because he tried too hard in *The Misfits*; Dick Powell gave his voice to cancer; and Tracy's health was failing. Who was left?

"Nobody . . . nobody . . . God damn!

"The Golden Age" by Robert Taylor was an article originally written for *Variety* and later published in *Film Fan Monthly.*

He expressed himself directly in this article and perhaps he was speaking for those few who were left— Crawford, Turner, Garson, Stewart:

243

No matter how old one is, the Golden Age of Hollywood was long ago. I hope I'm not talking tired because I refer to change. Many of the major people are still working today but they have all been transformed.

If today is still the 20th Century, the Hollywood of the 1930's and early 1940's was 200 years ago. In a sense it was baroque. There was a style of living and making motion pictures which no longer exists. It has been coldly modernized into something very factual, very efficient—and I'm afraid, not very much fun.

The creative and artistic management and the fabulous "showmen" still exist—there are a few—but they're largely working for themselves on a one-picture-every-two-years basis. Their great talent isn't directed toward a "program" of pictures—toward the management and betterment of a studio.

For some of us who were fortunate enough to have been a part of the Golden Age, however, the memory lingers on.

In my own case, I was part of the MGM "stable." We called Metro the campus—and even the seasons were semesters. Camaraderie was shared at work and at play, up and down the line, and the aspect of jealousy was virtually nonexistent—at least among the male stars.

There was nothing predictable, except perhaps sunrises and L. B. Mayer—and not necessarily in that order.

L. B. was the most important person in my career, as he was in hundreds of others. He was not a "desk jockey." He was constantly on the move around the lot—he knew every department—he knew the heads of every department—and he knew everyone's problems.

Gable was legend, he set the style and the pace. His cars, especially, drove the lesser lights, like myself, mad with envy. I remember two very distinctly—one a green Deusenberg convertible and the other a Darrin Packard Twelve which Carole Lombard had had built for him.

We associated with each other in those days for fun—not just publicity. The Trocadero was the clubhouse—and on Sunday nights, some outstanding wit was master of ceremonies, introducing for the first time on the West Coast such people as Martha Raye or Joe E. Lewis. Owner Billy Wilkerson would wander around accepting compliments on the wonderful food, wonderful entertainment

244

and wonderful service. And it was just that—wonderful!

People pop up in my memory. Many of them are gone. Wallace Beery was special. Lionel Barrymore had forgotten more about acting than most of us would ever know. Yet he was always—and strangely—shy—about voicing his opinions. However, if you asked him he could sketch a lesson on portrayal that was complete and perfect in a matter of seconds.

I recall visiting his stateroom on the Queen Mary after we finished *A Yank at Oxford*. I found him asleep in his chair—the ashes of his cigarette all over his chest, the butt extinguished by his own lips. He was a very tired man—and unwell—but none of us ever thought that such a marvelous, warm moment would ever leave us.

And good old Gary Cooper—"Coop" to just about everyone, whether they knew him or not. In my way of thinking, Coop was the handsomest man—certainly one of the two or three best actors—ever to honor the ranks of the motion picture business. And one of the most beautiful and talented ladies ever to grace a motion picture screen—Vivien Leigh.

The closeness and the pace never did create the terrible dose of imitation current today. Perhaps television is at fault—perhaps not, I honestly don't know. But at least in that long ago decade we had both poles.

I recall making *Magnificent Obsession* with Irene Dunne. John Stahl was directing. He approached the responsibility of a director in very much the same manner as I assume an atomic physicist approaches the handling of a bomb—with infinite care and painstaking slowness. It was not uncommon for us to do 30, 40, 50 takes on a relatively simple scene. At the time I was doing retakes on one of the *Broadway Melodies* and Woody Van Dyke was directing. Woody cut as he shot. He used his camera as though it were a six-shooter and he was the fastest gun in Hollywood. Actors rarely got more than one take on any scene, then the camera was moved rapidly to another set-up. It was, of course, going from the sublime to the ridiculous, but it seemed normal. It was the age.

It ended in the late 1940's with the unexplained but seemingly premediated murder of glamour. Television, taxes, actors pricing themselves to the skies—are all part-causes, but not the definite ones. I don't know really.

I can't explain the demise. Perhaps if someone could correctly explain the phenomenon of rock 'n' roll, Beatle haircuts and the beatnik wardrobe, we will start to understand. In any case, it was 200 years ago. [12]

12. Robert Taylor, "The Golden Age," *Variety*.

Chapter XIV

Taylor went to the nursing home to visit Ruth. The doctors said she was hanging on pretty nicely for an eighty-year-old woman, but that she would remain a vegetable until she died. He walked into her room which was white, airy and comfortable.

She seemed aware of his presence, but the nurse said Ruth would appear normal and look at someone as if to say something, but her words had no relation to the situation or person involved.

He asked if his mother knew who he was and was told it was very, very doubtful, but was asked to stay with her for as long as he wished.

He talked quietly to her (the conversation is unknown), but one can only assume Taylor spoke of Nebraska. She looked at him closely almost like a child would react to the story of Cinderella.

But she said nothing.

When he got up to leave he paused a few minutes to talk to the doctor, and when he had closed the door behind him, Ruth turned to the nurse and said, "Wasn't he a nice man?"

Driving home, Taylor remembered a conversation he had had with some old friends in Beatrice when he and his mother attended a funeral there. Ruth spoke about her weak heart and said she never did feel well and knew she would die soon. Taylor laughed; "Mother, you'll probably outlive us all!"

She did . . .

Savage Pampas, a Western set in Argentina and filmed in Spain, was rather like *Westward the Women,* but hardly comparable in the quality of the script or the acting. Again, the tough and unshaven Taylor led a group of women across the dangerous pampas. He was killed at the end and the only impressive part of the movie was his horse "riding off into the sunset."

While he was in Spain he wrote to his tailor, Nudie, about some new clothes:

Dear Nudie et al—
Urgent Smoke Signal from Gen. Franco's little hunting preserve! It looks likely that I'll be making a "pilot" film in Argentina for the Winchester-Western folks. We hope to shoot boar, puma, stag and maybe do some fishing. It ain't all wrapped up real neat yet so this info is on the confidential side until I get home, OK?
Need two pair of frontier pants made out of cotton twill with rivets but don't finish off the bottoms until I have a fitting. Also two shirts of the same material, but cut them a shade fuller, short sleeved and with the "action back."
And since these suits would be used pretty much on safari, I would also suggest that you send the material out to be washed and pre-shrunk *before* they are made. Where I might be goin' it is inevitable that they will be washed rather than dry cleaned.
This whole caper started out as a real SNAFU but it's slowly beginning to take shape. At least I'm reasonably sure of getting all my money this time!
It appeared for awhile Ursula would not be able to find a "reliable" to leave at home with the children, so she cancelled her reservations, but I talked to her this morning and she has found someone (A German lady who's old enough to know better!) so I'm expecting her late this week. I ain't no Casanova any more—and ain't seen anything in Spain which would raise my temperature too much, but fun's fun and somebody to come home to at nite is mighty important in these twilight years.
As soon as I get home I'll be out for a fitting and since under normal circumstances I can't hit my ass with both hands with a gun, shooting without a Nudie suit would be sheer disaster. I might ruin my whole film career and never get another job in my life!

As ever,
Bob

248

Taylor liked Nudie, who is the best Western tailor in the business. He liked to kid Nudie about the fact he was "goin' to a tailor who started out making G-strings for Gypsy Rose Lee." However, this statement was a factual one.

Nudie signs his checks "Nudie," and his wife, Bobbie, signs them "Mrs. Nudie." He owns twin Pontiac Bonnevilles that are decorated with silver pistols, stirrups, spurs, rifles and steer horns. Each car cost him $21,000.

Nudie's custom-made outfits cost anywhere from $300 and up. He made a $10,000 outfit for Elvis Presley, which was a 24-carat gold lamé tuxedo with matching gold shoes and tie.

Not only did Taylor like Nudie personally, but he thought his workmanship the best. He wrote to Nudie from wherever he was just to say "Hello." "Besides," Taylor said, "he's got two million bucks in the bank and has the best coffee in town. Maybe I should have gotten interested in G-strings instead of scripts!"

Taylor's relationship with Nudie was typical of his "personal touch" and down-to-earth manner he had with people he liked.

In January, 1966, Ronald Reagan announced his candidacy for Governor of California. He had been host of the television series *Death Valley Days*, and his contract ran through September, 1966. The opposing political party said his being exposed on television was unfair and they wanted equal time in California. To avoid conflict, several popular stars—John Wayne, Leon Ames, Walter Brennan, Clint Walker, Rory Calhoun and Robert Taylor—volunteered to fill in for Reagan until the end of his contract.

Reagan and Taylor had been good friends for a long time and after he became Governor of California Reagan's first stop whenever he was in Los Angeles was the

Ursulor Rancho. He put on sneakers and a pair of old pants, sat on the floor with Bob talking about anything but politics, and he enjoyed Bob's steaks grilled on the outdoor barbeque.

Taylor greeted his friends with warmth, but there were no phony kisses or embraces. He was approached only if he approached. Though many actors who worked with him said Taylor was not a personality one would tap on the shoulder, the few who knew him well all agreed that he was not really an untouchable. He gave this appearance only because he was reaching out to be loved and admired for himself, not for his fame. There was undoubtedly an air of "don't come near" about Taylor, but only because he was afraid he wouldn't know how to handle it. The majority of people stayed away and everyone misunderstood.

On the other hand, Ursula reached him deeply as did Tom Purvis and Ronnie Reagan, whom Bob made executor of his estate should anything happen to him.

In September, 1966, Robert Taylor signed as host, narrator and occasional star of *Death Valley Days*. Working on television this time gave him more satisfaction than it did when he starred in *The Detectives*. For one thing, he loved the atmosphere of the West and preferred Westerns in general. He said he liked doing television this time around. "One goes in and gets the job done with no time wasted as in the movie business."

It also kept him close to home because the films were shot on location in Arizona, Utah, New Mexico and Northern California. One day, as host, he filmed introductions and closings for thirteen shows, and left for home.

He wrote to Tom Purvis that things were looking up. *Death Valley Days* was a successful show and did not take up much of his time. He hoped to make movies— good or bad—but at least he had a steady income now and could be near Ursula and the kids.

He told the producer of the show, Bob Stapler, "When you come across a script that looks good for me, let me know." The first one picked for his approval called for a thirty-two-year-old man, but the story was perfect for

Taylor. Bob took one look at the first page, saw the age, and immediately turned it down.

"In fact," Stapler said, "Bob kept refusing scripts but not telling me why. He was an easy guy to work for and I knew he was anxious to star in several episodes—it was written in his contract—but he was sending the best ones back to me without comment. One day I approached him about it. Taylor said he was not going to play the part of a young man and that was that.

"I got the message but outsmarted him. I told my secretary when I found a good story for Taylor to simply change the age of the leading man to forty-five and from that time on he accepted every one!"

Taylor wore no make-up, loved the lines in his face and did his best to look unattractive at age fifty-four. However, he didn't like the squint lines around his eyes that he had gotten from working outdoors in the sun or indoors with hot brilliant lights shining directly in his eyes. He consulted a doctor and was told he didn't need an operation to remove these for another ten years, but Taylor said, "Let's do it now. I'm not too concerned about sagging or wrinkles, but these damn squint lines could keep me out of work."

He had them removed and didn't joke about it to the two or three people who were aware of the operation. Tom wrote, "You think you've got problems! I swore I'd never get bald or have a gut and now I've got both!" Taylor answered, "Balding and a pot belly isn't so bad. That's from lack of sex, start massaging somethin', old Bud, and I don't mean your head!"

Purvis has a picture of the back of Taylor's head with a lump behind his ear. "After Bob was divorced sometimes he'd go away on location and probably wouldn't see a decent-looking girl for weeks. I told him if he didn't get himself *a little* he might develop a lump on the back of his head. Few weeks later I received the photo and knew just what he meant!"

Appearing on weekly television brought Taylor's face before the younger generation who categorized him as a well-built, rather handsome middle-aged actor "who must have been something once." Their mothers and grandmothers said they only wished he would appear in something other than Westerns. "Why, in our day there *was* no one else!" The teen-agers liked him just as he was and couldn't picture him making love to Joan Crawford or Lana Turner. "He's just not the type, Mom!"

Letters poured in to the *Death Valley Days* offices, and Taylor said it was like being welcomed back again. If he had said a million times he was a lucky guy, he surely thought he was one now.

In 1966 he did *Return of the Gunfighter,* a TV movie, with his friend Chad Everett. He used his own saddle and guns, as was his common practice. If possible, he had his own horse transported to location also. He did most of his own stunts and asked for a stand-in for the sole purpose of providing a job for some struggling actor or stunt man.

During the filming of *Return of the Gunfighter* he retired to his bungalow every night and was not seen after dark. The temperature in Tucson was over 110 degrees and he hated it, despite the fact that most of his work had taken him to hot climates in San Fernando Valley, Spain, Africa, Arizona and Egypt. However, it was beginning to affect him now and although the whole cast in *Return of the Gunfighter* thought he had a woman stashed away, he was actually exhausted.

He usually brought his own lunch to work or stood in line with the other working men. He especially liked Chad Everett and said he hoped the kid would get the right breaks. The two became unusually close friends and Chad was one person Taylor welcomed to his home.

When Everett became an established actor on *Medical Center,* he said he did not deny the fact that he was trying to emulate Robert Taylor. "I've never seen such a professional!"

Taylor, however, did not look well. He was overweight and puffy. The publicity director for the film thought it best that Bob did not meet the press face-to-face in Tucson, knowing that any untouched photos would show Taylor as he was—too heavy and bloated. But when he approached Taylor about cancelling the press conference, Bob knew why instinctively.

"Why flaunt yourself, Bob? We'll postpone it until you've had a chance to take off a few pounds ..."

"Hell, no!" Taylor insisted. "I don't care—couldn't care less!"

At the completion of *Return of the Gunfighter* there were the usual two days of retakes involving an extra fee for Taylor. Unpredictable, as usual, about money, he refused the $2,000.

"This feature film for TV was 'out of the old MGM cat bin,'" one critic wrote, "but had a little something extra—that would be the old pro, Robert Taylor, who no doubt could have played the aging gunfighter blindfolded."

Taylor was not feeling well and rode his horse on the ranch with great effort. A year or so ago he could ride all day filming a movie, come home and saddle up for a few more hours.

He sold his plane and this put an end to his flying. He said, "Old Betsy is air weary and so am I." Ursula insisted he give up the plane for his family. Terry became ill in high altitudes and in low altitudes, so it wasn't fun for him anymore.

Taylor was known to fall asleep on moving vehicles— cars, boats, airplanes, etc.—almost before the motors started, but he came to the conclusion that was part of his nature, period. Sleeping was his way of hiding or escaping participation in small talk.

However these days he was *truly* tired, which made him cranky. He began to dig Ursula in front of friends almost as if to say, "I don't love her as much as everyone may think!"

She ignored it, but when she left the room he'd smile and rave about her, but always added, "Don't tell her what I said!" Art, who was very close to the situation, pretended not to notice Taylor's grouchy attitude. He knew his boss well enough by now to expect periods of gloom and discontentment, and didn't think Taylor's lack of energy was anything more than what every man goes through at fifty-five. And despite the fact that he took it easy more often than usual, Taylor looked good and was losing the excess weight which he attributed to drinking too much fluids in Tucson when he was working in the extreme heat.

Hall Bartlett (American International Pictures) signed

Taylor for *The Glass Sphinx* in Egypt, but Bob said he was sure this picture would be the lousiest. The crew was Italian and the cast consisted of one Swede (Anita Ekberg), several Spaniards, one Yankee and a bunch of Egyptians. "How the hell we ever get through dialogue scenes is a real mystery! But the big problem is purely a technical one. Anita Ekberg has an enormous pair of 'lungs'—and to find a camera lens which can hold HER LUNGS and MY ASS in the same scene is a difficult thing to solve!"

He returned to California and continued his work on *Death Valley Days*. While on location in Utah he ran into Barbara, but only for a brief minute, and neither said more than "Hello." They both seemed surprised to see each other and the expression on Bob's face was tense. That night he sat down with the boys and had a few drinks. Everyone carefully avoided any mention of Barbara, and then suddenly he said, "Do you realize I'm *still* paying her 15 percent of my salary? She doesn't need the God damn money, but I sure as hell do!"

Nothing more was said, but those who were at the table were shocked. They had assumed that she had waived alimony long ago since her television series, *The Big Valley,* was a popular one, and she had invested very well. In fact, she could have retired on her income from her business ventures alone. Socially she had not been linked with any man since her divorce from Taylor, but her friends said she was always attracted to young men who resembled Bob.

In 1967, after a brief appearance in *Where Angels Go . . . Trouble Follows,* Taylor flew to Spain to star in *The Day the Hot Line Got Hot* (American International Pictures—Commonwealth United Entertainment) with Charles Boyer. This spy-comedy was moderately successful and made money, but perhaps it is seen by more people on television today than viewed it on the movie screen.

Taylor's biggest thrill on his trip to Spain was sitting in the cockpit of the jet from London to Madrid. The Spanish crew offered to let him take over the controls for awhile, but he said he thought that was carrying the "good neighbor" policy a bit too far! He was like a little boy, studying the instrument panel, asking questions and taking notes. He told Tom later that he'd like to buy a small jet if they could raise the cash together, but "with my fat ass and your big gut, we'd never fit in the cockpit!"

Ursula joined him in Spain for ten days. Bob had been suffering through Spanish coffee saying it was difficult to breathe after the first gulp and it took him awhile to get his eyes uncrossed, but Ursula brought him a good supply of instant coffee which he always took with him to Europe.

He jotted a letter to Nudie about the food. "At lunch today I ran across some new 'leather' they have here in Spain. It's kinda brown on the outside—and pink in the middle—and I think they call it 'steak.' In any case it would, I'm sure, outlast anything you've ever used in boots. I'm not at all sure that it would take the 'dye' for some of those 'fag' colors you use in your boots, Nudie—but I'll guarantee you on the basis of the slab I worked my way through at lunch it would outlast anything you've ever tried for *soles*. GooooooooooooDam!!!!!!!"

He also wrote to Purvis, but this letter was far from amusing. He confided that he had had an x-ray of his chest and the doctors said his "boyhood" spot on one lung had grown bigger. Taylor said he wasn't surprised because *somehow* he knew he had lung cancer and wouldn't live too long. It was a frustrating letter because that was all Bob said, and when he arrived home he did not say anything further to Tom except that he had made some simple requests in his will. The preacher should not take more than five minutes and there was to be no sacred music at his funeral because it was too depressing . . . sentimental music was beautiful. His last request was that he be cremated.

Devil Make Care was his last movie . . .

With both children in school and his cabin in Wyoming sold, Taylor wanted to find some outdoor place not too far from Los Angeles where the family could go even on short school vacations. They had a family conclave: they all liked to swim and preferred still-water fishing.

255

Terry had two ambitions—to own a boat and to live in a trailer, so Bob went looking.

He bought a mobile home at the Lake Mohave Resort where he enjoyed fishing for bass and trout in the man-made lake: sixty-seven miles of Colorado water backed up between Hoover and Davis Dams. He bought two boats, a thirteen-foot Boston Whaler for Terry and a twenty-one foot Thompson inboard-outboard for himself.

His neighbors there were doctors, lawyers and a few industrialists, and none in show business. The resort was the kind of place where the children could run loose without any worry and Ursula had her warm climate and sunshine. As for Taylor, he knew the pilot's eye view of the Arizona desert and he didn't knock it, but he liked it better from where he sat fishing.

In February, 1968, he and Ursula went around the world on behalf of the Winchester people. As Honorary Director of the Winchester Claybird Tournament, Taylor accompanied the winning team to Hawaii, Australia, Thailand, Italy, Germany and England.

Winchester reported that they could not have found a better man for the job: "All his life Mr. Taylor has been deeply involved in outdoor sports—particularly shooting. He is a fine actor, an excellent shot and a gentleman. We feel his association with this Claybird Tournament will greatly add to the lustre of the shooting sports."

Taylor looked exceptionally well, tanned and cheerful. He said he felt great, but again showed signs of puffiness and fatigue.

He told the press he was delighted with the week he had spent in the Bahamas the previous October during the claybird finals and especially enjoyed the "round of skeet" with His Serene Highness Prince Ranier III of Monaco.

He was relaxed but gave Ursula credit for that because she was as organized as he was and having her with him put Bob at ease. He was interviewed but he spoke mainly about Winchester rifles and the Cowboy Hall of Fame, mentioning that Joel McCrea was the only living trustee, which he felt was quite an honor.

At the time, *Quo Vadis* (1951), in which Taylor starred with Deborah Kerr, was the most expensive movie ever made

As Colonel Tibbetts, the man who triggered the first atom bomb, Taylor starred with Eleanor Parker in *Above and Beyond* (1952)

A tumultuous reception greeted Taylor on his arrival in Great Britain

An official portrait taken in 1956 of Robert Taylor
and his bride of two years, Ursula Thiess

The mature Taylor

Taylor enjoyed skeet (clay pigeon) shooting

Terry, Robert, Ursula and Tessa Taylor, 1967
BRUCE BAILEY

One of Taylor's favourite photos, without the moustache he never liked, taken two years before his death

Taylor's image was a less glamorous one in the tv series 'Death Valley Days' (1967)

Ursula is comforted by her daughter Manuela after Robert Taylor's funeral (June 11, 1969)
Close friends Nancy and (then) Governor Ronald Reagan (he delivered the eulogy) follow

Was there any chance that he would be the second? Taylor shrugged it off. (In 1970 he was given the award of *Cowboy of the Century* posthumously, and was the only nonliving trustee of the Museum in the National Cowboy Hall of Fame.)

Taylor said he had no plans to make any movies and was satisfied with his television series, *Death Valley Days,* and with having his picture on the back of the Borax boxes! He answered questions about his glamorous leading ladies of the past and joked about doing a movie with Debbie Reynolds. "She was the cutest piece of femininity when I first saw her wiggling thru the MGM commissary. I think she was only fifteen years old, but she was wearing short, short shorts and she reallllly filled them out—in fact, she filled out EVERYTHING she was wearing purty good! I must admit I took a good look and got a stiff neck trying to follow her when she walked past me. Yeah, she was something, alright!"

Ursula stood tall, statuesque and beautiful—soft-spoken and swan-like in her movements. Bob said she wasn't jealous when he spoke about the gorgeous women he had made love to on the screen. He got a plug in about Tessa. "What a beautiful child she is! Both kids are blonde, would you believe that? Nobody would know they were mine!"

The Taylors arrived back at Ursulor Rancho with Bob complaining that the trip had been wonderful, but tiring. However, he started work immediately on *Death Valley Days.* Bob Stapler, the producer, noticed Taylor was not himself though he never let it affect his work. He had a slight persistent cough and on one trip back to Los Angeles from location, Stapler found an empty box of tissues under Bob's seat on the plane. "It was full when he started home and it was a short hop. . . ."

Ursula commented that no one was THAT tired ALL the time. He went to bed around 8:00 every night complaining about the heat or saying, "I HAVE to get up at dawn, don't I?" Trouble was, Ursula commented, Bob always was an early riser, but now he was making a point of it.

He began to drink more than his usual few drinks before dinner and added several during the evening.

257

Ursula said nothing, but when she caught him pouring one too many, he said, "It eases the pain of life."

In September, 1968, Taylor finished his work on *Death Valley Days* for the television season in Kanab, Utah. Waving good-bye to everyone, he said, "See ya down the hill!"

He was scheduled to do a "spaghetti Western" in Italy, but at the last minute it was cancelled. Ursula had been begging him for a year to have a complete physical check-up, but he insisted a good long vacation would fix him up just fine. However, he needed the money and was going to hunt around for another movie until resuming *Death Valley Days*. He reminded Ursula that he wasn't going to go through any more anxious days waiting for doctors to make up their minds whether he had a hernia or cancer!

Her pleading finally made him change his mind and the examination showed a mass on the right lung. Since he had had a spot there for years, the one that they had found in 1962, the doctors suspected Rocky Mountain Spotted Fever and suggested an operation. Taylor knew better because only two years previously he had confided in Purvis that his x-rays clearly showed there was a growth that was getting bigger.

Taylor said he'd think about the operation. Chatting with Art at the stables one day he asked, "What would you do? Would you let them cut YOU up?"

"No!"

Bob made up his mind to take his chances without surgery. Ursula disagreed and reminded him that he should think of his family, not only of himself.

In September, he was a pallbearer at Dennis O'Keefe's funeral. Those at the services noticed that Taylor was ashen and did not attend the gathering afterwards "for a drink." O'Keefe had died of lung cancer and it was written all over Bob's face that he knew he, too, was facing the same thing.

Ursula did not stop pleading with Bob about his having the operation, but he repeatedly said that his chances were better without going under the knife. If he did have cancer, there would be little time left once the surgeons got through with him. The discussions continued, and it was only for the sake of Ursula and the children that he reluctantly agreed. On October 8, 1968, a portion of his right lung was removed. It was announced to the public that he had Rocky Mountain Spotted Fever, and the doctors assured Bob that was all it was.

He was discharged, but Ursula took him home knowing that he had cancer.

In November he was sent back to the hospital for cobalt treatments and although the word *cancer* was not mentioned, Taylor knew he was its victim. His last tape to Tom Purvis on the day before Thanksgiving indicated his feelings. He made the recording with a tube from his throat to his lung:

Hello, Curly, Old Buddy. I'm a—I know way behind in this tape department, but in any case I appreciated yours and enjoyed 'em. Guess half a dozen times I've sat down at this darn machine thinkin' that I'd knock one out but always felt either too pooped or felt lousy—or almost as now, nothin' to talk about except my miseries and that wears pretty thin—even when you talk to yourself about it—wears pretty thin . . .

Anyway I'm . . . I'm kinda pooped tonight but I'll give you a rundown on what's been goin' on and what we HOPE for in the future. As you know, this damn fever just wouldn't let up and they didn't know what was causin' it and they figured the only way they had of findin' out was to go back in that damn lung—had to be there some place. So they chased me back to the hospital . . . a . . . about ten days ago and sent me down to the x-ray department and put me on some kind of rotating-gyro that kinda makes motion picture x-rays and they stuck needles into my gullet—God damn nearly made a new hole in the roof when they started that 'cause this was all without any anesthesia—a—then they pumped stuff into the lungs through my throat and through these needles—ah—tryin' to find out where there might be an abcess or something in that damn lung which would be sealed off and causin' the temperature. Well, sure as hell they found her—a pretty good-sized one . . . It was sealed off to the extent that no antibiotic coulda gotten to it.

They coulda pumped me full of that stuff for ten years and it wouldn'ta done any good.

Lost so much weight I went out to ol' pal, Nudie, in the Valley and had a coupla lounge suits made. Those God damn pants, Curly, I tell ya—when I get back on my feet I'm just gonna have to take these pants off, let 'em out a little bit and give 'em to Terry. God damn things wouldn't go around one leg before I got puny 'cause I'm holdin' on to all my old stuff.

I'm as breathless as a bride and I'm so God damn weak I can hardly get my pants on and I'm not kiddin'. Everytime I breathe this damn hose talks back to me! Guess I'm down to about 150 pounds . . . I just—Hell, when I get down, I'm just lucky if I get back up again.

Ursula's been—God Damn—this gal has been takin' care of the ol' man and the whole damn family, too. But if I ever get well, why *we'll* have a vacation, by God!

Ol' clothes don't fit, but I'm hanging on to all my old stuff 'cause when I get through payin' for these doctors, I ain't gonna have money for any new clothes. In fact I don't know where the money's comin' from now. God damn hospital room costs mè $100 a day— had round the clock nurses cause I *had* to have em. Ursula couldn't stay here—they wouldn't let her and I just couldn't even do nothin' so that's costin' me about $150 a day and that's gettin' a little old.

Soooo, I'm glad to be home and at least savin' that money. I ain't got a bita appetite—force myself to eat. Ursula makes up a batch of milk shakes with lots of eggs and milk and malt and I siphon off a small one of those every morning and in the afternoon, but I'm not eatin' cause I'm not hungry—but that will all change—generally speakin'—take a little time . . .

Yesterday before they sent me home they shot me down to radiology and gave me a dose of cobalt and I'll be takin' it now everyday for 14 more go rounds—then we'll see what happens. It should—if we're lucky—it should do the trick for at least a few weeks—few months—something like that. Naturally you have to check on it all the time—get a booster now and then, I guess . . . I don't know. But if you get 'er whipped once, usually it's for good. Sometimes they never get 'em . . . I don't know.

260

Well, Curly, I'm damn tuckered here. Haven't been doin' nothing all day. Came home, listened to the radio and took a little nap and that's about all. By God I just ain't got any strength at all. Anyhow, that's all the news I've got right now, ol' Bud. Wish there were more. Wish I could lie about some big fish I didn't catch but I can't even do that.

So . . . you all take care and I hope you have a great big juicy Thanksgivin' Day tomorrow. We're not doin' a damn thing. Art and his wife are comin' up from down at the barn and guess Mani will be over. No cobalt treatment tomorrow and that's a vacation, but I'll be back down there Friday morning.

So, you take care, old Bud. Glad you like your new Ford. They are nice, no kiddin'. Ford has come a long way and I think they're one of the nicest wagons on the market. I really do. I haven't driven a car in so God damn long I'll probably have to go to one of those driving schools . . . yeah, when I get back in to circulation I'll probably have to take a refresher course, but it will sure be worth it.

Incidentally if you hear some wheezing sounds as I'm talkin' here it's that damn tube talkin' back at us, but if it's doin' the job, I'm not goin' to complain. OK, may, you tell Vi . . . Damn cough! Comes once in awhile and you just can't do anything to stop 'em.

Anyway, you say hello to everyone and for God's sake, keep well. I have enough here for everybody so go about your business. I'll take care of that part of it. Have a good Thanksgivin', Old Buddy, and drop me a tape when you have time and I'll try to do better next time, OK?

Over and out . . .

Art said Taylor managed to walk around the stables when he was up to it, refusing to take pain pills though his discomfort showed clearly on his face. He did not talk about his illness and discussed only the goings-on around the ranch or cussed at Reeves about the damn tool shed. One of his biggest problems was deciding whether Terry should have a new bike, but he thought better of it until the old one fell apart.

Reporters were staked out on Mandeville Canyon

Road and Art spent most of his time making sure no one got near the Taylor property. When he drove Bob to and from the hospital it appeared as though Art were alone in the car—Taylor crouched down in the front seat.

"Fortunately no one could see the ranch from the main road," Art said, "and the gates could be locked. So Bob was able to get into the car without anyone observing him, but it was mighty tricky getting to the hospital which, fortunately, was not that far. We were always followed and it got to the point where I had to work out several plans with the doctors to get Bob in and out of the hospital without the press knowing about it."

Taylor did not want to be photographed, but at almost any hour of day or night, at least one reporter was seen hanging around the entrance to St. John's Hospital in Santa Monica. They questioned the doctors who would not reveal any information—not even that Taylor was making visits to the hospital or that he was seriously ill.

Two operations followed the major one—and back home he'd come. He refused to stay in the hospital unless it was absolutely necessary. He constantly asked permission for Ursula to take over the duties of the night nurse, but the doctors couldn't let her. Even then, he persisted, but was turned down.

On December 3 the newspapers announced the truth:

ROBERT TAYLOR CONFIRMS IT: HE HAS LUNG CANCER

Robert Taylor, one of Hollywood's most enduring stars, confirmed rumors today. He is undergoing treatment for lung cancer. He has been appearing in the television series, *Death Valley Days,* but his working schedule will be sharply curtailed now.

He said he was in no pain but that he is very weak and has lost about 30 pounds.

Some movie colony friends had feared the worst when the 57-year old actor's right lung was removed eight weeks ago. But doctors said a number of small tumors found in the removed tissue were not malignant. Taylor said his wife knew differently. He told newsmen, "I didn't say

262

anything then because it is a very private matter, isn't it? It's one John Wayne role nobody wants! It was a tremendous shock, of course. When I went into surgery I didn't know, but they found tumors in the right lung and that was it! I have to get a lot of rest and that's the hardest part for me. But, I've got to face it. I'm putting myself and all my faith in the hands of my doctors."

Tom wired Ursula: Did she need him? The reply was, "Bob's message from the hospital stay where you are. We'll come to see you in time. Love Ursula."

Taylor had been admitted to St. John's shortly before Christmas and was in serious condition. On Christmas Day, the doctor called Ursula at home to tell her Bob had terminal cancer.

There was no hope.

Ivy Mooring, Ursula's best friend, was with her when the doctor telephoned. "She put down the receiver slowly and told me the news. I wanted her to cry, but she didn't. Her eyes showed total disbelief. I wasn't going to talk about miracles because I think I knew from the beginning Bob's situation was a hopeless one, and Ursula was not a fool. She was every bit the realist, but she did not want to believe that Bob was going to die."

Ursula made up her mind she would be with Bob every minute. She blamed herself for what had happened, and their many arguments about whether he should have the operation crept back into her mind. Maybe if he had done what he truly wanted to do—take his chances without surgery—he would not have had to suffer so much and watch himself deteriorate. This was the one thing he did not want to happen. He had watched Dick Powell and Dennis O'Keefe fade away, and it tore him to pieces. O'Keefe had laughed to the end, telling Bob he'd be up and "screwing the first piece of ass" even if it was one of the chubby nurses.

Also Taylor said he didn't want the children to watch him die, but Ursula would have to tell them now about their father. She did not tell Tessa immediately, but she was open with Terry who said, "I understand." Ursula told him not to say anything to Puss Puss and that she would be with his father at all times. Uncle Art would have to take over now.

A heavy smoker since he was a kid, Taylor quit smoking before his operation. He had given it up in 1962, but went back to chain smoking. Though he told Purvis (and for some reason Tom agreed) that he did not think cigarettes had caused his illness, he made television pleas on behalf of the American Cancer Society.

In January, Taylor returned to Ursulor Rancho not knowing he had terminal cancer. He had a telephone interview with Ivor Davis and Ursula said, "My husband is giving a beautiful performance—the greatest of his lifetime."

His wife said that her husband was putting up a good front for a private audience. "Bob is not the kind of man to cry the blues."

Taylor talked matter of factly about his disease almost as if he were chatting about a cold in the head. He sounded cheerful and optimistic when he said, "I think I've got it beaten but I know it's going to be a long haul to recovery and I know it's worth any amount of patience and care to get well again. The word cancer is initially very frightening, of course, but it no longer need necessarily evoke the terror it once did. The doctors say my chances are good. One good thing about this surgery —I was getting too heavy and needed to lose weight anyway!"

Ursula concluded the telephone interview and said, "We're not a particularly religious family, but a very optimistic one. We're all in this together and that'll get us through." [13]

The one thing that bothered Taylor the most was not being able to hunt and fish, but he found it too tiring even to clean his guns.

There was laughter in the house and everyone continued their same pattern of living, pretending that conditions would improve. Ursula, Terry and Art were the only ones who knew they would not. Nancy Reagan was a constant visitor, always helping out.

John Wayne kept in touch, trying to give Bob strength.

13. Ivor Davis, *Los Angeles Times*, January 12, 1969.

"When they told me I had lung cancer it was like being belted across the gut with a baseball bat, but I licked it!"

Dale Robertson was a frequent guest, as were Chad Everett and his wife Shelby, who gave Ursula a hand.

Rhonda Fleming came over to the ranch, put on an apron and helped Ursula in the kitchen. She often prepared the meals.

Barbara Stanwyck dropped by occasionally—still collecting her alimony. Observers said she appeared to be under a terrible strain and looked as if she were heavily sedated on her visits.

And then there were hundreds of letters.

Reporters, unable to get a glimpse of Taylor, continued to telephone him for comments. They kept a stake-out on the main road and at the hospital, still trying to find out what Taylor's chances were. They pestered the doctors and nurses, who remained silent. They tried to stop Art when he was driving through the gates or Ursula or anyone who knew Taylor.

Heavy rains hit Los Angeles in February, 1969, and there was a report that Mandeville Canyon Road would be flooded. Taylor was at home and shrugged off the weather threats, but Ursula feared he might take a turn for the worse. She would be unable to get him to the hospital, and the doctors might not be able to get through to the ranch. Bob was running a fever, not too high, but this usually indicated a return visit to the hospital. She decided to take him there immediately.

Bob put up a fight, but Art took over this time! "C'mon, Bob, why do anything foolish now when things are going so well." In any event, he was ready to use a little "gentle force" if necessary and Bob got ready to return to St. John's.

Art was preparing to put him into the car when a truck drove up to the house, and he noticed a man hiding in the back.

"Don't come out yet, Bob. Stay put."

He walked over to the rear of the truck and looked at the man who was trying to pretend he wasn't there. "I don't know who you are, Mack, but you'd better get out of here, and I mean right now—or I'll tear your hide off!"

It was a reporter, and he admitted it. He had been trying to get a look at Taylor for months and this seemed like the only way. Art made a move to jump into the back of the truck when the driver yelled that they were leaving. The rain was coming down and mud was everywhere. Every minute was valuable. Art was getting nervous watching the truck speeding down the road. He got Bob into the car and started for the hospital. There was a tie-up on the canyon road—cars were spread out all over the road. Art got out of the car while Taylor crouched in the back on the floor. The reporter whom he had threatened minutes before approached Art, who stood guard at the car. "I'm losing my patience, you bastard!" The man apologized, saying his city editor wanted news about Robert Taylor, and all attempts had failed. Meanwhile he was trying to look over Art's shoulder to see if Taylor was in the car.

Reeves said, "I let that bastard go because I HAD to get Bob to the hospital before the flooding got any worse, but my temper had reached the limit, and I used control that I didn't think I had!"

Taylor remained at the hospital, checking every hour to find out if the rains had stopped. He checked out as soon as he heard "the road home" was open. His desire to be at the ranch was an obsession. He drove everyone crazy on the medical staff. He never asked for anything or complained but just demanded, "When the hell can I go home?" One of the nurses said Taylor was easygoing except for his desire to be with Ursula and the children on the "farm."

On February 25th he wrote to Purvis. There would be other letters, but as far as Bob and Tom were concerned, this was the final one.

Dear Curley,
Yeah, I know . . . I've been neglecting my ole buddy—and I'm sorry. But I just ain't felt like writin' or tapin' or nothin' of late.
My day consists of eatin' a little—sleepin' a little—watchin' some TV—and hurtin' a lot.

Thank God for pain pills these days and shots—otherwise I'd be goin' out of my skull.

The Doc's tryin' to make me think everything's O.K., but I know different. I'm losin' this one, Curley—and as lousy as I feel and as fast as I'm goin' broke, I'd just as soon it would hurry up and come to an end fast. It'd be better for Ursula and the children and everybody.

This has been the worst winter I've ever seen in California. Fortunately we've had no serious damage to any of our buildings but the place has really been torn up. Mandeville itself is a real disaster area and it's still raining. From now on, Ole Bud, I wouldn't plan on hearin' from me. If things get a lot better you can bet your ass I'll break out the recorder and shoot you a tape. If they get worse Ursula will, I'm sure, be in touch.

Meanwhile we hope all goes well with all of you—our love to everyone—take good care—and good fishin'.

Always,
Dilly

"Good fishin'," was Bob's way of saying Good Bye, and Tom knew it!

In March, Bob Stapler, producer of *Death Valley Days*, received a call from Taylor. "I'm lettin' you out of your contract. I doubt I will be able to work this year."

Stapler replied, "Get off it, Bob. We can postpone filming until August." Then he asked Bob if he'd like to do a day's work. This was strictly a gesture on Stapler's part. There was no work, and he knew Taylor would never make it on location again, but he went out to the ranch with some of his TV crew and they did some tapings, and in general created as many things as possible for Taylor to do, assuring him that he was needed and they expected him to return to *Death Valley Days* during the summer when he was feeling better. "We'll take it slow, of course . . . and don't worry about starring in anything until you're really in tip top shape. We will limit your work to a few introductions and closings for awhile."

Stapler left the ranch in tears, but Taylor was in a good mood and he felt much better than he had in a long time. He had actually done a few hours work and surely Stapler wouldn't have gone to all that trouble for nothing. He felt needed again, and this day was the greatest he had had during his illness. Ursula considered Stapler's act one of the finest hours during those tragic months. For several days Taylor showed signs of improvement, at least in spirit. The cobalt affected him in strange ways, too, lifting him up mentally sometimes, but Stapler's "day of work" was no illusion.

In April, Ivy Mooring noticed Bob's mail piling up and offered to have her secretary answer his letters. She said, "You know, Bob, when I was down and out after the war you offered me a job and one of my duties was to do your correspondence, but you always typed better than any professional stenographer, and I never did get the chance to earn a day's pay. The least I can do is make up for it now."

Ivy Mooring, now a Doctor of Psychiatry, came to California from England shortly after World War II. Because it was difficult getting into the United States at that time, David Niven did a favor for Ivy and her husband by giving them jobs on his household staff, granting them entry to the United States. However, Niven's wife, playing a game with the children at Tyrone Power's house, accidentally fell down a flight of stairs, and when she died, Niven's life was considerably upset and he indicated to Ivy and her husband that it might be best for them to seek employment elsewhere.

Taylor, a close friend of Niven's, suggested she work for him and Barbara as a "household organizer" (correspondence, errands, shining shoes and any other odd jobs), but it was actually a gesture on Bob's part because he really didn't need her assistance at all.

Ivy's husband became seriously ill with a cancerous brain tumor, and he was sent to a nursing home in England to live out his life as a vegetable. Whenever Taylor was assigned to do a movie there he put Ivy on the MGM payroll "To take care of my typing" so that she would be able to visit her dying husband.

Thus, the relationship began. Ivy continued going to college and worked for Bob, and often spent time caring for Ruth. She became a psychiatrist, worked on President Kennedy's staff for the mentally retarded.

When her first husband died, she remarried and settled in Los Angeles. Ursula and Ivy became very friendly: as Dr. Mooring describes their relationship, "We are just like sisters."

Ivy said Bob always did the work he had hired her to do—especially his correspondence—and she put him at ease when she said she would handle his letter-writing for him during his illness. "After all," she said, "I got paid for doing it. Don't you think it's time I did my work at long last?"

Bob dictated three form letters: one to his fans, one to his business associates, and the other to his very close friends. He signed each one personally.

April, 1969

Dear Curly—

Believe me old Buddy I'd be happy to let Ursula take care of my letter writing for me, however, I've been married to her fifteen years now and I still can't even decipher her shopping list. She writes even worse than you do and I know you'll admit that's pretty bad. Therefore, you'll just have to settle for an occasional note from me until I feel like going back to work on the tape recorder.

My third trip to the hospital was the roughest of the bunch and I sure hope that they're through carving on me for awhile. I've lost more weight and just don't feel like I could take anymore of that nonsense.

The doctors all seem optimistic, and I wish that I could be, too, however I somehow just don't trust them too much or feel that they know all there is to know about my case.

We sure have enjoyed your periodic newsy little notes and apologies for not having replied much sooner—that will get better as we go along. Ursula is fine as are the children and I am hopeful of being well enough to take them all to the River as soon as school is out.

Your idea of making a little jaunt to California sure was a good one, old Buddy, and I guess you know there just ain't anybody I'd rather see than you; however, the way I'm feeling now makes me think that you might just be

wasting your time. Maybe we can do it a little later on
. . . either there or here. Sure do hope so.

Always,
Dilly

Tom knew Taylor didn't type this one. *Curley* was
misspelled, for one thing, and it was too formal—almost
as if it had been a news release.

In May, Taylor was back in St. John's. The doctors
told Ursula the time had come. He would go into a coma
. . . and then the end. Terry took the news like his father
would have wanted him to with no tears. Tessa withdrew
and remained silent. They did not visit Bob in the hospital, but he asked Art to buy Terry that new bike he
wanted. Art drove home from the bicycle shop by way
of the hospital and asked Terry if he would like to see
his father.

The boy didn't answer but Art said, "Your mother
would be very pleased."

Ursula was pleased, and of course, Taylor was pleased
but Terry did not know what to say and leaned heavily
on Art for support. He thanked his dad for his new bike,
the one he never would have gotten if Taylor had been
in good health, but which was a last gesture to his son.

In his last days Taylor spoke of nothing but Ursula.
When she was not in the room he persistently expressed
his desire that everyone look after her. He never spoke
to her about what she was going to do when he was no
longer around, rather about the good summer coming up.

Dale Robertson, who would eventually replace Taylor
in *Death Valley Days,* came to the hospital but was only
able to control his emotions for a very brief time. He
walked out into the corridor, but Art had to take him
into a private room. "I just can't believe it!"

Meanwhile friends were frantically calling Bob's business manager regarding his estate. He had willed 50
per cent to Ursula and the children, and 50 per cent to
Ruth, now a vegetable who never knew her son was dying.
But there was no cash. The major operation in October
had cost $25,000 and the others close to it. Barbara was

270

still billing the Taylor estate for alimony which was her way of possessing Bob to the end.

It was suggested that the ranch be mortgaged, but nothing was done, and Ursula would be left with 113 acres worth $1 million and little else until hopefully she could sell the property.

Tom received another form letter. Dilly said he was still trying to put on some weight, but that could change at any time. The kids were doing well at school—Tessa had straight A's, but Terry couldn't care less. He said if he wasn't able to go to the desert in June, he'd get a practical nurse and send Ursula and the kids.

Chapter XV

At the time of Taylor's hospitalization, twenty-four-year-old Michael Thiess was living in a motel but spending weekends at the ranch while he was recuperating from hepatitis. Previously he had been in Camarillo State Hospital under heavy sedation; though he was still taking drugs under the doctor's care, they were slowly decreasing the dosage.

Because he was not trusted with large amounts of sedatives, Ursula had been taking his drugs to him at the motel during the week.

On May 24th he and his sister, Manuela, were together on the ranch, but because he was acting peculiarly, the psychiatrist told Art to keep a close eye on him. The following day he returned to the motel and on Monday, May 26th, Ursula found her son dead. She immediately called his doctor who summoned the police. Art rushed to the scene where Ursula was talking with detectives.

After several hours of extensive questioning, she collapsed.

She had been under a terrible strain for over a week, dashing to the hospital, back home, to and from the motel where Michael was, and worried every minute that Bob would need her. She wanted to be with him during this critical period.

The newspapers hinted that an overdose of drugs had caused Michael's death, and it was an apparent suicide. A year ago he had attempted to take his life by cutting his wrists.

Police listed Michael as a "struggling actor" who after a year in prison in Germany for trying to kill his father, George Thiess, returned to the United States where he was convicted five times on charges ranging from assault and battery on a policeman to possession of marijuana.

Michael was never mentally stable and whatever life he had was wasted. Feelings were a mixture of regret and relief. Manuela, who believed in ghosts, said her brother would return as a spirit and "get her" because she had refused to speak to him the day before he died.

On Tuesday, Taylor's condition worsened and Ursula was by his bed continually while her son's funeral was being arranged. Bob had been told of Michael's death and insisted that he go home after the services on Thursday. The doctors refused but said that Ursula could remain with him at the hospital on Tuesday and Wednesday nights. Taylor argued. He wanted to be with his wife on the ranch—alone. She would need him more than ever, but in an atmosphere other than a hospital room. To convince Ursula he said, "The 'farm' is the only home I've ever really had and I want to see it—just one more time . . ."

The press remained at the entrances of St. John's knowing Taylor was there, but also aware that he might attend the funeral of his stepson. They had been told when he did leave, "he would walk out!"

The memorial service for Michael was a quiet one with only fifty people attending. Ursula arrived and her composure was remarkable. She was grieving for the loss of Michael but her greatest emotion during the service was that of fear—fear that she might not be with Bob at the end.

Michael's hippie friends attended the impersonal funeral. Ursula, spending most of her time with Bob, had not been able to arrange a proper service that might have lent some warmth to the tragic burial of a young boy. The minister mispronounced his last name and his message could have been about anyone, because he had not been briefed.

Some of Michael's friends who attended were there to work their voodoo of "spells and magic" for his new existence as a ghost.

Ursula invited these hippies to the ranch after the funeral. They had never been permitted there before, but Manuela played hostess to her brother's chums while Art served—in another part of the house—the group who were paying their respects on behalf of Ursula and Bob.

Taylor's refusal to take "no" for an answer to his going home one last time gave the doctor no alternative but to tell him the brutal truth—the disease had reached his bones and tissues. Shortly after he was told, Art walked into his room. Taylor winked and said, "Well, I guess Old Dad's had it!" Art was so shaken he couldn't speak, but Bob said he wanted to be taken home immediately, which brought Art back to his senses. "If Bob hadn't said *that*, I think I would have bawled like a baby."

Taylor's insistence on coming home presented problems. The first, of course, was his grave condition, and the other—the many newsmen who were waiting outside for a glimpse of Robert Taylor "walking out" of St. John's. But nothing would change Bob's mind. He said he did not want to be taken to the ranch in an ambulance or have attending nurses.

His doctor, who had been fighting off reporters for days, was told that *if* Bob left the hospital it *had* to be kept a complete secret. There was a discussion between Ursula, Art and the doctor, and they decided to grant Bob his wish but only if he had nurses in attendance day and night. Ursula said Bob did not want them because of the money involved, but the doctor said it would be this way or Taylor would remain in the hospital.

Art worked out a plan. Taylor would be taken out the refuse exit to a prearranged spot where he would be waiting to take his boss home. But at the last minute Bob became extremely weak and had to be placed on a stretcher and taken out of the emergency exit to the ambulance.

They somehow managed to avoid the press completely. Taylor was terribly concerned that he might be photographed and said he couldn't understand why there were so many reporters assigned to cover his dying. Maybe at one time in his life it might have been worthy of print, but why now did they find his whereabouts so important?

He was taken home after Michael's funeral and stayed for several days. His presence in the house was not good

274

for the children because they saw him unable to cope mentally and physically, but Ursula, numb with strength, stayed by his side. Bob wanted her to care for him and resented the presence of nurses. Though his excuse for not wanting them there in the first place was the financial burden, he truly wanted to be alone with Ursula—wanting to say so many things, but not saying them.

When Michael died, Taylor gave up his fight. He could succumb now that Ursula had been relieved of one burden anyway. His great love for her, and the awareness that she would be tested to the fullest when he was gone, was on his mind more than the fear of death. How much more would she have to take? Would Manuela snap out of her troubles?

When he spoke to Art it was always, "Ursula . . . Ursula . . . Ursula . . ."

He was taken back to the hospital and on Thursday, June 5th, exactly one week following Michael's funeral, Ursula was again taken from Bob's bedside. She went to Terry's grade school graduation. "I wanted to be with my husband, but Terry needed me for a little while . . . if anything had happened to Bob when I wasn't there . . ."

Shortly before Taylor lapsed into a coma, he spoke privately to Ronald Reagan: "I only have one request right now. Tell Ursula, be happy . . ."

On Saturday, June 7, 1969, the newsmen printed the news that Taylor was fighting for his life. He was not in pain, since the disease had reached his nerve centers several days ago.

The following morning Ursula and Art stood over him. The nurse, who said she had prayed she would not be on duty when Bob died, was so upset, she was unable to take his blood pressure. Art had to take over, but it really didn't matter.

Robert Taylor simply closed his eyes.

"A few years ago a friend of mine shot a large cock pheasant and seconds later, he himself fell dead.
I always thought that if anybody woulda told me that was the way I was gonna die, I'd be happy as a bird dog . . ."

275

Robert Taylor Eulogy

June 11, 1969
Governor Ronald Reagan

How to say farewell to a friend named Bob. He'd probably say, "Don't make any fuss. I wouldn't want to cause any trouble."

How to speak of Robert Taylor—one of the truly great and most enduring stars of the Golden Era of Hollywood. What can we say about a boy named—well, a boy from Nebraska with an un-Nebraska-like name of Spangler Arlington Brugh?

Perhaps that's as good a starting point as any. A young man, son of a Nebraska doctor, coming to California—to Pomona—for his last years in college, and from there the story reads like a script from one of those early musicals. And it happens to be the last person in the world who would have thought that great fame was in store for him.

There was the college play, the talent scout, the most improbable of all—the coincidence of timing that found him in an MGM casting office on the day that had been picked for the testing of a prospective actress. Who can we get to do the scene with her? What about that kid in the outer office. When the test was over, they didn't hire her, they hired him. And I suppose that would be first-act curtain.

And the second act followed the same pattern—almost a repeat. A newly signed contract player getting a minor role in a picture. No one remembers who had the principal roles—most have even forgotten the title of the picture. But when it was previewed, everyone wanted to know who was Robert Taylor—a young man with the name that sounded like one the studio would think up and become instead Robert Taylor—a name with a kind of honest Midwest sound.

MGM was a giant and the home of giants. It had the greatest stars in an era when Hollywood was a Mount Olympus peopled with God-like stars—Gable, Grant, Montgomery, Coleman, Cooper, the Barrymores. And there were Goddesses to match—Garbo, Shearer, Craw-

276

ford, Irene Dunne. Bob Taylor became one of the all-time greats of motion picture stardom. Twenty-four years at the same studio, MGM, alone. Thirty-five years before the public. His face instantly recognizable in every corner of the world. His name, a new one—a household word. And all of this came to be one sudden dazzling burst. To simply appear in public caused a traffic jam. There has never been anything like it before or since—possibly the only thing that can compare it—Rudolph Valentino, and why not? Because on all Mount Olympus, he was the most handsome.

Now there were those in our midst who worked very hard to bring him down with a label, "Pretty Boy," and of course there's that standard Hollywood rule that true talent must never be admitted as playing part in success of the individual who is too handsome or too beautiful. It's only in the recent years of our friendship that I've been able to understand how painful all of this must have been to him—to a truly modest man—because he was modest to the point of being painfully shy. In all of the years of stardom, he never quite got over being genuinely embarrassed at the furor that his appearance created. He went a long way to avoid putting himself in a position where he could become the center of attention. And in these years I have learned—and not by any complaints from him—complaining wasn't part of him—but I have learned of something else that must have been hard for him to bear; the idea that just a handsome face was responsible for his success—that he wasn't truly an actor. Because Bob had one intolerance: he had no patience with those who came into the business with the idea that they could short-cut hard work and substitute gimmicks for craftsmanship.

He respected his profession and he was a superb master of it. He took a quiet pride in his work. He was a pro, and the "Pretty Boy" tag couldn't begin to survive roles like *Magnificent Obsession, Camille, Waterloo Bridge, Johnny Eager, Quo Vadis.*

It takes a rare and unique actor to be believable, as he was believable—in costume epics like *Ivanhoe, Knights of the Round Table,* and also at the same time as a fighter in *The Crowd Roars* and the almost psychopathic *Billy the Kid.* Some of his pictures live on as true classics, and generally, the standard is so high in retrospect it would appear his modesty caused this industry to underrate the calibre of this man who was truly a star among stars.

And yet, none of this is what brought us together here today.

Perhaps each one of us has his own different memory, but I'll bet that somehow they all add up to "nice man." Mervyn LeRoy, who directed so many of his great pictures, speaks of his always showing consideration for everyone who worked with him. Artie Deutsh said he never worked in a company where he wasn't well-loved, well-liked, even beloved by his cast and crew.

His quiet and disciplined manner had a steadying affect on every company he was ever in and at the same time, throughout the country, there are hundreds of men who remember him because he taught them to fly. He sought combat in World War II as a Navy flier and he wound up teaching others—and I'll bet he taught them well.

There was no caste system in his love of humanity.

Today I am sure there is sorrow among the rugged men in the Northwest who run the swift water of the Rogue River and who knew him as one of them. There are cowpokes up in a valley in Wyoming who remember him and mourn—mourn a man who rode and hunted with them. And millions and millions of people who knew him by way of the silver screen, and they remember with gratitude that in the darkened theatre he never embarrassed them in front of their children.

I know that some night on the late, late show I'm going to see him resplendent in white tie and tails at Delmonico's, and I am sure I'll smile—smile at Robert Spangler Arlington Brugh Taylor, because I'll remember how a fellow named Bob really preferred blue jeans and boots. And I'll see him squinting through the smoke of a barbeque as I have seen him a hundred times.

He loved his home and everything that it meant. Above all, he loved his family and his beautiful Ursula—lovely Manuela, all grown up!—little Tessa; Terry, his son, a young man in whom he had such great pride.

In a little while the hurt will be gone. Time will do that for you. Then you will find you can bring out your memories. You can look at them—take comfort from their warmth. As the years go by, you will be very proud. Not so much of the things that we have talked about here—you are going to be proud of simple things. Things not so stylish in certain circles today, but that just makes them a little more rare and of greater value. Simple things he had like honor and honesty, responsibility to those he worked for and who worked for him—standing up for what he believed and, yes, even a simple old-fashioned love for his country, and above all, an inner humility.

I think, too, that he'd want me to tell you how very much he loved your mother. What happiness she brought him and how wonderful she is. The papers say he was in the hospital seven times—actually he was out of the hospital seven times. He needed the strength that he could only get from being in that home so filled with her presence. He spoke to me of this just a few days ago. It was uppermost in his mind and I am sure he meant for me to tell you something that he wanted above all else. Ursula, there is just one last thing that only you can do for him—be happy. This was his last thought to me.

I don't pretend to know God's plan for each one of us, but I have faith in his infinite mercy. Bob had great success in the work he loved and he returned each day from that work with the knowledge there were those who waited affectionately for the sound of his footsteps.

APPENDIX

THE FILMS OF

ROBERT TAYLOR

Roxy Theatre
August 3, 1934

HANDY ANDY
Fox 1934

Director—David Butler
Story based on the play *Merry Andrew* by Lewis Beach
Screenplay—William Counselman and Henry Johnson

Andrew Yates—Will Rogers
Ernestine Yates—Peggy Wood
Fleurette—Conchita Montenegro
Janice Yates—Mary Carlisle
Doc Burmeister—Roger Imhof
Lloyd Burmeister—Robert Taylor

Reviews—Robert Taylor makes the most of the part of the
young man who is in love with Mary Carlisle.

THERE'S ALWAYS TOMORROW
Universal 1934

Director—Ed Sloman
Story—based on a novel by Ursula Parrott
Screenplay—William Hurlbut

Joseph White—Frank Morgan
Alice Vaile—Binnie Barnes
Sophie White—Lois Wilson
Janet—Louise Latimer
Helen—Eliz Young
Harry—Alan Hale
Arthur—Robert Taylor
Ella—Margaret Hamilton

Taylor—not reviewed

Role—Frank Morgan is touching as the husband rejected by
his family and Taylor is his son.

A WICKED WOMAN
MGM 1934

Director—Charles Brabin
Storly—Anne Austin
Screenplay—Florence Ryerson and Zelda Sears

Naomi Trice—Mady Christians
Rosanne—Jean Parker
Naylor—Charles Bickford
Yancey—Betty Furness
Curtis—William Henry
Ed Trice—Paul Harvey
Gram Teague—Zelda Sears
Bill Renton—Robert Taylor
Peter—Sterling Holloway

Taylor—not reviewed

Role—A tearjerker about a woman who kills her brutish
husband. Taylor is a friend of the family.

BURIED LOOT
(made 1934)   MGM 1935

Director—George B. Seitz
Narration—Bill Tannen

Robert Livingston
Jas. Ellison

The first of forty-eight two-reelers in MGM's *Crime Does
Not Pay* series (1935–1947).

Taylor plays a bank clerk who embezzles $200,000.

SOCIETY DOCTOR
(made 1934)   MGM 1935

Director—George B. Seitz
Screenplay—Based on the play *The Harbor* by Theodore
     Reeves

Dr. Morgan—Chester Morris
Madge—Virginia Bruce
Dr. Ellis—Robert Taylor
Mrs. Crane—Billie Burke

Reviews—*Society Doctor* is played in spotless white and
     with an appropriate sense of glamour and nobility
     by Chester Morris, Virginia Bruce and a promis-
     ing newcomer, Robert Taylor.
     Billie Burke as the foolish widow gives the best
     performance in the cast and a young unknown
     named Robert Taylor gives a good account of
     himself in spite of his matinée idol looks.
Role—   A trifle about life in a city hospital. In a support-
     ing role as an interne, Taylor received his first
     attention.

WEST POINT OF THE AIR
MGM 1935

Producer—Monta Bell
Director—Richard Rosson
Story—James K. McGuinness and John Monk Saunders
Screenplay—Frank Wead and Arthur J. Beckhard

Big Mike—Wallace Beery
Little Mike—Robert Young
General Carter—Lewis Stone
Skip—Maureen O'Sullivan
Dare—Rosalind Russell
Joe Bags—James Gleason
Pettis—Henry Wadsworth
Jaskerelli—Robert Taylor

Review—No comment on Taylor
Role— Taylor had a very brief appearance as a flying cadet

TIMES SQUARE LADY
MGM 1935

Producer—Lucien Hubbard
Director—George B. Seitz
Story—Albert Cohen and Robert Shannon

Steve—Robert Taylor
Toni—Virginia Bruce
Margo—Helen Twelvetrees

Reviews—"Entertaining"
        "A bit of light divertissement"
        —Taylor not reviewed

Role—   A light film about Broadway and crooked lawyers
         with Virginia Bruce as a blues singer and Taylor
         the night club host who befriends her

June 2, 1935
Loew's State Theatre

MURDER IN THE FLEET
MGM 1935

Producer—Lucien Hubbard
Director—Ed Sedgwick
Story—Ed Sedgwick
Screenplay—Frank Wead and Joe Sherman

Lt. Tom Randolph—Robert Taylor
Betty Lansing—Jean Parker
Mac O'Neill—Ted Healy
"Toots" Timmons—Una Merkel
Victor Hanson—Jean Hersholt

Role—   A fair actioner about a battle cruiser with Taylor
         as a lieutenant.

Reviews—Looking at the matter rationally, you know per-
        fectly well that Mr. Taylor is too valuable a prop-
        erty to be drowned like a rat.
        Taylor is satisfactory in a colorless role.

BROADWAY MELODY OF 1936
MGM 1935
(only movie in which Taylor dances)

Producer—John W. Considine, Jr.
Director—Roy Del Ruth
Story—Moss Hart
Screenplay—Jack McGowan and Sid Silvers
Music and Lyrics—Nacio Herb Brown and Arthur Freed

Bert Keeler—Jack Benny
Irene Foster—Eleanor Powell
Bob Gordon—Robert Taylor
Kitty Corbeet—Una Merkel
Snoop—Sid Silvers
Ted—Buddy Ebsen
Lillian Brent—June Knight
Frances Langford—herself

Role—   Taylor, as a theatrical producer, sings and dances
(the only time in his career he did so).

Reviews—Taylor gives a sterling performance and handles
his role with disarming naturalness.
Robert Taylor is handsome, masculine and should
go far.

MAGNIFICENT OBSESSION
Universal 1935

Director—John M. Stahl
Story—based on a novel by Lloyd C. Douglas
Screenplay—George O'Neill, Sarah Y. Mason and Victor
       Heerman

Helen Hudson—Irene Dunne
Bobby Merrick—Robert Taylor
Tommy Masterson—Charles Butterworth
Joyce Hudson—Betty Furness

Role—   Taylor's performance as the playboy who wins
        the affection of an older woman (Dunne) lifted
        him to stardom.

Reviews—Mr. Taylor plays the reformed wastrel with such
        aggressive charm that the only word for his per-
        formance is "cute."

April 10, 1936
Capitol Theatre

SMALL TOWN GIRL
MGM 1936

Producer—Hunt Stromberg
Director—William A. Wellman
Story—based on a novel by Ben Ames Williams

Screenplay—John Lee Mahin and Edith Fitzgerald

Kay Brannan—Janet Gaynor
Bob Dakin—Robert Taylor
Priscilla—Binnie Barnes
Dr. Dakin—Lewis Stone
George—Andy Devine
Elmer—James Stewart

Role—   City-boy Taylor marries Gaynor while intoxi-
         cated. Re-made in 1954 as a musical with Jane
         Powell and Farley Granger.

Reviews—Janet Gaynor emerges as a more mature actress
         and Robert Taylor practically reaches stardom with
         his spontaneous performance. Mr. Taylor, the
         current personality boy of the screen, performs
         amicably enough but I am still sceptical about his
         great histrionic equipment.

         Mr. Taylor and Miss Gaynor are a pleasant co-
         starring combo, and if Metro heard the cooing
         from the feminine contingent in yesterday's audi-
         ence, they probably will be teamed again.

June 11, 1936
Radio City

PRIVATE NUMBER
Fox 1936

Director—Roy Del Ruth
Story—re-make of Cleves Kinkead's play *Common Clay*
Screenplay—Gene Markay and William Conselman

Richard Winfield—Robert Taylor

288

Ellen Neal—Loretta Young
Wroxton—Basil Rathbone
Gracie—Patsy Kelly
Smiley Watson—Joe Lewis

Role— Story of the clandestine marriage of a rich college student (Taylor) to the family maid (Young)

Reviews—*Private Number* starts off like the perfect summer idyll with Loretta Young, the maid, winning the notice of Robert Taylor, the scion, in artless fashion. Believe it or not, the picture is well acted throughout. Mr. Rathbone is as hateful as Miss Young is charming and Mr. Taylor is manly to a fault.

Handsome and assured, Mr. Taylor gives a restrained performance calculated to make feminine hearts flutter.

August 14, 1936
Capitol Theatre

HIS BROTHER'S WIFE
MGM 1936

Producer—Lawrence Weingarten
Director—W. S. Van Dyke
Story—George Auerbach
Screenplay—Leon Gordon and John Meehan

Rita—Barbara Stanwyck
Chris—Robert Taylor
Prof. Fahrenheim—Jean Hersholt
"Fish-Eye"—Joseph Calleia

Role—   Taylor, a medical student, rejects Stanwyck for jungle research. She marries his brother as revenge.

Reviews—The beautiful Mr. Robert Taylor, the loveliest screen hero of the season, the entrancing juvenile who causes young women to swoon and strong men to snarl, turns out to be the austere scientific genius who discovers the cure for Spotted Fever. Mr. Taylor never forgets his charm. Film theatres want to have the reactions of their audiences reported so I may note that the Taylor admirers at the Capitol yesterday afternoon laughed at their hero's dramatic meeting with his married brother.

In offering this report we are being bold enough or cowardly enough to admit that words of a critic are of no weight against the enormous popularity of Mr. Taylor. We are convinced we should be scolded, clawed and kicked for implying he can be anything less than sublime. Still roguishly risking this abuse, we must admit to certain reservations about him. Mr. Taylor is just not the type to be exposed to heat, fever bearing ticks and Metro's special effects.

Top Ten Grossing Film   September 5, 1936
                                          Capitol Theatre

THE GORGEOUS HUSSY
MGM 1936

Director—Clarence Brown
Story—based on a novel by Samuel Hopkins Adams
Screenplay—Ainsworth Morgan and Stephen Morehouse
            Avery

290

Peggy Eaton—Joan Crawford
"Bow" Timberlake—Robert Taylor
Andrew Jackson—Lionel Barrymore
John Eaton—Franchot Tone
John Randolph—Melvyn Douglas
"Rowdy" Dow—James Stewart

Role— A star-studded fictionalization about Andrew Jackson's Peggy Eaton. Taylor is the Navy lieutenant who marries her and is killed on their wedding night.

Reviews—A colorful and heart-warming saga of American history. The new matinée idol, Robert Taylor, plays "Bow" Timberlake with considerably more power than he has shown up to now.

Top Ten Best

January 22, 1937
Capitol Theatre

CAMILLE
MGM 1937

Director—George Cukor
Story—From Alexander Dumas's *La Dame Aux Camélias*
Screenplay—Zoe Akins, Frances Marion and James Hilton

Marguerite—Greta Garbo
Armand—Robert Taylor
Monsieur Duval—Lionel Barrymore
Nichette—Elizabeth Allan

Role— Tragedy of love affair between Marguerite (Garbo) and Armand (Taylor) to end in the death of Camille.

291

Reviews—You could hear a few tear drops in the Capitol Theatre during the exquisite pathetic scene when Camille dies in the arms of her lover, Armand. As a matter of fact, "tear dropping" could be heard all over the movie house during the more poignant scenes. It came at times like a rush of water through the flood gates. There wasn't a dry eye in the theatre when the picture ended and there was a sound of sniffing and scrambling for handkerchiefs.

Robert Taylor plays Armand with considerable reserve. He must have felt instinctively that he would be overshadowed by Garbo. And he modestly steps away from the center of the stage allowing Miss Garbo to bask in the full glory of the limelight.

Mr. Taylor, curly-haired, tender-eyed and full of health became a wholesome Armand Duval. His final visit to the dying Marguerite was hailed with balcony cheers precisely like those that greet the arrival of the United States Cavalry to the settlers besieged by the Indians except they were uttered by ecstatic females instead of small boys. This is a spontaneous tribute to Taylor and he has implied therapeutic values. That he failed to save her life was not for want of passionate kissing.

The kissing, by the way, is pretty hot stuff in this picture. There were times I thought they were going to bite each other. Instead, after baring their teeth, they didn't.

Miss Garbo's performance is amazing. She was so marvelous that she breathes life into the story. Mr. Robert Taylor seemed alright. I couldn't see why so many people speak ill of the handsome fellow.

As Armand, Robert Taylor is ofttimes handsome and always modish but never deeply moving. His is a studied performance throughout—from the consciousness of his first smile to his carefully

292

posed embraces. He brings little to the character.

Robert Taylor is surprisingly good as Armand.
—a bit on the juvenile side at times, but certainly
not guilty of the sin of many Armands in the
past—callousness.

Mr. Taylor, inexperienced, is good. His Armand
is dashing and well-tempered and his love scenes
are certainly making the pulses beat more quickly.
Garbo, in no sense of disparagement, has brought
out his talent that to date has not been shown.

Mr. Taylor's performance as Armand will delight
his feminine followers, but he is no match for
Garbo. In some of their torrid love scenes, he
seems about to swoon.

It appears as if Miss Garbo frightens young Taylor. He seemed to be a reluctant Armand.

April 15, 1937
Capitol Theatre

PERSONAL PROPERTY
MGM 1937

Producer—John W. Considine, Jr.
Director—W. S. Van Dyke II
Story—based on the play *The Man in Possession* by H. M.
    Harwood
Screenplay—Hugh Mills and Ernest Valja

Crystal Wetherby—Jean Harlow
Raymond Dabney—Robert Taylor
Claude Dabney—Reginald Owen

Clara—Una O'Connor

Role— A comedy about two brothers—Taylor and Owen —who vie for the affections of an American widow (Harlow).

Reviews—Were it not again a libel against the calling, it might be said that Mr. Taylor is excellently cast, as he is as utterly incapable of expressing an idea, feeling or emotion as the most rigidly traditional of head servants is supposed to be.

Grateful fans by the herd will doubtless storm the portals all week and have a simply elegant time in the company of the peerless Mr. Taylor and the ineffable Miss Harlow. As the French say, however, *"Pas pour je."*

May 27, 1937
Radio City

THIS IS MY AFFAIR
Fox 1937

Producer—Kenneth Mac Gowan
Director—William A. Seiter
Screenplay—Allen Rivkin and Lamar Trotti

Lieutenant Richard L. Perry—Robert Taylor
Lil Duryea—Barbara Stanwyck
Jock Ramsay—Victor McLaglen
Bat Duryea—Brian Donlevy
President Theodore Roosevelt—Sidney Blackmer
Ed—John Carradine

Role— A large-scale picture about bank robberies in the

294

Middle West. Taylor is a government undercover agent.

Reviews—*This Is My Affair* is agreeable entertainment even if Mr. Taylor is in it.

They couldn't disguise Mr. Taylor. Although he has the rank of lieutenant, assumes a hero's stature and has a reservation in Arlington Cemetery, Mr. Taylor is still Mr. Taylor, for which the feminine contingent undoubtedly will be grateful.

The big news for the fans is that Mr. Taylor and Barbara Stanwyck are paired as hero and heroine. The former does a fairly creditable job with the role of secret service ace and he makes love to Miss Stanwyck persuasively. Neither she nor Mr. Taylor know much about counterfeiting an emotion—at least neither of them steals the show from the other.

Not even Mr. Taylor can out-glamour that glamourous era—the turn of the century.

September 2, 1937
Capitol Theatre

BROADWAY MELODY OF 1938
MGM 1937

Producer—Jack Cummings
Director—Roy Del Ruth
Story—Jack McGowan and Sid Silvers
Screenplay—Mr. McGowan
Music and Lyrics—Nacio Herb Brown and Arthur Freed

Steve Raleigh—Robert Taylor
Sally Lee—Eleanor Powell
Sonny Ledford—George Murphy
Caroline Whipple—Binnie Barnes
Peter Trot—Buddy Ebsen
Alice Clayton—Sophie Tucker
Betty Clayton—Judy Garland

Role— A musical with good songs, but little plot. Taylor
is a theatrical producer.

Reviews—Mr. Taylor seems to walk through his part with
a suggestion of diffidence although his natural
sympathy never fails while Mr. Murphy, in a supporting role, is ingratiating and proves an excellent dancer.

LEST WE FORGET
MGM 1937
A Will Rogers Memorial

Directors—Henry Hathaway, E. Mason Hoffer, Richard
Thorpe, Harry Lowd

A Will Rogers memorial short in which Robert Taylor, Gary
Cooper, Harry Carey and Allan Jones make brief appearances.

A YANK AT OXFORD
MGM 1938
Filmed in England

Producer—Michael Balcon
Director—Jack Conway
Story—Leon Gordon, Sidney Gilliat and Michael Hogan
Screenplay—Malcolm Stuart Boylan, Walter Ferris and
George Oppenheimer

Lee Sheridan—Robert Taylor
Dan Sheridan—Lionel Barrymore
Molly Beaumont—Maureen O'Sullivan
Elsa Craddock—Vivien Leigh
Dean of Cardinals—Edmund Gwenn

Role— Taylor is a cocky American athlete who indis-
creetly falls for a coquette (Leigh). The first of
the roles which "roughed up" Taylor.

Reviews—The intention of MGM has been hinted at in publicity releases of *A Yank at Oxford*, now at the
Capitol Theatre. Robert Taylor's more rugged
aspects were to be developed in order to counter-
act damaging impressions based on his startling
beauty and effect on maidens.

The movie has scarcely begun grinding when Robert
is shown in track regalia running a forty-seven
second quarter mile without breathing heavily.
And there, peeping manfully from the upper edges
of his track shirt, is hair! Quite a mattress, if I
may say so.

To say that Robert Taylor is the least powerful
link in the picture would be to admit prejudice
against his personality and his work. Besides, he
isn't bad. A few others might have been better,

297

but disregarding handicaps of fatal beauty and that slight stiffness of the acting muscles, he is all right. I'll go further and say that this is Robert Taylor's best effort to date. Having said that on several occasions I am beginning to be more aware of the distance involved in Robert's moving from down there to up there.

Concerning the question of whether the picture should be recommended only to Robert Taylor fans, my best guess is that others will find much to enjoy also. Even the anti-Taylor contingent need not avoid the picture for fear of conversion. They will be gratified to see the romantic beast in Robert break into the open, a couple of times, and the rest of the time his physical prowess will supply that wonderful and subtle taint of un-reality which is the delight of all good haters...

Mr. Taylor, still not much of an actor, is more a human being, less of a conscious beauty in this one picture, *A Yank at Oxford*. The athletic sequences are handled with dash and excitement from the first sleek appearance of Sheridan (Taylor) to the last swift boat race between Cambridge and Oxford. These scenes, by the way, settle that burning question which occupied so much news-paper space—the insistence that Taylor reveal his chest.

Taylor ceases to be the Cinema's Leading Ex-ponent of Oscillation and becomes a two-fisted man's man—a regular guy whose broad shoulders pull a mean oar at Oxford and who steps along right smartly on the cinder track with commend-able form.
No fooling, Robert really looks fine. The girls will sigh with renewed rapture! The boys will sneer but admit that he certainly has what it takes. There is no overlooking the fact that Taylor alone makes *A Yank at Oxford* entertaining. He puts verve and vitality into a wisp of a story. His smile is disarming, his laughter infectious. So go tell the girls that all is forgiven. Robert is beauti-

ful, all right, but he's top man in the virility club, also. This film marks the first step in the campaign to deemphasize Taylor's good looks and almost strictly feminine appeal. It is eminently successful in this objective and enjoyable screen fare to boot.

A Yank at Oxford turns out to be an uncommonly diverting show. It can't be the story because we've read the one about the old college spirit before. And it can't be Robert Taylor for we still regard that widow's peak with cynicism the feminine contingent rightly defines as envy. And it can't be the track and crew events our Mr. Taylor of Oxford carries off with such Nebraskan aplomb. But we even found ourselves rooting for Mr. Taylor in the Oxford-Cambridge crew races. Subconsciously that might have been because we were glad to see him overseas!

The fact that this picture is a shrewd American blend is not so important as Hollywood rates, but as the personality of Mr. Taylor. Laboring under the stigma of being thought pretty, the actor has done his best to confound the "have you any hair on your chest?" hecklers, by becoming belligerently virile. In his new starring assignment he runs, rows and throws a mean right with scarcely a trace of the posturing matinée idol. Judging on this performance it is my suspicion that Mr. Taylor may be an actor.

Looks very much like a Robert Taylor year. *A Yank at Oxford* is his best picture and Robert should thank his lucky stars because when he left for England several months ago, the pendulum could very easily have swung the other way.

THREE COMRADES
MGM 1938

Producer—Joseph Mankiewicz
Director—Frank Borzage
Story—based on a book by Erich Maria Remarque
Screenplay—F. Scott Fitzgerald and Edward Paramore

Erich Lohkamp—Robert Taylor
Patricia Hollman—Margaret Sullivan
Otto Koster—Franchot Tone
Gottfried Lenz—Robert Young
Alfons—Guy Kibbee

Role—   A beautiful film about three veterans who run an auto-repair shop in post-war Germany. Taylor is the idealistic one and Sullivan his tubercular wife.

Reviews—Robert Taylor was good occasionally but more often merely acceptable. He has his moments of sincerity, but shares them with those suggesting again the charming well-fed, carefully hair-groomed leading man of the glamour school of The Cinema.

In general, Taylor, Young and Tone were accepted as "Splendid."

Robert Taylor has never been better in a role for which he is obviously not suited.

THE CROWD ROARS
MGM 1938

Producer—Sam Zimbalist
Director—Richard Thorpe
Story—George Bruce
Screenplay—Thomas Lennon, George Bruce and George
       Oppenheimer

Tommy McCoy—Robert Taylor
Jim Cain—Edward Arnold
Brian McCoy—Frank Morgan
Sheila Carson—Maureen O'Sullivan
Johnny Martin—William Gargan
Vivian—Jane Wyman

Role—   Taylor plays "Killer McCoy," an ethical boxer
        amid the crooked.

Reviews—The campaign to make Robert Taylor a man's
        man, has been carried to somewhat extreme
        lengths in *The Crowd Roars*. Not content with
        mussing up his hair, the offering asks the prettiest
        of the motion-picture idols to portray a murderous
        pugilist with a racketeer's philosophy.
        Let it be noted at once that Mr. Taylor plays a
        tough guy with considerable persuasion. If you
        are interested in just how virile he can be, you
        will find the show intriguing. Mr. Taylor plays
        the pug seriously and with a good deal more
        command than he has mustered in the past.

        We are glad to note that the story has a surprising
        amount of content and characterization for a
        picture involving Mr. Taylor, who in the past has
        been regarded as having to lift dead weights of
        footage with the unaided profile. For the rest, any

picture with a prize fight for a climax is unfair
to organized criticism . . .

The Crowd Roars, one of the greatest prize fight
pictures ever to hit the screen, puts Robert Taylor
to the fore. As a human hero, he takes his place
with Gable among the screen greats. Everything
MGM had hoped to accomplish with Taylor has
been more than achieved in this story and from
now on there will be no stopping him with male
as well as female audiences.

Capitol Theatre
January 26, 1939

STAND UP AND FIGHT
MGM 1938

Producer—Mervyn LeRoy
Director—W. S. Van Dyke II
Story—Forbes Parkhill
Screenplay—James M. Cain, Jane Martin and Harvey Fer-
gusson

Captain Boss Starkey—Wallace Beery
Blake Cantrell—Robert Taylor
Susan Griffith—Florence Rice
Amanda Griffith—Helen Broderick
Arnold—Charles Bickford
Crowder—Barton MacLane

Role—   A bankrupt aristocrat (Taylor) fights the elements and stagecoacher Beery in order to build
a railroad across the Cumberland Gap.

302

Reviews—The performance of Mr. Taylor, while mannered
and pompous in spots where it shouldn't be, is
generally authoritative.

Mr. Taylor gives a fine performance as the society
gentleman demonstrating clever acting finesse.

Capitol Theatre
May 4, 1939

LUCKY NIGHT
MGM 1939

Producer—Louis D. Lighton
Director—Norman Taurog
Story—Oliver C. Laxton
Screenplay—Vincent Lawrence and Grover Jones

Cora Jordan—Myrna Loy
Bill Overton—Robert Taylor
Joe Hilton—Joseph Allen
Calvin Jordan—Henry O'Neill
Mrs. Briggs—Marjorie Main

Role— A rich girl (Loy) meets an unemployed paint
salesman (Taylor) on a park bench. A gambling
spree, hasty marriage and complicated domestic
life, in an embarrassingly bad script, follow.

Reviews—Mr. Taylor is aggressively dashing but he scarcely
fits the role of an introspective rebel against con-
ventions.

LADY OF THE TROPICS
MGM 1939

Producer—Sam Zimbalist
Director—Jack Conway
Screenplay—Ben Hecht

Bill Carey—Robert Taylor
Manon de Vargnes—Hedy Lamarr
Pierre DeLaroch—Joseph Schildkraut
Nina—Gloria Franklin
Father Antoine—Ernest Cossart

Role— Taylor steps off a yacht in the Orient and falls in love with a half-caste (Lamarr)

Reviews—Hedy Lamarr is more beautiful than Robert Taylor—if you can believe that!

It was not a good picture but it stars the two most beautiful people on the screen.

Mr. Taylor gives a rather wooden performance in the earlier sequences. Later he is more capable—bringing his "American" to life with considerable persuasion.

December 14, 1939
Capitol Theatre

REMEMBER?
MGM 1939

Producer—Milton Bren
Director—Norman Z. McLeod
Story and Screenplay—Corey Ford and Norman Z. McLeod

Jeff Holland—Robert Taylor
Linda Bronson—Greer Garson
Sky Ames—Lew Ayres
Mrs. Bronson—Billie Burke
Mr. Bronson—Reginald Owen

Role—   A situation comedy with Taylor and Ayres vying
for Garson.

Reviews—*(Hollywood Press)* "It may have been the very
desolation of *Remember?* when it was released
that began appealing to our sense of fair play. We
have it, if you dig down deep enough. Whatever it
was, I know that you could feel the Hollywood
mood toward Taylor changing from that day on.
What lays in the future for him, none of us can
prophesy, but it seems that he has taken too much
punishment!"

Taylor labored at it!

This is the kind of picture in which Mr. Taylor
appears to his best advantage.

FLIGHT COMMAND
MGM 1940

Producer—J. Walter Ruben
Director—Frank Borzage
Story—Commander Harvey Haislip and John Sutherland
Screenplay—Wells Root and Commander Harvey Haislip

Ensign Alan Drake—Robert Taylor
Lorna Gary—Ruth Hussey
Squadron Commander Bill Gary—Walter Pidgeon
Lieutenant Commander "Dusty" Rhodes—Paul Kelly
Lieutenant Jerry Banning—Sheppard Strudwick
Lieutenant "Mugger" Martin—Red Skelton

Role— A story about Navy fighting planes with Ensign Taylor falling in love with the Commander's wife (Hussey) and then saving the life of the Commander (Pidgeon)

Reviews—Taylor is a real star—there is no question about that. His part in the movie isn't easy to play.

WATERLOO BRIDGE
MGM 1940

Producer—Sidney Franklin

Director—Mervyn LeRoy
Story—based on Robert E. Sherwood's play of the same
  name.
Screenplay—S. N. Behrman, Hans Rameau and George
  Froeschel

Myra—Vivien Leigh
Roy Cronin—Robert Taylor
Lady Margaret Cronin—Lucille Watson
Kitty—Virginia Field
Mme. Olga Kirowa—Maria Ouspenskaya
The Duke—C. Aubrey Smith

Role—   Story about a soldier (Taylor) who falls in love
         with a ballerina-turned-prostitute (Leigh). Tay-
         lor's *favorite film.*
Reviews—Vivien Leigh is indescribable. Robert Taylor, too,
         turns in a surprisingly flexible and mature per-
         formance as the young officer, although his activ-
         ity is mainly confined to being enthusiastic.

         A dance by two lovers in a candlelit cabaret the
         night before his departure for the front will live
         in tender memory. In fact all of *Waterloo Bridge*
         spans a dream-world of sentiment.

         Mr. Taylor is not by any means one of my fav-
         orites, but he is of staunch assistance in this film
         enterprise. He plays the role with sincerity and
         restraint. MGM has exploited the showmanship
         values of having the impersonator of Scarlett
         O'Hara together with one of Hollywood's top
         glamour boys, which helps to keep the film from
         becoming maudlin. *Waterloo Bridge* has solid act-
         ing throughout . . .

ESCAPE
MGM 1940

Producer—Mervyn LeRoy
Director—Mervyn LeRoy
Story—based on the novel *Escape* by Ethel Vance
Screenplay—Arch Oboler and Marguerite Roberts

Countess Von Treck—Norma Shearer
Mark Preysing—Robert Taylor
General Kurt Von Kolb—Conrad Veidt
Emmy Ritter—Nazimova
Fritz Keller—Felix Bressart
Dr. Ditten—Philip Dorn
Ursula—Bonita Granville

Role— Taylor, an American, plots the escape of his mother (Nazimova) from a concentration camp.

Reviews—Robert Taylor, as the young American, plays with becoming self-possession but with a hint of obtuseness which is bad. Neither he nor Miss Shearer are given anything very convincing to say.

It doesn't seem that either Miss Shearer or Mr. Taylor do much to further the production artistically, despite their pull at the box office. Taylor is too monotonously intense for comfort.

BILLY THE KID
MGM 1941

Producer—Irving Asher
Director—David Miller
Suggested by—*The Saga of Billy the Kid*, a book by Walter
        Noble Burns
Screenplay—Gene Fowler
Story—Howard Emmett Rogers and Bradbury Foote

Billy Bonney—Robert Taylor
Jim Sherwood—Brian Donlevy
Eric Keating—Ian Hunter
Edith Keating—Mary Howard
Dan Hickey—Gene Lockhart

Role—   Taylor's first Western. He played the title role.

Reviews—Taylor gives a distinguished performance in the
title role—the stature of the outlaw who left little
but memories behind him. Also he rides well and
handles his left-hand draw very well. There is no
romantic interest for him this time.

The general physical make-up of the gun-slinger
as interpreted by Robert Taylor is admirable—
makes *Billy the Kid* a colorful film.

A great deal more is seen of Mr. Taylor than anything else in this film. Mr. Taylor in a forbid-
dingly black and shiny cowboy suit—Mr. Taylor
at medium distance flashing a smile—Mr. Taylor's face in intimate close-ups with his jaw set
firm and his steely eyes looking about sharply for
any movement at all untoward—vaguely he gives
the impression of a kid in a new cowboy suit!

The magnificence of Robert Taylor, which is al-

ways something special to behold, falls into pale
inconsequence alongside the glories of the great
outdoors in Metro's flashy, technicolored Western,
Billy the Kid.

Capitol Theatre
September 4, 1941

WHEN LADIES MEET
MGM 1941

Producer—Robert Z. Leonard and Orville O. Dull
Director—Robert Z. Leonard
Story—Rachel Crothers
Screenplay—S. K. Lauren and Anita Loos

Mary Howard—Joan Crawford
Jimmy Lee—Robert Taylor
Clare Woodruff—Greer Garson
Rogers Woodruff—Herbert Marshall
Bridget Drake—Spring Byington

Role—   A comedy about two women (Garson and Craw-
          ford) who unknowingly love the same man (Mar-
          shall). Taylor portrays the happy-go-lucky play-
          boy who introduces the two women and succeeds
          in "getting the girl" (Crawford).

Reviews—Robert Taylor does all right—in fact, he does
          surprisingly well as the bouncing newspaper writer
          whose job and whose ardor are conveniently rogue.

          Taylor has most of the real action and a great
          deal of the comedy to interpret and he is rarely
          at a loss.

310

JOHNNY EAGER
MGM 1942

Producer—John W. Considine
Director—Mervyn LeRoy
Author—James Edward Grant
Screenplay—John Lee Mahin and James Edward Grant

Johnny Eager—Robert Taylor
Lisbeth Bard—Lana Turner
John Benson Farrell—Edward Arnold
Jeff Hartnett—Van Heflin (Oscar)
Jimmy Courtney—Robert Sterling
Garnet—Patricia Dane
Mae Blythe—Glenda Farrell

Role— Taylor is the gangster (Johnny Eager) who destroys himself when he falls in love with the girl he frames (Turner). Heflin stole the picture and won an Oscar for his performance as Jeff.

Reviews—Taylor is terrific and his "tough-guy" is *really* tough. He pulls no punches.

It is hard to figure out why MGM wanted to flash another facet of its already faceted Mr. Taylor. Let it be said right away that it is Mr. Taylor's best "facet" to date! Such fatal beauty as his is much better taken with mussed up hair and a convincing snarl. In fact, Mr. Taylor, though the admiration comes grudgingly, you're o.k.!

The New York Times complimented Taylor for being a man, but went on to say, "We can't believe that he is a ruffian. That widow's peak still gives him away."

311

Give Mr. Taylor credit for a gallant, if unsuccessful, attempt at a tough role.

Such a clean-cut young man [Taylor] is out of place amid the dark and forbidding characters who naturally inhabit gangster films.

July 16, 1942
Capitol Theatre

HER CARDBOARD LOVER
MGM 1942

Producer—J. Walter Ruben
Director—George Cukor
Story—based on an original play by Jacques Deval.
Screenplay—Jacques Deval, John Collier, Anthony Veiller
and William H. Wright

Consuelo Croydon—Norma Shearer
Terry Trindale—Robert Taylor
Tony Barling—George Sanders
Chappie Champagne—Frank McHugh
Eva—Elizabeth Patterson
Judge—Chill Wills

Role— Taylor portrays Miss Shearer's "Cardboard" Lover. An earlier version produced by Buster Keaton in 1932 was called *The Passionate Plumber*.
Fable about a lady who employs an ardent gentleman to pose as her personable male secretary (papier-mâché) in order to pique the bounder she loves.

Reviews—Bad movie! It was a disappointment, especially since it is Miss Shearer's farewell to movie-making.

312

Mr. Taylor, who had finally gotten somewhere as an actor, is back where he began . . . as a piece of well-dressed furniture . . . compelled to make the most inane remarks!

Mr. Taylor makes something of an engaging character.

May 11, 1943
Capitol Theatre

STAND BY FOR ACTION
MGM 1942

Producer—Robert Z. Leonard and Orville O. Dull
Director—Robert Z. Leonard
Story—from an original story by Captain Harvey Haislip, U.S.N., and R. C. Sheriff
Screenplay—George Bruce, John L. Balderston and Herman J. Mankiewicz
Suggested by the story *A Cargo of Innocence* by Laurence Kirk

Lieutenant Gregg Masterson—Robert Taylor
Rear Admiral Stephen Thomas—Charles Laughton
Lieutenant Commander Martin J. Roberts—Brian Donlevy
Chief Yeoman Henry Johnson—Walter Brennan
Audrey Carr—Marilyn Maxwell
Commander Stone M.C.—Henry O'Neill
Chief Boatswain's Mate "Jenks"—Chill Wills

Role—   Taylor is a society yachtsman who becomes a Navy officer

Noel Coward's superior picture *In Which We Serve* was the English counterpart of *Stand By for Action*.

313

Reviews—Mr. Taylor—how shall we say?—is not impressive
in a very fatuous role. It would—if one could—
be better to laugh this picture off, but too many
folks will take it seriously.

Robert Taylor is not at all bad as the patronizing
young lieutenant who learns what it is to be in
active service. This picture is worth seeing!

Capitol Theatre
June 3, 1943

BATAAN
MGM 1943

Producer—Irving Starr
Director—Tay Garnett
Story—unofficial remake of *The Lost Patrol*—RKO 1934
Screenplay—Robert D. Andrews

Sergeant Bill Dane—Robert Taylor
Lieutenant Steve Bentley—George Murphy
Corporal Jake Feingold—Thomas Mitchell
Corporal Barney Todd—Lloyd Nolan
Captain Lassiter—Lee Bowman
Leonard Purchett—Robert Walker (screen debut)
Felix Ramirez—Desi Arnaz
F. X. Matowski—Barry Nelson
Gilbert Hardy—Philip Terry

Role— A candid film about Bataan. Taylor is the sergeant
who is last to die.

Reviews—Taylor is magnificent as the Sergeant. The acting
is exactly what it should be in *Bataan*. Taylor is
believable as the Sergeant who takes over the

rather motley crew and then digs his own grave before his final skirmish with the Japanese.

Taylor's acting will remain in our memory for a long time without a doubt. His role as the Sergeant is by far the most intriguing, without a trace of the softness his roles once allowed him. Handsome Bob looks with disdain from the beginning to the end.

This time at least the studio hasn't purposely "prettified" the facts of war—they made it true and ugly in every detail.

Mr. Taylor is believable though he does dash around a bit too much with a dark scowl.

Excellent film!

THE YOUNGEST PROFESSION
MGM 1943

Taylor made a brief guest appearance.

SONG OF RUSSIA
MGM 1944

Producer—Joseph Pasternak
Director—Gregory Ratoff
Story—Leo Mittler, Victor Trivas and Guy Endore
Screenplay—Paul Jarrico and Richard Collins

John Meredith—Robert Taylor
Nadya Stepanova—Susan Peters
Boris—John Hodiak
Hank Higgins—Robert Benchley
Petrov—Felix Bressart

Role—   An American conductor (Taylor) tours Russia.

Reviews—One never believes that Mr. Taylor is a conductor, especially when his baton is out of rhythm.

Mr. Taylor makes a very good impression as a young American caught in Russia by love and war.

THE FIGHTING LADY
Cod and U.S. Navy 1944

Oscar-winning documentary about fourteen months in the life of a U.S. warship.

Taylor's role—Narrator (during Taylor's navy duty)

Reviews—Alton Cook: "Taylor's is a stern, self-effacing

voice with no trace of the movie star."

November 28, 1946
Capitol Theatre

UNDERCURRENT
MGM 1946

Producer—Pandro S. Berman
Director—Vincente Minnelli
Story—Thelma Strabel
Screenplay—Edward Chodorov

Ann Hamilton—Katherine Hepburn
Alan Garroway—Robert Taylor
Michael Garroway—Robert Mitchum
Prof. Hamilton—Edmund Gwenn
Sylvia Burton—Jane Meadows
Lucy—Marjorie Main

Role—   Taylor's first movie after his return from service.
           Taylor is a businessman who kills a man to steal
           his invention, then attempts to kill his own wife
           (Hepburn) when she falls in love with his brother
           (Mitchum)

Reviews—Taylor's performance has new presence and dig-
        nity . . . handsome, forceful maturity . . . strong
        performance.

        It certainly is great to have Bob Taylor back on
        the screen after his war service. He portrays little
        of the jitteriness that hits many returning actors
        and he does a marvelous job. His varying of

moods from charming to dangerous is quite. striking.

December 25, 1947
Capitol Theatre

THE HIGH WALL
MGM 1947

Producer—Robert Lord
Director—Curtis Bernhardt
Story—Suggested by a play by **Alan R. Clarke and Bradbury Foote**
Screenplay—Sidney Boehm and Lester Cole

Steven Kenet—Robert Taylor
Dr. Ann Lorrison—Audrey Totter
Willard I. Whitcomb—Herbert Marshall
Helen Kenet—Dorothy Patrick
Mr. Slocum—H. B. Warner

Role— A psychiatrist (Totter) helps a war veteran (Taylor) prove himself innocent of killing his wife.

Reviews—Taylor gives a "workmanlike" performance as a sullen, secretive mental patient.

Who would the chief maniac be but our old friend, Robert Taylor, who can look fiercer than any nut we know.

THE BRIBE
MGM 1949

Producer—Pandro S. Berman
Director—Robert Z. Leonard
Story—based on a short story by Frederick Nebel
Screenplay—Marguerite Roberts

Rigby—Robert Taylor
Elizabeth Hintten—Ava Gardner
J. J. Bealer—Charles Laughton
Carwood—Vincent Price
Tug Hintten—John Hodiak

Role—   Taylor is a Federal Agent who falls in love with
a honky-tonk singer (Gardner) while investigating
a smuggling ring in the Caribbean.

Reviews—Taylor is somewhat bemused by the early sequences, in which he soliloquizes about honor and
infatuation in the manner made famous by Laurence Olivier in *Hamlet*, but he is very good indeed
when violence moves into a tremendous crescendo.

THE CONSPIRATOR
MGM 1950 (filmed in England)

Producer—Arthur Hornblow, Jr.
Director—Victor Sarille
Story—based on a novel by Humphrey Slater
Screenplay—Sally Benson and Gerard Fairlie

Major Michael Curragh—Robert Taylor
Melinda Greyton—Elizabeth Taylor
Captain Hugh Ladholme—Robert Flemyng
Colonel Hammerbrook—Harold Warrender
Joyce—Honor Blackman
Aunt Jessica—Marjorie Fielding

Role— An American girl (Elizabeth Taylor) discovers her husband (Taylor) is a communist agent and has been ordered to kill her.

Reviews—Robert Taylor and Elizabeth Taylor are the two most beautiful people on the screen.

Taylor as a British Army Major spying for Soviet Russia, and Elizabeth Taylor as his American wife, were "working under a considerable handicap" because of the script.

Miss Taylor and Mr. Taylor are capable of doing better!

AMBUSH
MGM 1950 (A Sam Wood Production)

Producer—Armand Deutsch
Director—Sam Wood
Story—Luke Short
Screenplay—Marguerite Roberts

Ward Kinsman—Robert Taylor
Captain Ben Lorrison—John Hodiak
Ann Duverall—Arlene Dahl
Lieutenant Linus Delaney—Don Taylor
Martha Conovan—Jean Hagen
Major Breverly—Leon Ames

Role— The U.S. Cavalry vs. the Apaches. Taylor is a
Scout for the Army.

Reviews—Taylor handles his role expertly and with restraint.

Taylor, playing a civilian Scout for the Army,
gives an excellently restrained performance of a
frontier-sophisticated tough guy.

DEVIL'S DOORWAY
MGM 1950

Producer—Nicholas Nayfack
Director—Anthony Mann
Story—based on a screenplay by Guy Trasper

Lance Poole—Robert Taylor
Verne Coolan—Louis Calhern
Orrie Masters—Paula Raymond
Rod MacDougall—Marshall Thompson
Red Rock—James Mitchell
Zeke Carmody—Edgar Buchanan
Mrs. Masters—Spring Byington

Role—   Taylor is a Shoshone Indian who wins the Congressional Medal of Honor at Gettysburg and
returns to Wyoming to help his family save their
land.

Reviews—Robert Taylor may strike you as a rather peculiar
choice to play a full-blooded Indian, but give the
man credit for a forceful performance.

Indeed, his is the only role that is not a stereotype.

Top Ten Grossing Film
Ten Best Film Daily Award

QUO VADIS
(Filmed in Rome)

Producer—Sam Zimbalist
Director—Mervyn LeRoy
Story—from a Henry Sienkiewicz novel
Screenplay—John Lee Mahin, S.N. Behrman, Sonya Levien

Marcus Viniqius—Robert Taylor
Lygia—Deborah Kerr
Petronius—Leo Genn
Nero—Peter Ustinov
Ursus—Buddy Baer
Poppaea—Patricia Laffan
Peter—Finley Currie
Pedicurist—Lia DiLeo
Extras—Sophia Loren, Elizabeth Taylor

Role—   Taylor portrays a Roman Officer who falls in love
with a Christian (Kerr)

Reviews—A money-making spectacle rather than a critical
success.

Mr. Taylor and Miss Kerr in their performance
appear anything but inspired.

WESTWARD THE WOMEN
MGM 1952

Producer—Dore Schary
Director—William Wellman
Story—Frank Capra
Screenplay—Charles Schnee

Buck—Robert Taylor
Danon—Denise Darcel
Ito—Henry Nakamura
Maggie—Lenore Lonergan
Jean—Marilyn Erskine
Patience—Hope Emerson
Laurie—Julie Bishop

Role—   Part Western—part burlesque, but authentic. Taylor is a wagonmaster leading 200 women to California—and husbands.

Reviews—There is that about Mr. Taylor's toughness that is as clear and brittle as a pane of glass!

A picturesque novelty.

IVANHOE
MGM 1952
(Filmed in England)

Producer—Pandro S. Berman
Director—Richard Thorpe
Story—from Sir Walter Scott's novel
Screenplay—Noel Langley
Adaptation—Aeneas Mackenzie

Ivanhoe—Robert Taylor
Rebecca—Elizabeth Taylor
Rowena—Joan Fontaine
DeBois Guilbert—George Sanders
Wamba—Emlyn Williams
Sir Hugh De Bracy—Robert Douglas
Cedric—Finlay Currie

Role—   Taylor portrays Ivanhoe

Reviews—Robert Taylor portrays a sturdy and forthright
          Ivanhoe!

Top Ten Best

January 30, 1953
Mayfair Theatre

ABOVE AND BEYOND
MGM 1952

Producers—Melvin Frank and Norman Panama

Directors—Melvin Frank and Norman Panama
Screenplay—Melvin Frank and Norman Panama and Beirne
         Lay, Jr.
Author—Beirne Lay, Jr.

Colonel Paul Tibbets—Robert Taylor
Lucey Tibbets—Eleanor Parker
Major Uanna—James Whitmore
Major General Vernon C. Brent—Larry Keating
Captain Parson—Larry Gates
Marge Bratton—Marilyn Erskine
Major Harry Bratton—Stephen Dunne

Role—   Taylor is the pilot who heads our atomic bomb-
         ing of Japan. A semi-documentary, it dissipated its
         impact in domestic scenes between Taylor and
         Parker (Mrs. Tibbets).

Reviews—Taylor plays his role with "set jaw" and determi-
         nation—a man with a singleness of purpose.

         Taylor's best performance to date.

I LOVE MELVIN
MGM 1953

Director—Don Weis

Taylor's Role—Cameo

RIDE VAQUERO!
MGM 1953

Producer—Stephen Ames
Director—John Farrow
Screenplay—Frank Fenton

Rio—Robert Taylor
Cordelia Cameron—Ava Gardner
King Cameron—Howard Keel
Jose Esqueda—Anthony Quinn
Father Antonio—Kurt Kaszner
Sheriff Parker—Ted De Corsia

Role—   Taylor portrays an outlaw

Reviews—Nothing could have been as static as the dusty
        shenanigans of the clattering of such urban buck-
        aroos as Robert Taylor, Ava Gardner and Howard
        Keel, and mercifully some fine Technicolor back-
        grounds.

        Robert Taylor is required merely to look somber
        and shoot fast. The movie trots along at a good
        pace and in colorful style.

ALL THE BROTHERS WERE VALIANT
MGM 1953

Producer—Pandro S. Berman
Director—Richard Thorpe
Story—Ben Ames Williams
Screenplay—Harry Brown

Joel Shore—Robert Taylor
Mark Shore—Stewart Granger
Priscilla Holt—Ann Blyth
Silva—Keenan Wynn
Fletcher—James Whitmore
Quint—Kurt Kaszner
Captain Holt—Lewis Stone

Role— Taylor, the good brother, and Granger, the bad, meet up with pearls, whales and mutiny.

Reviews—Mr. Taylor is in the nature of one great big walking scowl as the brave and honorable shipmaster who defies his mutineers.

It is not sadistic, it is simply bloodthirsty in the popular story-style!

KNIGHTS OF THE ROUND TABLE
MGM 1954
(Filmed in England and Ireland)

Producer—Pandro S. Berman
Director—Richard Thorpe
Story—Based on Sir Thomas Malory's *Le Morte D'Arthur*
Screenplay—Talbot Jennings, Jan Lustig and Noel Langley

Lancelot—Robert Taylor
Guinevere—Ava Gardner
Arthur—Mel Ferrer
Morgan-Le Fay—Anne Crawford
Modred—Stanley Baker

Role— Taylor portrays Lancelot

Reviews—As Sir Lancelot, Taylor is a fine-looking specimen of a knight and he acts with bravery and bravura, but he has no genuine life.

Robert Taylor is a trim, military Lancelot.

VALLEY OF THE KINGS
MGM 1954
(Exteriors filmed in Egypt)

Director—Robert Pirosh
Story—Suggested by historical date in *Gods, Graves and Scholars* by C. W. Ceram, Robert Pirosh and Karl Tunberg

Mark Brandon—Robert Taylor
Ann Mercedes—Eleanor Parker
Philip Mercedes—Carlos Thompson
Hamed Backour—Kurt Kasznar
Taureg Chief—-Victory Jory

Role—   Taylor portrays an archaeologist

Reviews—"Very Good"

Taylor has a role with a bit of meat on it!

September 17, 1954
Paramount

ROGUE COP
MGM 1954

Producer—Nicholas Nayfack
Director—Roy Rowland
Story—based on a novel by William P. McGivern

Screenplay—Sydney Boehm

Christopher Kelvaney—Robert Taylor
Karen Stephenson—Janet Leigh
Dan Beaumonti—George Raft
Eddie Kelvaney—Steve Forrest
Nancy Corlane—Anne Francis

Role—   Taylor is a crooked cop who reconsiders when his
         brother (Forrest) is killed.

Reviews—A well-done melodrama, produced and directed
        in a hard, crisp style and very well acted by Robert
        Taylor in a somewhat disagreeable role. He plays
        it with a cold determination that gives some real-
        ism to the sullied character that was outlined in a
        tight, colloquial script.

        Taylor handles his tough guy role with ease—
        never sneering more broadly or hitting harder
        than necessary.

February 23. 1955
Loew's Neighborhood Theatres

MANY RIVERS TO CROSS
MGM 1955

Producer—Jack Cummings
Director—Roy Rowland
Story—Steve Frazee
Screenplay—Harry Brown and Guy Trosper

Bushrod Gentry—Robert Taylor
Mary Stuart Cherne—Eleanor Parker
Cadmus Cherne—Victor McLaglen

331

Fremont—Jeff Richards
Shields—Russ Tamblyn
Esau Hamilton—James Arness
Luke Radford—Alan Hale, Jr.

Role— A tom-girl (Parker) romantically pursues a frontiersman in 1798 Kentucky.

Reviews—"Slap-stick in buck-skin"—Taylor as Bushrod Gentry displays a "sense of humor" in trouping the role of a trapper. This movie is truly slapstick —anyone had to walk out chuckling at the hectic battle in which Taylor and Eleanor Parker "best" some Indians.

November 23, 1955
Mayfair

QUENTIN DURWOOD
MGM 1955
(Filmed in England and France)

Producer—Pandro S. Berman
Director—Richard Thorpe
Story—based on a novel by Sir Walter Scott
Screenplay—Robert Ardrey

Quentin Durwood—Robert Taylor
Isabelle, Countess of Marcroy—Kay Kendall
King Louis XI—Robert Morley
Hayraddin—George Cole

Role— Filmatization of Sir Walter Scott's novel of feudalistic France. Taylor is Durwood.

Reviews—Taylor, as usual, acquits himself with valor.

332

Once more, Robert Taylor is playing the heroic role of a high-minded champion of fair ladies. This is beginning to be a trifle dull.

Mr. Taylor and "the boys" at MGM did much better by Sir Walter when they made *Ivanhoe*.

April 30, 1956
Loew's State

THE LAST HUNT
MGM 1956

Producer—Dore Schary
Director—Richard Brooks
Story—based on a novel by Milton Lott
Screenplay—Richard Brooks

Charles Gilson—Robert Taylor
Sandy McKenzie—Stewart Granger
Woodfoot—Lloyd Nolan
Indian Girl—Debra Paget
Jimmy—Russ Tamblyn
Peg—Constance Ford

Role— Taylor portrays a Buffalo hunter who eventually goes mad.

Reviews—*The Last Hunt* is an unusual Western because its characters have some depth—Taylor plays his role well as the—not so much villain—but as a psychopath. He is "spooked" by the buffaloes his mean streak is always there—in his thoughts and his smallest actions..

D-DAY, THE SIXTH OF JUNE
Fox 1956

Producer—Charles Brackett
Director—Henry Koster
Screenplay—Ivan Moffat and Harry Brown

Brad Parker—Robert Taylor
John Wynter—Richard Todd
Valerie—Dana Wynter
Colonel Timmer—Edmond O'Brien
Brigadier Russell—John Williams

Role— Taylor is a U.S. Air Force Captain in the same
task force as the husband of the woman he loves.

Reviews—Taylor and Todd are two of the most solemn "suit-
ors" in the business.

A soft and sticky story of a wartime love affair
in London.

September 26, 1956
Loew's State

THE POWER AND THE PRIZE
MGM 1956

Producer—Nicholas Nayfack
Director—Henry Koster

334

Story—based on a novel by Howard Swiggett
Screenplay—Robert Ardrey

Cliff Barton—Robert Taylor
Miriam Linka—Elizabeth Mueller
George Salt—Burl Ives
Guy Eliot—Charles Coburn
Mr. Carew—Sir Cedrick Hardwicke
Mrs. George Salt—Mary Astor

Role—   Taylor is an ethical businessman pitted against
         unscrupulous giants of the industrial world.

Reviews—Even Mr. Taylor, who runs to statuary looks these
        days, is convincingly ardent and courageous as the
        temporarily diverted tycoon.

        Taylor is earnest and likeable as the fair-haired
        boy!

September 6, 1957
Loew's State

TIP ON A DEAD JOCKEY
MGM 1957

Producer—Edwin H. Knopf
Director—Richard Thorpe
Story—Irwin Shaw
Screenplay—Charles Lederer

Lloyd Tredman—Robert Taylor
Phyllis Tredman—Dorothy Malone
Paquita Heldon—Gia Scala
Bert Smith—Martin Gabel
Jimmy Heldon—Jack Lord

335

Role— Taylor is a neurotic pilot who gets involved with a smuggling gang.

Reviews—Taylor is grim and moody.

Robert Taylor's stint as the strangely beset aviator is restrained and effective enough to lend credence to some of the long-winded introspective scenes, and his appearance is properly wan and overwrought.

June 6, 1958
Odeon Theatre

THE LAW AND JAKE WADE
MGM 1958

Producer—William Hawks
Director—John Sturges
Story—based on a novel by Marvin H. Albert
Screenplay—William Bowers

Jake Wade—Robert Taylor
Clint Hollister—Richard Widmark
Peggy—Patricia Owens
Ortero—Robert Middleton
Rennie—Henry Silva

Role— A reformed outlaw turned lawman (Taylor) and his wife (Owens) are kidnapped by the lawman's ex-partner (Widmark). A gunfight and Comanche attack follow.

Reviews—Robert Taylor plays the good guy solemnly!

336

Mr. Taylor, looking grim and mature, carries conviction as the lawman.

March 20, 1958
Loew's State

SADDLE THE WIND
MGM 1958

Producer—Armand Deutsch
Director—Robert Parrish
From—a screenstory by Thomas Thompson
Screenplay—Rod Serling

Steve Sinclair—Robert Taylor
Tony Sinclair—John Cassavetes
Joan Blake—Julie London
Clay Ellison—Royal Dano
Mr. Deneen—Donald Crisp

Role— Taylor as a reformed outlaw (again) opposes his gun-happy brother.

Reviews—An intelligent little Western drama.

Three stars are consistently good.

Taylor has turned in a thoughtful performance but it is to Mr. Parrish who directed, and Mr. Serling, that most of the credit should go.

PARTY GIRL
MGM 1958
(A Euterpe Production)

Producer—Joe Pasternak
Director—Nicholas Ray
Story—Leo Katche
Screenplay—George Wells

Thomas Farrell—Robert Taylor
Vicki Gaye—Cyd Charisse
Rico Angelo—Lee J. Cobb
Louis Canetto—John Ireland
Jeffry Stewart—Kent Smith

Role—   For the love of a girl (Charisse) Taylor, a crooked
lawyer, goes straight.

Reviews—As the true blue legal spokesman for the mob,
Robert Taylor makes the most of a fairly stereotyped series of situations. He is a grim but stalwart operator who is as convincing as might be
expected in a well-worn role.

THE HANGMAN
Paramount 1959
(Taylor's first independent film)

Producer—Frank Freeman, Jr.
Director—Michael Curtiz
Screenplay—Dudley Nichols

MacKenzie Bovard—Robert Taylor
Buck Weston—Fess Parker
Selah Jennison—Tina Louise
Johnny Bishop—Jack Lord

Role— Taylor is a U.S. Marshal obsessed with hunting down a killer.

Reviews—One of Robert Taylor's chief assets has always been his quality of conviction. He contributes a great deal of this to his role, but it is a hollow figure despite cursory attempts at providing reasons for his being a "hangman."

THE HOUSE OF SEVEN HAWKS
MGM 1959
A David E. Rose Production
(Exteriors shot in Holland)

Producer—David E. Rose
Director—Richard Thorpe
Story—From the novel *House of the Seven Flies* by Victor
    Canning
Screenplay—Jo Eisinger

John Nordley—Robert Taylor
Constanta—Nicole Maurey
Elsa—Linda Christian
Hoff Commissar Van Der Stoor—Donald Wolfit
Wilhelm Dekker—David Kassoff

Role— A passable suspenser with Taylor involved in
        intrigue over a fortune lost by retreating Nazis.

Reviews—Mr. Taylor, is, as always, competent in his role
        of romantic adventurer.

        The picture's one distinction is that Robert Taylor
        as the Skipper, with a minimum of material, can
        still show his successors how a dull job may be
        well done.

        Taylor does a good job with his characterization.

340

KILLERS OF KILIMANJARO
Columbia, 1960
A Warwick Production (Owned by Taylor)
(Filmed in Kenya, Africa)

Producer—Irving Allen and Albert R. Broccoli
Director—Richard Thorpe
Story—Based on the book *African Bush Adventures* by
J. A. Hunter and Daniel P. Mannix

Adamson—Robert Taylor
Jane—Anne Aubrey
Pasha—John Dimech
Hook—Anthony Newley
Gunther—Martin Boddey

Role— As an engineer, Taylor fights for a railroad from
Mombasa to Lake Victoria (South Africa)

Reviews—*Killers of Kilimanjaro* is a travelogue as well as
an adventure picture.

Taylor walks bravely through a role which re-
quires little of him except to stare imperturbably
in the face of danger.

THE MIRACLE OF THE WHITE STALLIONS
Buena Vista 1963
Walt Disney Production
(Filmed in Austria)

Producer—Walt Disney
Director—Arthur Hiller
Story—Autobiography by Colonel Alois Podhajsky
Screenplay—A. J. Corothers

Colonel Podhajsky—Robert Taylor
Verena Podhajsky—Lilli Palmer
General Tellheim—Curt Jurgens
Rider Otto—Eddie Albert
Major Hoffman—James Franciscus

Role—   Story of the director of the Lipizzan stallions,
Colonel Podhajsky (Taylor)

Reviews—A beautiful picture and stirring and suspenseful
is the story of the evacuation of the Lipizzan
stallions from Vienna before the arrival of the
Russians, who are not averse to dining on horse
meat.

Mr. Taylor, looking weather-worn and weary,
makes the Colonel a rather dull sort, so fanatic
about horses that he scarcely seems a man.

Robert Taylor, weathering prettily with the years,
seems more and more able to portray hard-bitten
men. This, for an actor who used to be too beautiful for words, is high praise.

CATTLE KING
MGM 1963

Producer—Nat Holt
Director—Tay Garnett
Screenplay—Thomas Thompson

Sam Brassfield—Robert Taylor
Sharleen—Joan Caulfield
Johnny Quatro—Robert Loggia
Clay Mathews—Robert Middleton

Role— Taylor is a rancher in this Western about cattle-
men and the National Trial Act in the 1850's

Reviews—*Cattle King* really holds your attention!

Robert Taylor, to be sure, has little more to do
than look sullen and woodenly stands by his
principles.

The altitude of Cheyenne is 6,101 feet above sea
level. The heights attained by *Cattle King* are considerably lower. Blame the role they've handed
Robert Taylor. He's cast as a land baron with
starch in his veins and custom-fitted clothes on his
back. His brows are perpetually knit.

Taylor gives a solid performance, and to the film's
credit, there is no actor in Hollywood who sits a
horse so well.

A HOUSE IS NOT A HOME
Embassy 1964

Producer—Clarence Greene
Director—Russell Rouse
Story—book by and about Polly Adler
Screenplay—Russell Rouse and Clarence Greene

Polly Adler—Shelley Winters
Frank Costigan—Robert Taylor
Lucky Luciano—Cesar Romero
Casey Booth—Ralph Taeger
Sidonia—Kaye Ballard
Harrigan—Broderick Crawford

Role—   Taylor is the racketeer who is Polly Adler's backer.

Reviews—Robert Taylor gives the professional touch to an underworld character.

Something was missing in this picture and to be blunt about it, the missing ingredient is sex! There is hardly a suggestion of it. It may or may not discourage impressionable young girls from a life of sin, but it certainly is enough to keep anyone away from the movie!

THE NIGHT WALKER
Universal 1965
A William Castle Production

Producer—William Castle
Director—William Castle
Screenplay—Robert Bloch

Irene Trent—Barbara Stanwyck
Barry Morland—Robert Taylor
Howard Trent—Hayden Rorke
Dream—Lloyd Bochner
Joyce—Judith Meredith
Hilda—Rochelle Hudson

Role— Stanwyck is plagued by night-walking ghost, Taylor.

Reviews—Robert Taylor gives the professional touch to the role of the lawyer of the blind husband.

William Castle has two old pros enriching the quality of his new eerie suspense thriller, *The Night Walker*. Barbara Stanwyck and Robert Taylor, coming out of semi-retirement from films, are the invaluable assets in the Universal release.

The whole thing would not be worth reporting if it didn't have Barbara Stanwyck in the role of the somnambulistic sufferer and Robert Taylor as her husband's lawyer who tries to help.

Miss Stanwyck, silver-haired and seasoned, does lend an air of dignity to the otherwise unbelievable woman and Mr. Taylor, lean and wrinkled, does at first make the lawyer seem something more

345

than the spurious character he finally turns out to be.

Local Theatres
June 15, 1966
(World Première, Orlando, Florida)

JOHNNY TIGER
Universal 1966
Nova-Hugh Productions

Producer—R. John Hugh
Director—Paul Wendkos
Screenplay—Paul Crabtree and R. John Hugh

Dean—Robert Taylor
Doc—Geraldine Brooks
Barbara—Brenda Scott
Johnny—Chad Everett
Billie—Marc Lawrence

Role—   Taylor portrays a school teacher of Seminole In-
        dian children in Florida.

Reviews—Robert Taylor assumes the character of the white
        educator of Seminole Indians with a serious mien
        and a stubborn unbending attitude. It is a worthy
        piece of acting.

        Mr. Taylor may be slightly obtuse as an educator,
        but he handles his role naturally and with ease.

346

SAVAGE PAMPAS
Prades Productions—1967
(Filmed in Spain)

Producer—Hugo Fregonese

RETURN OF THE GUNFIGHTER
MGM 1967
Made for television

Producers—Maurice and Frank King
Director—James Neilson
Screenplay—Robert Buckner

Robert Taylor
Chad Everett
Ana Martin
Mort Mells
Lyle Bettger
John Davis Chandler

This feature film for TV was right out of the old MGM oat bin, but it had a little something extra—that would be the old pro, Robert Taylor, who no doubt could have played the aging gunfighter blindfolded.

HONDO
MGM 1967
Made for television

Cameo

THE GLASS·SPHINX
American International
Released abroad in 1968

Producer—Fulvio Lucisano
Director—Luigi Scattini
Screenplay—Louis M. Heyward

Robert Taylor
Anita Ekberg
Giana Sarra
Jack Stuart
Angela del Pozo

WHERE ANGELS GO . . . TROUBLE FOLLOWS
Columbia 1968

Cameo

THE DAY THE HOT LINE GOT HOT
Commonwealth United Entertainment
AIP 1968 Filmed in Spain

Producer—Alexander Salkind
Director—Etienne Perier
Screenplay—Paul Jarrico

DEVIL MAKE CARE
Feature Film Corp. of America
1968

Television

THE DETECTIVES
ABC-TV 1959–1961

ROBERT TAYLOR'S DETECTIVES
NBC-TV 1961–1962

STAR SPANGLED CITY
Two-Part Color Special
Robert Taylor and family tour Washington, D. C.
NBC-TV 1965

DEATH VALLEY DAYS
Syndicated
Host and Occasional Star
1966–1968

349